Research methods
in personality

THE CENTURY PSYCHOLOGY SERIES

Richard M. Elliott, Gardner Lindzey & Kenneth MacCorquodale

Editors

FRANKLIN C. SHONTZ
The University of Kansas

Research methods in personality

New York

APPLETON-CENTURY-CROFTS
Division of Meredith Publishing Company

To Nancy

PREFACE

When this book was first conceived, its purpose was to be primarily educational. Too many students, who wished to perform research in personality, had appeared too frequently with ever-recurring problems of design and methodology, which they were, for some reason, totally unable to resolve independently. Their questions were distressing, for one would not have supposed that their training had left them in any way inadequate to the tasks they faced. They had all been exposed to course work in experimental psychology, and it was evident that they knew how to conduct research in learning, perception, and other familiar laboratory subjects. Furthermore, they knew a good deal about personality, for they had read the customary books and heard the usual lectures; many were working in clinical placements, where firsthand experience enabled them to integrate the abstractions of the classroom with the realities of the diagnostic and treatment situation. Yet, they could not perform acceptable research in personality.

The basic trouble was that they could not use their knowledge of laboratory methods for coming to grips with the kinds of research problems they wished to attack. They had discovered that life is not what happens in the laboratory and that human beings, for the most part, cannot be treated like experimental animals; but they did not know what to do about it. There was nothing for it but to conclude that something was indeed lacking in the training of these generally bright and promising students of psychology. This book therefore began as an effort to provide that something, as an attempt to help such students bridge the gap between what they had been taught research ought to be and what they wanted it to become: the study of personality processes in situations with probable real-life significance.

That is how it began, but not how it ended. As work on the various chapters progressed, it became increasingly evident that the task at hand was not merely to eliminate the harassment that results from having to deal repeatedly with the same deficiencies in research designs; nor was it to apologize for what seemed at first sight to be basic inadequacies in available methods for personality research. In fact, the task soon became that of unraveling the whole complex web of the scientific process, not in general philosophical terms, but with specific reference to the study of organized human behavior and experience. More, it became that of developing and rationalizing a steadily growing conviction that personality research inherently requires solutions to methodological problems that are in some ways unique.

Whether this book has succeeded in satisfying the comprehensive purposes that finally evolved for it, is not to be judged here. But if it has not, there are perhaps others who will be stimulated by its contents to achieve its objectives more effectively.

No such work as this is the product of a single person, and it is impossible to recognize publicly everyone who influenced it. Special thanks are due to Mrs. Ruth Fellnagel and Mrs. Anita Zimbrick, who kept on typing, with seemingly infinite patience, through apparently endless revisions of the manuscript. Mrs. Mary Cook was extremely helpful in constructing the index of names and in preparing material for the printer. Gardner Lindzey also deserves special acknowledgment for his help in suggesting important clarifications and reorganizations of some very complex ideas. Finally, a heavy debt of gratitude is owed to the many students, whose interest in personality research made the need for this book evident, whose endurance enabled them to sit through a full oral presentation of the manuscript, and whose genuine enthusiasm for its contents made its completion possible.

In the book itself research examples are cited freely. The sources, from which these examples were drawn, have been double-checked in an effort to minimize the possibility of descriptive error. Considerable effort has been exerted to assure reportorial accuracy, for it would be regrettable, indeed, if overeagerness to illustrate a point resulted in misrepresenting any serious investigator's scientific activities. A writer bears full responsibility for his perceptions as well as for his ideas; and though neither can be expected to be perfect, the reader may be assured that this author has conscientiously tried to minimize his faults.

F.C.S.

CONTENTS

Research methods
in personality

1
Theory and research

The purpose of this volume is to examine critically a variety of research methods currently employed in the study of personality. The obvious justifications for such an undertaking are that it is necessary and that it has not been successfully completed elsewhere.

In the past half century, personality theories have multiplied and been elaborated to the extent that it is now almost impossible to describe them all, separately and in detail, in any work of manageable proportions. As inconvenient as the situation has become, however, it has led to important conceptual advances. To survey the field requires that theories be classified; and the very process of classification has tended to clarify similarities and differences among various schools of thought. Hall and Lindzey (1957) have contributed significantly to the development of a clear view of the subject matter of personality by concluding their authoritative survey of personality theories with an extremely lucid chapter summarizing and describing the key issues on which theorists tend to differ (pp. 538-558). Lazarus (1963, pp. 51-72) has also noted the overwhelming diversity of points of view in this field and has attempted to simplify matters by reducing conceptual variations to three basic "frames of reference" (trait and type; stimulus-response; phenomenology) under which specific theories of personality may be subsumed. Another useful addition to the literature is the collection of papers titled *Personality: Readings in Theory and Research*, edited by Southwell and Merbaum (1964). This volume contains theoretical, research, and critical papers, representing eight important general conceptions of personality. Although no individual point of view is done full justice in the necessarily cursory treatment such a book provides, the reader is given an impression of the variety of approaches that are currently in vogue. More importantly, he is exposed to well-selected illustrations of the scientific process, from theoretical conception through empirical confirmation to critical evaluation.

It is evident that the increasingly necessary, comprehensive approach to personality theory has placed the modern psychologist in a good position to gain an overview of the concepts available to him. His detailed examination of specific theoretical ideas may then follow sensibly from a well-organized beginning. Regrettably, no such possibility is open to the psychologist who wishes to examine the growing body of research reports relevant to the subject of personality.

Recent years have produced an accelerating demand for the accumulation of objective evidence in support of proposed theories of behavior. Psychologists have come to feel that the finely articulated explanations of human functioning, which have been constructed over the past fifty years, are too speculative and stand upon empirically shaky and observationally insecure foundations. Many textbooks on personality now place special stress upon the empirical aspects of their subject. Some suggestive titles are *Personality: A Behavioral Science* (Baughman & Welsh, 1962); *Personality: An Experimental Approach* (Lundin, 1961); and *Personality and Behavior* (Gordon, 1963), described on the dust jacket as "an integrated presentation of personality against a background of experimental research." Compilations of reports of important research in personality have been published by Sarason (1962) and by Mednick and Mednick (1963); and collections of this type are certain to increase in popularity as the literature grows. The clear trend is for present-day personality theorists to exert far greater effort than their predecessors to develop bodies of systematic empirical evidence to support their points of view. Bulging scientific journals strain to carry the continually expanding flow of accounts of research this effort produces.

Despite the concern for and proliferation of empirical investigations of personality processes, no single publication, to the author's knowledge, has yet devoted itself exclusively to the analysis of research methods, per se, as they are and ought to be employed in this field of study. Perhaps the lack of availability of such a source accounts, in part, for the rather poor quality of many investigative efforts. Research on personality is often remarkably inconclusive, and it may well be that it is so because those who execute it lack an adequate understanding of methodological possibilities and limitations. Theoretical problems are often ill-suited to empirical methods, and meaningful questions are often attacked in scientifically meaningless ways.

The close examination of research methods in personality may therefore be expected to serve several useful purposes. Besides merely summarizing possible scientific strategies, it may provoke a more critical attitude toward the design, execution, and interpretation of empirical investigations. A sharper consciousness of the significance of methodological decisions may assist the student of personality not only in deriving maximum meaning from empirical results, but also in recognizing weaknesses that are often inherent in the research designs he selects. A greater sensitivity to methodological nuances may increase his ability to communicate investigative ideas, findings, and implications more clearly to others. An aroused interest may lead to efforts to improve existing methods so that their deficiencies are overcome or minimized. Finally, an increased awareness of the importance of methodological issues may instigate the initiation or development of new or previously ignored methods with scientific potentialities that have as yet gone unrealized.

THE NATURE OF PERSONALITY

The analysis of research methods may proceed satisfactorily even on the basis of a rather sketchy characterization of the nature of personality. All that is required is an approximate identification of the preferences and interests of personality theorists and a delineation of certain biases that may influence the assessment of investigative strategies. This is not an appropriate place for a scholarly and comprehensive definition of personality, but it is well to consider the matter briefly before detailed discussion of research methodology is begun.

The Range of Human Behavior

Psychopathology. For all practical purposes, personality theory had its start in Freud's concern with the causes and treatment of psychological disturbance. Its history, therefore, reflects a heavy emphasis on phenomena observed most readily in the psychiatric clinic or the therapist's office. It is a mark of Freud's genius that, despite his major concern for psychopathology, he was able to formulate a general and fully comprehensive theory of human personality; but it is not hard to see why this theory was marked by an almost exclusively pathological, or defensive, interpretation of everyday human functioning.

Freud's notion that normal behavior represents less severe, or more socially acceptable, manifestations of the same processes that operate in "mental illness" was more than just a brilliant insight; it forged a strong conceptual link that joined the therapeutic skill of the practicing clinician with the growing scientific respectability of academic psychology. Psychoanalysis furnished the personologist with some of his most powerful techniques for discovering the secrets of normal and abnormal behavior; for decades it was agreed that mental disorders provide, as it were, a magnifying glass, through which healthy behavior-determining processes can be observed and studied. Many of the most popular personality tests of the past 25 years grew out of this assumption. Even such methodologically contrasting devices as the *Rorschach* and the *Minnesota Multiphasic Personality Inventory* could gain acceptance as general measures of personality because, despite their differences, both had demonstrated their usefulness as diagnostic instruments in the clinical situation.

To this day the study of personality remains closely tied to the examination of the behavior of psychologically troubled persons. Any theory that makes no provision for explaining such phenomena must be judged at the outset to be incomplete. Research on problems of a clinical nature is now not the only concern of the personologist; but it is clearly a task of major importance to him.

Unusually effective behavior. A sharp contrast to the pathology-centered point of view is afforded by those more recent theories of personality that begin by studying the characteristics of people who behave with unusual effectiveness. The best example of this approach is the work of Maslow (1954; 1962), who based his conception of personality on the study of particularly well-organized and creative behavior. His focus on "peak experiences" stressed the peculiar psychological properties of exceptionally productive and integrative human activities.

Especially effective behavior is as "abnormal" as especially ineffective behavior, and for the personologist it is as impossible to disregard the one as it is to ignore the other. There are many research reports on subjects such as creativity that rightly deserve a place alongside studies that are classically identified with the field of personality. These investigations have their conceptual source in concern for the highest levels of human functioning, and they make as legitimate a claim upon the personologist's interest as do the studies of neurotic and psychotic disorders.

Normality. Aside from approaches that are designed essentially for explaining atypical or extreme individuals and conditions, there also exist serious efforts to approach normality on its own terms. Between the personologist's concern for exceptionally well-functioning and for exceptionally poorly functioning individuals, lies his interest in more ordinarily encountered persons and events. In 1953, Gordon Allport restated two points that he has stressed for years: first, that normal and abnormal psychological processes are not continuous, and second, that the proper study of normal personality is direct inquiry into the conscious motives and purposes of normal subjects. Tests such as the *Edwards Personal Preference Schedule,* the *Allport-Vernon Study of Values,* and Strong's *Vocational Interest Blank* are thus rightfully identified as relevant to the study of personality, although they were not designed primarily to detect psychiatric disturbances. Similarly, researches on level of aspiration, on the frustration-aggression hypothesis, on perceptual defense, on nonpathological psychological stress, and similar matters are studies of personality, although they do not usually examine extreme or exceptional conditions.

It is apparent, then, that the study of personality cannot be identified with an exclusive concern for particular groups of people or levels of adjustment; it encompasses the whole range of organized human activity. Specific theories and methods may, in practice, be most useful within relatively narrow limits. Still, personality theories are designed to explain both the typical and the atypical; whatever their source, most are intended to be maximally inclusive in this regard.

Personality as Consistency

The science of personality is sometimes said to comprise the study of individual consistencies across time and tasks. This statement is appealing in its simplicity, but it is inadequate as an identification of the purview of personality theory. For one thing, it fails to recognize that personologists, more than most others, have consistently acknowledged the importance of inconsistency and change in human behavior (Lazarus, 1963, pp. 37-45). This acknowledgment is evidenced by their emphasis upon processes of development, their stress on the importance of conflict and ambivalence in the determination of behavior, their faith in the efficacy of psychotherapy, and their recurrent recognition of the fact that growth toward complete integration is a never-ending process.

It is indeed true that personologists often study response consistencies; but it would be erroneous to presume that the reality of personality is in any way verified by the observation of these phenomena. Indeed, the mere existence of either stability or instability of responses no more proves nor disproves the existence of personality structures than intelligent behavior proves that the behaver has intelligence or stupid behavior proves that he lacks it.

The difficulties with the contention that personality is personal consistency become even more apparent when one considers certain concrete problems, such as those involved in evaluating the reliability of projective techniques. Psychometric reliability is largely a measure of the internal consistency and temporal stability of test responses. Consistency and stability, however, are not necessarily characteristics that the student of personality most desires from measuring instruments. It would be a violation of the purposes of an examination such as the Rorschach, for example, to demand consistency of responses from a person who is himself internally distraught and conflicted. It would be equally unacceptable to require temporal stability of response from individuals whose personalities are characterized by temporal fluctuation or who are in the process of drastic personal change. Indeed, the essence of a good projective instrument is its sensitivity to the fluidity of the processes reflected in subjects' responses. It has, therefore, been extremely difficult to discover methods of test-evaluation that satisfy both the demands of traditional psychometrics and the requirements of the personality theorist. (Surveys of attempts to assess the reliability and validity of the Rorschach may be found in Holzberg [1960] and in Harris [1960]. See also Holtzman, Thorpe, Swartz, and Herron [1961] for a brief critique of the Rorschach and for a description of a new ink blot test designed to possess more favorable psychometric properties.)

Consistency and inconsistency of behavior cannot be ignored. Indeed, they are the phenomena that personality theories are designed to explain. The ideal theory of personality enables the psychologist to predict the occurrence of both constancy and change, of consistency and inconsistency. Such a theory specifies what is to remain constant, what is to change and how these changes will manifest themselves, what is to be consistent with what, and how specifically predicted inconsistencies are to be recognized and identified. It states the rules by which predictions may be made, by specifying the significance of relationships among relevant variables existing in explicitly described configurations.

That is a lot to ask of any theory, and it is more than is provided by the theories of personality currently in existence. It is a goal, but as such it may serve as an organizing principle for ensuing discussions. At least it makes clear the preferences and predilections that are implicit in the presentations to follow.

Mediation and Organization

Put most directly, the study of personality is identified by its concern for inferred mediating processes that account for organization in the behavior of the individual person.

Whatever laws or principles the personologist proposes, whatever regularities he discovers, the ultimate value of his ideas is determined by their applicability to concrete cases (Lewin, 1935, pp. 41-42). The student of personality is as much concerned with uniquenesses as with similarities among people. The psychoanalytic literature, for example, is for the most part a literature of case histories. Goldstein's organismic psychology was developed out of detailed analyses of only a few cases of brain-damaged veterans. Rogers' conceptions of the nature of personality were buttressed empirically primarily by detailed transcriptions of individual therapeutic hours. Lewin's complex conception of hodological space was designed, in part, to provide conceptual tools for the analysis and understanding of the individual life situation. Even factor analytic approaches, like Cattell's, are usually directed toward the construction of measuring instruments for evaluating the patterning of relevant forces or qualities that characterize particular persons. The same is true of actuarial devices, such as the MMPI. All the tests and psychometric instruments used in personality assessment, in the clinic or elsewhere, are intended to assist the psychologist in drawing conclusions about the individual case.

This feature of personality theory is felt by some to imply a contradiction of purposes. It is sometimes argued that the study of the individual as a self-contained universe (the *idiographic* approach) is antithetical to the study of groups for the purpose of discovering laws and processes that apply to all persons (the *nomothetic* approach). But there is really no problem here, for the purpose of the science of personality is, admittedly, to discover and study laws that apply to all human beings. The distinction between the idiographic and the nomothetic approaches is itself wholly artificial, and it has been well said that these "mischievous and difficult terms" serve no useful purpose in our scientific vocabulary (Holt, 1962).

The personality theorist certainly does not follow the lead of the student of learning, perception, or motivation. He does not carve out for himself a particular class of reponses (he would call them *part processes*) and then proceed to examine or analyze out the simpler variables that account for them. Personality theory is more likely to be concerned with how learning, perception, and motivation are organized in the overall structure of the person. Instead of seeking simpler variables with which to explain part processes, it postulates more inclusive and complex variables that cut across these processes. Thus, although he recognizes the possibility for change, the personologist ordinarily expects the well-functioning individual to display coherency in a variety of psychological functions. The field-dependent person (Witkin, Lewis, Hertzman, Machover, Meissner, & Wapner, 1954), for example, is characterized by a recognizable style of behavior that is manifested in many different things he does. Field dependence is not just perception; though it is a way of perceiving, it is reflected in learning and motivation as well. Similarly, ego strength is neither learning nor intelligence, although the psychoanalytic theorist may well claim that the ability to learn (and to do a lot of other things) effectively is a function of ego strength. Self-actualization is not analyzable into parts or elements; nonetheless, it is a mode of existence that clearly characterizes some persons more than others, and thus the concept may be useful to the personality theorist.

Goldstone and Goldfarb (1964) have stated that acceptance of the concept of personality is tantamount to advocating "a frontal assault upon *the person*" (their italics) as an "integration of all of the attributes of cognition, conation, sensation and perception, motivation and learning." These authors are not happy with the global approach. They feel that existing theories of personality "are not theories at all" and that the study of this subject "would require a separate science of the person with its own methods and language" (p. 177). The last two points are moot, but the general characterization of personality theory that Goldstone and Goldfarb present is concise and reasonably accurate. Its implications are not to be avoided.

GENERAL METHODOLOGICAL ISSUES

Wholes and Parts

A possible misconception. A great deal is said about the importance of the *whole person* and about the *organized individual*, as the focus of concern of personality theory. It is imperative to avoid any suggestion that the study of personality denies the importance or reality of the part processes that compose it. To accept such a statement would be very much like asserting that the study of faces denies the importance or reality of noses, eyes, and mouths, that the study of gross anatomy denies the existence of cells, or that an interest in cakes denies the legitimacy of an interest in eggs, butter, and milk. It would be as unsatisfactory to accept this notion as it would be to assert its opposite, which would, in effect, deny the existence of faces, gross anatomies, or cakes, because all these entities can be analyzed into relatively simpler and more elementary constituents. The concept of personality is *molar* by definition, and it differs fundamentally from concepts like association, learning, and perception (at least in the psychophysical sense of that word). But the study of personality does not depreciate a legitimate interest in other aspects of behavior. It merely calls for the use of research methods that are suited to its special requirements.

Research strategies and goals. An example may help clarify some of the general characteristics and problems of personality research. Suppose that a personologist wishes to study the psychologically relevant properties of molar entities, such as faces. He may begin by attempting to discover meaningful classifications of his subject matter. The classes may be grossly qualitative (Negroid, Caucasian, or Mongoloid; angular or rounded), or they may be quantitative (rated attractiveness). Whatever classes are chosen, they should refer to the whole face, rather than to the parts that compose it. The investigator may then move in either of two directions. He may approach his subject descriptively, by studying relations between overall class membership of the face and the characteristics of particular parts that make it up (*cf.*, Brunswik, 1949). Thus he may arrive at the conclusion that skin color, eye structure, and properties and color of hair are correlated with judgments of overall facial characteristics. Another possibility is to begin with the classes as such and to attempt to make predictions about other events that might occur because various samples of faces have the properties peculiar to them. For example, the investigator might predict, on the basis of a knowledge of social stereotypes, that a group of Negroid faces will, on the average, be more frequently judged "sensuous" by prejudiced Caucasians than will samples of other types of faces.

The first approach would specify with increasing precision the particular combinations of parts that go into the structure of faces of different sorts. Thus, a possible product of this type of research would be specific measures of facial characteristics that would permit more sensitive and objective classification or assessment of individual faces. The second type of research would enable the investigator to make general statements about the implications of having a particular kind of face. If the two methods are combined, so that increasingly sensitive measures are employed for testing more and more precisely stated hypotheses, it follows that the end product of a coordinated research program should be statements about relationships between molar facial characteristics and other, more specific, variables. These statements will apply not merely to grossly defined samples but to particular faces.

Similarly, the student of global aspects of personality begins with the identification of some general features of organized behavior and then studies the constituent parts of the features or attempts to predict their significance for behavior in future or new situations. Even in this work, however, his study of part processes remains firmly embedded in a pervasive concern for molar entities; for it is this concern that identifies the ultimate interest of the personologist.

It must be admitted at the outset that personalities are elusive entities. Certain existing theories provide gross classification schemes, by which genotypic personality structures may be divided into groups or arranged along continua. Often, however, little is known about the organizational characteristics of the part processes that define these classes; indeed, there is often doubt about the nature of the part processes themselves. Inductive or descriptive research can aid in providing sensitive and accurate measurements of molar personality characteristics and in yielding insights about their organizational properties and the nature of their constituent parts. Predictive research can lead to the testing of hypotheses about relations between molar personality characteristics and specific behaviors. These hypotheses must remain gross and inapplicable to the individual, however, until the two methods are used together in a systematic and mutually supportive way (cf., Cronbach, 1957).

The Place of Theory in Research

Influence of operationism. Perhaps no single development in the philosophy of science has had as profound an effect on psychological research as the doctrine of operationism. It would be superfluous to describe the tenets of this point of view in any detail, for almost every student of psychology is exposed to them early and often in his educational career. Briefly, operationism advocates identifying the content of science with specific procedures, carried out by the investigator as he measures or controls variables in the conduct of research. It thereby reduces scientific concepts to sets of instructions for producing and observing empirical phenomena.

In a fully operationized science, every statement is capable of direct verification, because all acceptable definitions of terms can be translated into repeatable and performable research activities or conditions. Speculative theorizing is replaced by operational analyses, which have "the validity of actual experience" (Bridgman, 1945). Such an ideal science is fully precise, and the possibility of concealed contradiction is eliminated.

Many psychologists hoped that the doctrines of operationism would serve to stabilize and unify the study of human behavior by providing a common set of criteria by which all research and theory might be unequivocally evaluated. Unfortunately, however, the attempt to reduce many meaningful psychological processes to sets of statements describing only specific research operations provoked at least as many disputes as it settled.

An overzealous insistence upon a consistent application of operationistic principles in psychology has important consequences that deserve a moment's consideration. On the positive side, it fosters programs of research that seek to identify the simplest possible behavior processes. It encourages the study of pure stimulus-response relations, because these are most readily brought under direct experimental control. It advocates carefully instrumented laboratory research, because only in the laboratory is it possible to isolate and manipulate stimulus and response processes and to bring about behavioral uniformity in all subjects. The "rule of one variable" and the "law of parsimony" are usually the cardinal principles by which it proposes to judge all scientific enterprise.

On the negative side, a rigidly applied operationism fosters the conclusion that organizational constructs, of the type employed in the study of personality, are too vague and poorly defined to merit serious scientific consideration. It leads to a rejection of the study of mediating processes, because these are not readily tied to specific measurement operations that exhaust their theoretical meaning. It minimizes the value of the study of behavior in natural situations, because these pose almost insurmountable problems of control. It commonly views individuality of response as a bothersome and inconvenient source of error in research data. In short, it hands down the verdict that the study of personality is, at best, premature, or, at worst, unscientific.

One form of response to these consequences has been to assume an equally extreme anti-operationistic attitude. Accordingly, operationism has been taken to task by some for its devaluation of theory, its decontextualization of responses, its artificiality, its mechanization of organismic processes, its oversimplification of situations that are inherently complex, and its failure to deal effectively and directly with matters that ought to be of most pressing concern to psychology: real persons in real situations (Dembo, Leviton, & Wright, 1956, especially pp. 4-14; Maslow, 1954; Morrow, 1956; Morrow, 1957; Scheerer, 1958).

The pros and cons of operationism as a guiding philosophy for psychology were discussed in detail a good many years ago, in a special symposium held in 1945 (Langfeld, 1945). The interested reader may wish to pursue the matter further by consulting this authoritative and still instructive source. Suffice it to say that the present general trends seem to be to accept the notion that operationism performs a useful service, but to reject the contention that the only useful theoretical constructs are those that can be wholly identified with specific laboratory procedures.

Feigl (1945) appears to be the major spokesman for the view that is most broadly favored at this time. He feels that the operationistic approach is most beneficial when it is applied to the description of directly observed events and to the generation of empirical laws that state relationships among such events. At the same time, he reserves for theory the task of higher order integration and explanation of relevant phenomena. A theory is a set of logically related assumptions, with predictive implications that can be tested by systematic observation of empirical facts.

Few psychologists deny that it would be desirable to have all relationships between constructs and operations (rules of correspondence) so clearly specified that any hypothesis could be clearly judged to be true or false by the conduct of a few well-conceived experiments. The conflict among psychologists often appears to lie less in the ideals to which investigators aspire than in their judgment of the readiness of their science to achieve them.

Concepts and variables. In his book on psychological research, Underwood (1957) identified five conceptual levels at which psychologists operate in explaining behavior (pp. 195-233). At the first level, concepts are identified solely with the operations an investigator performs on the experimental situation; level 1 concepts apply only to independent variables and do not refer to subjects' responses. Level 2 concepts define behavioral phenomena; that is, they refer to responses that appear under operationally specifiable conditions. Level 3 concepts are operationally identical with those at level 2, but they are characterized by the ascription of causal status to the concept. They are often more central, in that a process or state is put inside the organism and is then used to explain its behavior. Frustration, for example, is often viewed, not as a type of response that is observed under specifically manipulable conditions, but as an internal condition of the organism that causes it to behave as it does.

Level 4 concepts are postulated processes, proposed to incorporate a variety of phenomena into a single comprehensive abstraction. They are not tied to specific stimulus or response variables; instead, they combine several lower-level concepts into an inclusive theoretical unit. Level 1, 2, and 3 concepts are isomorphic with specifiable operations and observations and are therefore valid by definition; but level 4 concepts are hypothetical in nature and must be put to the test of deductively generated research before they can be considered acceptable as theoretical constructs. Level 5 concepts are summarizations, dealing with the interaction of other postulated processes; they are not common in psychological theory.

Obviously, personality is not something that is readily reduced to highly specific operational definitions. The concepts that concern the personality theorist are not usually those of levels 1, 2, or (often) 3. They bear most similarity to those of levels 4 and 5, in that they tend to be inclusive and are not wholly tied to specific manipulations of environmental or organismic variables. Their function is to explain molar relations among lower-level variables, and they are commonly central in character. For these reasons personality research is generally deductively conceived, and it often requires an investigator to rely on what Feigl calls *confirmation* (i.e., partially incomplete or indirect empirical evidence) rather than *verification* (i.e., a clear-cut empirical judgment of the truth or falsity) of hypotheses. It also reflects acceptance of the dictum that specific behaviors or stimulus situations "may serve as (probabilistic) indicators of central (i.e., mental) states, but they cannot be identified with them" (Feigl, 1959).

Vitalization of constructs. A particularly serious criticism is frequently leveled at the constructs that are employed in many theories of personality. The observation is that such theories commonly tend to make living things out of mere abstractions. Thus the person is thought to possess (or better, "to be possessed by") a body image, an ego, or a personality. The *self*, for example, tends to exist independently of the behavioral consistencies that justify its postulated existence (Lowe, 1961). Underwood (1957) characterized such concepts as "spooks, or pixies or elves" and noted that they tend to get out of control and to pursue unpredictable lives of their own. The ego tends to become a soul-like entity that resides within the province of a hidden, mental existence. It deals with and is the representative of reality, although it is not equivalent to reality and does not necessarily represent it with a high degree of validity. It is also under a variety of inner strains, and it may react to these unobservables far more strongly than to the stimulus pattern provided by the environment. Its actions therefore cannot be anticipated, and its behavior is inherently unpredictable. Thus, the ego may be said to be an executive, a decision maker; but the theorist is left with no basis for specifying or manipulating the conditions under which particular decisions will be made.

It is impossible to imagine a science of psychology that seriously proposes theoretical constructs which are permitted to live their own lives and make decisions that in principle could not be predicted even with the fullest possible knowledge of the conditions under which they were made. Few personality theorists would admit to such intentions. Constructs, like self and ego, are necessary; the problem is to avoid animating these theoretical abstractions without yielding up their integrity or the theorist's legitimate interest in the relatively global organization of psychological processes in the particular individual.

Theoretical models. Ultimately the solution to the problems of concretization and vivification lies in the attitudes that personologists take toward the concepts they employ. Fortunately, certain formal devices are available that can help to keep before them the proper status of their ideas. These devices are called *models*, and they constitute representations of processes studied, rather than descriptions of entities possessing concrete existence. Lachman (1960) identified the model as a system that is separate from theory but represents theoretical constructs and their relationships to each other. It provides rules for inference and for the interpretation of data.

The value of a model stems from the fact that its components possess a "quasi-real structure" that serves purely methodological purposes. That is, they are presumed to represent correlates of "real" things but they are not thought to be descriptive of the things themselves. They are "as-if" constructions that have only "theoretical existence," and they are employed only insofar as their use facilitates the conduct and interpretation of research (Meissner, 1958). Just as a slide rule constitutes a model of an abstract number system and may be manipulated in such a way as to enable one to predict the outcome of specific logical (or correlated empirical) operations, the model stands for, makes explicit, and facilitates the use of the concepts from which it was derived.

A model is a permanently tentative construct, and its use is consistent with the philosophy that science is not founded on unique and obvious truths, from which all real facts can be derived. The bottom of the ladder of science is not composed of "necessary and obviously acceptable" axioms. It contains postulates, "statements which, *for the purposes at hand,* are simply assumed to be true" (Weaver, 1964; italics added). The statements are themselves conveniences; they may be accepted, rejected, or replaced by others that are preferred in their stead. Models can provide a vehicle for such postulates for the personality theorist, if he wishes to take advantage of their possibilities.

Churchman, Ackoff, and Arnoff (1957) called the model "a representation of some subject of inquiry" and identified its primary function as explanatory, rather than descriptive. Of the three types of models they proposed, the analogic seems the most serviceable to psychology. Analogues, such as flow charts, are particularly useful in representing "dynamic situations, that is, processes or systems" (pp. 157-162), and personality theorists should find the "communication model" especially intriguing (pp. 69-104). It is not likely that personality models will soon reach the stage of sophistication employed in Operations Research, which is the main subject of interest to Churchman, Ackoff, and Arnoff. Their work strongly suggests, however, that this approach to conceptual thinking has important possibilities for the improvement of psychological inquiry.

It is not appropriate to consider further the nature, properties, and uses of models in science. It is a complex subject that goes beyond the scope of the present volume. It is perhaps enough to note that their use is generally favored, although a few authorities still remain unconvinced of their value. There are arguments to be made for and against models, and the controversy has been outlined by Meissner (1960). These issues will not soon be resolved to everyone's complete satisfaction; but if models are indeed as useful as they seem, it is a virtual certainty that they will be employed, objections notwithstanding.

The potentialities of properly constructed and employed models of personality systems and processes have been mentioned only because they offer the theorist an approach that aids in avoiding the tendency to mistake theoretical constructs for descriptions of nature. It is not necessary, in fact it may not even be desirable, for every theory of personality to be expressed in the form of a flowsheet, a mechanical contrivance, or a set of mathematical formulas. It is imperative, however, that theoretical constructs assume their proper place in the conduct of scientific work and that alternative explanatory possibilities be recognized for what they are and dealt with accordingly.

References

ALLPORT, G. W. The trend in motivational theory. *Amer. J. Orthopsychiat.*, 1953, 25, 107-119. Also in G. W. Allport, *Personality and social encounter*. Boston: Beacon Press, 1960. Pp. 95-109. (In Mednick & Mednick, pp. 63-74 [see below].)

BAUGHMAN, E. E., & WELSH, G. S. *Personality: A behavioral science.* Englewood Cliffs, N.J.: Prentice-Hall, 1962.

BRIDGMAN, P. W. Some general principles of operational analysis. In H. S. Langfeld (Ed.), Symposium on operationism. *Psychol. Rev.*, 1945, 52, 246-249, 281-284.

BRUNSWIK, E. *Systematic and representative design of psychological ex-*

periments. Univer. Calif. Syllabus Series, No. 304. Berkeley: Univer. Calif. Press, 1949.

CHURCHMAN, C. W., ACKOFF, R. L., & ARNOFF, E. L. *Introduction to operations research.* New York: Wiley, 1957.

CRONBACH, L. J. The two disciplines of scientific psychology. *Amer. Psychologist,* 1957, *12*, 671-684.

DEMBO, TAMARA, LEVITON, GLORIA L., & WRIGHT, BEATRICE A. Adjustment to misfortune—a problem of social-psychological rehabilitation. *Artificial Limbs,* 1956, *3* (2), 4-62.

FEIGL, H. Operationism and scientific method. In H. S. Langfeld (Ed.), Symposium on operationism. *Psychol. Rev.,* 1945, *52*, 250-259, 284-288.

FEIGL, H. Philosophical embarrassments of psychology. *Amer. Psychologist,* 1959, *14*, 115-128.

GOLDSTONE, S., & GOLDFARB, JOYCE L. Adaptation level, personality theory, and psychopathology. *Psychol. Bull.,* 1964, *61*, 176-187.

GORDON, J. E. *Personality and behavior.* New York: Macmillan, 1963.

HALL, C. S., & LINDZEY, G. *Theories of personality.* New York: Wiley, 1957.

HARRIS, J. G., JR. Validity: The search for a constant in a universe of variables. In Maria A. Rickers-Ovsiankina (Ed.), *Rorschach Psychology.* New York: Wiley, 1960. Pp. 380-439.

HOLT, R. R. Individuality and generalization in the psychology of personality. *J. Pers.,* 1962, *30*, 377-402. (In Southwell and Merbaum, pp. 276-298 [see below].)

HOLTZMAN, W. H., THORPE, J. S., SWARTZ, J. D., & HERRON, E. W. *Ink-blot perception and personality.* Austin: Univer. Texas Press, 1961.

HOLZBERG, J. D. Reliability re-examined. In Maria A. Rickers-Ovsiankina (Ed.), *Rorschach psychology.* New York: Wiley, 1960. Pp. 361-379.

LACHMAN, R. The model in theory construction. *Psychol. Rev.,* 1960, *67*, 113-129.

LANGFELD, H. S. (Ed.) Symposium on operationism. *Psychol. Rev.,* 1945, *52*, 241-294.

LAZARUS, R. S. *Personality and adjustment.* Englewood Cliffs, N.J.: Prentice-Hall, 1963.

LEWIN, K. *A dynamic theory of personality.* New York: McGraw-Hill, 1935.

LOWE, C. M. The self-concept: fact or artifact? *Psychol. Bull.,* 1961, *58*, 325-336.

LUNDIN, R. W. *Personality: An experimental approach.* New York: Macmillan, 1961.

MASLOW, A. H. *Motivation and personality.* New York: Harper & Row, 1954.

MASLOW, A. H. *Toward a psychology of being.* Princeton, N.J.: Van Nostrand, 1962.

MEDNICK, MARTHA T., & MEDNICK, S. A. *Research in personality.* New York: Holt, Rinehart and Winston, 1963.

MEISSNER, W. W. Nonconstructural aspects of psychological constructs. *Psychol. Rev.,* 1958, *65*, 143-150.

MEISSNER, W. W. Intervening constructs—dimensions of controversy. *Psychol. Rev.*, 1960, *67*, 51-72.

MORROW, W. R. Psychologists' attitudes on psychological issues: I. Constrictive method-formalism. *J. gen. Psychol.*, 1956, *54*, 133-147.

MORROW, W. R. Psychologists' attitudes on psychological issues: II. Static-mechanical-elementarism. *J. gen. Psychol.*, 1957, *57*, 69-82.

SARASON, I. G. *Contemporary research in personality*. Princeton, N.J.: Van Nostrand, 1962.

SCHEERER, M. On the relationship between experimental and non-experimental methods in psychology. *Psychol. Rec.*, 1958, *8*, 109-116.

SOUTHWELL, E. A., & MERBAUM, M. *Personality: Readings in theory and research*. Belmont, Calif.: Wadsworth, 1964.

UNDERWOOD, B. J. *Psychological research*. New York: Appleton-Century-Crofts, 1957.

WEAVER, W. Scientific explanation. *Science*, 1964, *143*, 1297-1300.

WITKIN, H. A., LEWIS, HELEN B., HERTZMAN, M., MACHOVER, KAREN, MEISSNER, PEARL B., & WAPNER, S. *Personality through perception*. New York: Harper & Row, 1954.

2
Terms and principles

In addition to problems that derive from general theoretical predilections and philosophical biases, such as those discussed in the
previous chapter, there are difficulties to be anticipated with respect
to the use of words. It is essential that key terms be applied consistently and that they have explicit meanings which do not deviate
markedly from generally accepted definitions. For the most part, the
need is not to devise original expressions or to attach broader implications to existing terms; it is, rather, to delimit and restrict the
interpretation of words already in common use. The danger lies in
expressing more than was intended, not less. Such words as *research,
experiment, method, procedure, measure, test, examination, technique,* and *control* are critical to the discussions that follow, and
their definitions generally are unspecified in the scientific literature.
It is therefore necessary to consider the meanings that are ascribed
to them for present purposes.

Research and Data

In ensuing discussions, the term *research* refers to attempts to
collect empirical observations for the purpose of answering scientific
questions. It does not refer to library research, such as might be
carried on by the student of literature who wishes to trace various
influences on his favorite author. In common parlance the latter use
of the term may be admissible, but it does not serve a necessary
purpose in the present context and is not so employed.

Data. There are limits placed on the kinds of empirical observations (*data*) that can be considered acceptable in research. Perhaps the least useful data are those that are anecdotal in character. A story about the remarkable personality change that occurred in Aunt Minnie following her automobile accident may (or may not) be interesting, but it cannot serve as evidence for or against a scientific proposition. Events in which an individual or his close friends or relatives are personally involved are not likely to be reported either fully or accurately; second- or third-hand stories are even more strongly suspect. Popularly available news reports and similar sources must usually be rejected as scientific evidence, unless the investigator's purpose is to study reportorial distortion, propaganda, or bias, per se.

Explicitness. The usefulness of particular data to the purposes of science may often be evaluated in terms of their *explicitness*. Highly explicit data have maximal informational content, and details of the procedures by which they are collected are publishable and repeatable. Experimental data are usually highly explicit because controlled experimentation demands specification of all conditions that are relevant to the conduct of an investigation. By contrast, anecdotal evidence is notoriously lacking in explicitness.

Case studies sometimes display relatively little detailing of procedures and data, but it is possible to introduce explicitness into this type of research as a means of increasing its acceptability as evidence. Any device that collects or conveys information in a standardized and objective way serves the purpose. For example, detailed transcriptions of behavioral events may be provided by trained observers, or subjects' responses to unstructured situations may be directly recorded on tape or sound film. Scores from the components of a battery of psychological tests are also highly explicit.

A certain minimum level of explicitness is required in any research because it is always necessary to provide some assurance that data are objective, that is, that they reflect actual events with reasonable accuracy. At times the acceptable minimum may appear to be rather low, as in an article by Shontz (1957) which cited seven clinical cases as illustrations of motivational patterns found in patients with chronic physical illnesses. The information presented on each case amounted to no more than seventy-five words, and the reader was left to accept on faith the objectivity of these brief thumbnail descriptions. In purely theoretical articles the demand for explicitness may not be high, because case reports that are used only for illustrative purposes are seldom offered as positive proof of particular propositions. The training and integrity of the author usually provide a sufficient basis for assuming that minimal standards of accuracy have been met. In such presentations of theory, however, the citation of specific cases clearly implies the author's belief that his point of view would gain further support if additional acceptable data were collected. It is only from such data that the ultimate value of his theory can be finally judged.

Experimental and Descriptive Research

In this book the term *experimentation* refers to a particular kind of research. It identifies those method classes in which the levels of one or more (independent) variables are altered, so that the effects of these changes on other (dependent) variables may be evaluated by the investigator. Experimental research is frequently contrasted with *descriptive* research, in which existing situations are examined with a minimum of effort to determine how they are influenced by the levels of specific variables.

It is important that the differences between these types of research be clearly understood. In particular, it is critical to note that experimentation does not simply mean laboratory research and that description does not necessarily mean naturalistic observation. Many laboratory studies are not actually experiments but are descriptions of events that take place under highly controlled, constant conditions; and many experiments take place outside the confines of the laboratory. The two approaches are by no means incompatible. Indeed, some of the most important and valuable experiments in personality are those that describe people's responses (dependent variables) to naturally occurring events that change their real-life situations (independent variables) in important ways.

The selection of either a natural or a laboratory setting for the conduct of an empirical investigation has important implications for the precision with which results can be obtained and evaluated. It may also determine the degree to which a research can be considered appropriate for the study of personality processes. But the selection of a particular setting, alone, does not identify the research as experimental or descriptive in character.

Method, Procedure, and Design

The term *method* refers to a general and abstract statement of the strategy the scientist adopts in attacking a research problem. *Procedures* are the specific activities or tactics used in the execution of research. A research *design* is a statement of how procedures are organized and integrated for the purpose of answering scientifically meaningful questions.

Procedures reflect, and are derived from, designs; and to the extent that a design is complete and properly implemented, the two terms are, for all practical purposes, equivalent. A formal distinction is maintained primarily to permit discussion of those cases in which expected coincidences fail to appear. Although there are many possible sources of discrepancy in relating procedures to designs, control groups are especially likely to pose problems. An ambiguous research plan may recognize the need for a control group or for "appropriate control groups," but it frequently happens in personality research that one such group is not enough or that it is not immediately apparent what groups are appropriate.

The value in differentiating between designs and procedures derives, then, from the fact that defects in one are often responsible for, or traceable to, faults in the other. The ideal research begins with definite and specific purposes that are expressed in a carefully related design which clearly serves the aims of the investigation and unambiguously dictates the procedures to be followed. Purpose, design, and procedure therefore should be, but often are not, both public and congruent.

The combination of purpose, design, and procedure are ordinarily thought of as comprising the *method* of a specific research. Present concerns, however, are with single investigations only insofar as they illustrate the general classes or types of approaches to the solution of scientific problems. It is therefore desirable to use the word *method* to refer to the classes or types, themselves, rather than to particular studies. The characteristics of a given method identify similarities among a group of investigations that belong together for important reasons. It will be shown that methods are differentiable largely, though not exclusively, on the basis of the degree and type of control exerted over relevant variables. For the moment, it is important only to note that a meaningful classification of investigative approaches is possible and that the term *method* refers to the types that emerge from this grouping.

Measure, Test, Examination, and Technique

The subject of measurement is complex. A thorough analysis of the philosophical and mathematical foundations upon which the entire concept of psychometrics rests (Stevens, 1951) would carry this discussion far afield. To avoid involvement, it is best to take a pragmatic view of the matter and to identify as *measures* all quantitative indices of the types employed in the research reports that are used as examples in this book. The next chapter is devoted to the specifically methodological problems of measurement in personality research. If statistical theory were the primary focus of present concern, broader consideration of the basic logic of quantification in psychology would have to be included. Since statistical techniques and procedures are de-emphasized in all ensuing chapters, however, elaborate preliminary treatment of this aspect of the subject is not necessary and will not be attempted.

Tests, examinations, and *techniques* comprise the various approaches to measurement in personality research. *Tests* are characterized by the fact that the conditions under which measures are obtained are, as nearly as possible, constant from subject to subject. Standard intelligence tests, properly administered, provide good examples of the type of procedure that identifies these devices.

In general a test yields relatively few quantitative indices, and all tests are clearly subject to the specific statistical requirements (e.g., demonstration of substantial reliability and validity) that apply to traditional psychometric devices. The most important feature of tests, as far as the present discussion is concerned, is their emphasis upon maximally rigid control of the stimulus situation to which subjects are exposed.

In a manner of speaking, every controlled research involves testing; for it is presumed that identical conditions exist for subjects in the same research group. When treated subjects are compared with control subjects, conditions affected by the treatment differ; but within the treatment and control groups, conditions are expected to be identical for all subjects. Measures obtained within experimental groups are therefore appropriately identified as "test results."

The term *examination* is relatively more loosely applied than the term *test*. An examination may be as unstructured as the clinical interview that a psychiatrist conducts in his office. Although certain general principles of procedure may be followed in such an interview, the psychiatrist remains free to pursue leads suggested by what the subject says; and he may do so in any of a variety of ways. Projective devices are usually examinations rather than tests, for the conditions of their administration are often standard only in the sense that they are designed to permit the natural complexities of the stimulus and of organismic situations to operate with a minimum of outside interference.

In practical or applied situations it is most common for the results of examinations to be used qualitatively rather than quantitatively; but examination data can be converted to numerical indices when necessary. The conversion almost always involves more human mediation between response and score than is required by psychological tests. Judges or raters, trained in the use of a standardized and reliable scoring scheme, must usually be called upon to express, in quantitative form, important psychological characteristics that are directly or indirectly manifested in the examination record. Sometimes these judges must draw complicated inferences from the data before they can assign appropriate scores. When this happens, the resulting numerical indices are as much a function of the judges' characteristics as of the subjects'. It is therefore evident that the true measuring instrument in these cases is not the examination, per se, but the raters who apply the scoring scheme and who assign numbers to the data. Mediated quantification through the use of judges is common in personality research. Measures obtained in this way can be extremely useful, but they must be explicit and reliable, and they must have sufficient content validity (chapter 3) to be convincing.

The term *technique* is used here in a more specific way than usual. Ordinarily a technique is almost any device, test instrument, examination, research procedure, or design that an investigator employs. Here, however, the term is used mainly to identify groups of measurement operations which possess structural or formal continuity but which are not limited to particular item contents. Some obvious examples of techniques are the semantic differential (Osgood, Suci, & Tannenbaum, 1957) and the Q sort (Stephenson, 1953). Although the rating scales of the semantic differential are more or less fixed, the subject may, presumedly, be asked to describe almost any meaningful semantic concept with the instrument. Similarly, in Q sort there are few restrictions on the content of the items that may be included or on the things that the subject may be asked to describe.

Once specific items and contents have been decided upon, it becomes legitimate to consider a specific semantic differential or Q-sort array to constitute a test or an examination. The term *technique*, therefore, refers to the general approach rather than to particular instruments. The use of judges' ratings of examination data to obtain quantitative measures constitutes a technique. The projective approach, in general, is a technique as well; but specific projective instruments with fixed contents, such as the TAT, are best referred to as examinations.

Controls

Control consists of systematically manipulating, randomizing, or holding constant sets of stimulus, organismic, or environmental conditions. Its underlying purpose is to reduce the number of alternatives that can be accepted as explanations for subject behavior in a given observational situation. Anecdotal evidence obviously lacks control. By contrast, an experiment on conditioning that uses a colony of inbred rats as a source of subjects; that carefully identifies each theoretical variable with particular maze characteristics, feeding schedules, or experimenter behaviors; and that eliminates, holds constant, or purposively randomizes the operation of as many other variables as possible (e.g., time of day when experimental runs take place, stimulus properties of the experimenter, and order of administration of treatments) is very highly controlled.

A proper understanding of the nature and purposes of control is essential to the discussions that follow. The various research strategies that are taken up in detail in later chapters are distinguished largely in terms of their different uses of and attitudes toward controls. It is therefore imperative that this important concept be thoroughly understood.

Uses of controls. Controls in psychological research are directed toward three kinds of situations and events. First, they are exerted in order to manipulate *independent variables,* that is, to alter in systematic fashion the psychological factors presumed to be responsible for, or to influence significantly, subjects' responses to the research situation.

Second, they are used to hold within acceptable limits other variables that might influence responses but that are not relevant to the purposes of the study. That is, they hold essentially stable the *conditions* under which the research takes place. Sometimes, in more complex experimental designs, research conditions are systematically varied and take on the status of independent variables. Manipulations of this sort often serve purposes that are actually secondary to the major point of the study, however. In these cases, they may be considered to produce a *sample of conditions* under which the effects of a primary independent variable are investigated.

When there are two or more equally important independent variables, it is frequently possible to analyze the study as if it were several researches rather than one. The first research would be thought of as having *A* for the independent variable and *B* and *C* as conditions. The second would be thought of as having *B* for an independent variable and *A* and *C* as conditions, and so forth. In personality researches at higher orders of organization, the number of interacting independent variables becomes very large and analysis is extremely involved. Designs of this sort are procedurally efficient, but they are exceedingly complex and are not treated exhaustively in this book.

Finally, controls are exerted upon the situation in which the *dependent variable* is observed or measured. The dependent variable is the phenomenon the investigator seeks to understand; it is the psychological process that the research was designed to predict or explain in the first place.

The use of the term *control,* with reference to dependent variables, may require some explanation. At first glance, it might seem inappropriate to exert control in the response situation. It is, after all, the response that is generally predicted by the theory under investigation; and it would seem unfair to manipulate the outcome of a research by exerting controls over the very processes by which the adequacy of that theory is to be evaluated. Actually, of course, it is not the magnitude of the response that is controlled; for response values must remain free to vary as a function of the antecedent conditions and processes that determine them. It is, rather, the observational situation that is regulated, as in a test, either by limiting the type of subject behavior that is possible in that situation or by restricting the observational process itself. The former case would be exemplified by the typical rat maze, which limits the number of ways in which the animal may behave; for instance, it makes escape impossible. The latter case would be exemplified by an unstructured interview, in which the subject is free to express himself in a variety of ways but in which only a limited range or aspect of his behavior is recorded and evaluated by raters or judges. Standard psychological tests often combine restrictions on response type with limitations on observer sensitivity to behavioral variety. Limitations such as these are properly termed *controls,* but it should be remembered that they are exerted on the response situation, not on the actual response which interests the investigator.

Controls and Concepts

It is possible for controls to bear a *direct,* a *remote,* or an *indirect* relationship to the concepts and variables that are important to a given investigation. A direct relationship is more purely operational than a remote relationship; and the latter is, in turn, more operational in character than the indirect relationship.

Direct controls. A direct relation between concept and control implies that the concept of interest is specifically and exhaustively identified with operations, procedures, and physical conditions in the research situation itself. For example, in a study on the judgment of emotion from facial expression, a high degree of direct control of independent variables would be exerted if the concept of facial expression were equated with concrete properties of particular facial characteristics. Pictures of faces might be put together from components, constructed to provide systematic variations in a few specific stimulus characteristics (e.g., corners of mouth up, down, or straight; eyes open, squinting, or closed) while holding constant or eliminating other conditions (e.g., general head shape, sex, skin color, size of ears, and environmental context).

This example does more than illustrate the direct relation between concept and control; it shows that direct control does not necessarily yield the most productive research on personality. A sizable body of literature on the judgment of emotional expression already existed in 1938 (Woodworth, 1938), and it was apparent even then that meaningful experimental results did not appear when maximum direct control was exerted on the stimuli presented for judgment. Emotions are naturally occurring events that take their significance largely from the context of the situation in which they occur. It is not surprising, then, that success in appraising emotional expression was found to be evidenced only when judges had far more complex information about the circumstances under which the emotion was aroused than strict laboratory procedures allowed.

The difficulties involved in studying such apparently unanalyzable phenomena as emotions have led one prominent authority to omit the subject from his textbook on general psychology. This author's view was that the concept is ambiguous and unfit for inclusion in a discussion of the science of human behavior (Kendler, 1963, p. 263). As the term is commonly used, however, emotions are of major concern to the personality theorist. Emotions are notorious for the way they affect thinking, memory, learning, perception, and other important psychological processes. Indeed, they provide excellent examples of precisely the kinds of mediating and organizational influences that are implied by the definition of personality.

Remote controls. *Remote* relationships between controls and concepts are characterized by a conceptual distance between the properties or procedures of the research situation and the variables that are of primary concern to the investigator. The remote relationship is inferential, and remote controls do not exhaust the meanings of the concepts or constructs that they are designed to manipulate. They are always employed in research that deals with central, rather than peripheral, psychological variables; hence, as might be expected, they are used with considerable frequency in research on personality.

The actual physical conditions or procedures of a research that uses remote controls may be identical to those used in a research that employs direct controls, for the distinction between the direct and remote relationships is often entirely a matter of the intentions of the investigator. For instance, if a given set of controlling environmental conditions is defined as *stress,* then the relationship is direct. If the same set of controlling conditions is said to *arouse stress,* the relationship is remote. It is easier to make this distinction in principle than in practice, for research workers commonly fail to make clear which type of control they intend to employ. The importance of doing so may be conveyed by pointing out certain differences in procedural implications.

If *stress* is defined in purely situational terms (i.e., controlled directly), then all subjects exposed to the defining situation must be presumed to be under equivalent stress, and all must be included in the analysis of research results. If stress is defined as a central variable and the supposedly stressful situation is considered to operate as a remote manipulation of an internal state, then only those subjects who actually evidence stress need be included in the analysis of research results. Those who do not respond to the stress-arouser may be eliminated from the study before the data are further analyzed. Of course in these circumstances an independent test of stressful response to the situation must be used as the basis for deciding which subjects actually underwent stress.

Remote controls may be used to manipulate independent variables, as in the example above, or research conditions. Their use does not differ much in the two cases. For example, most experiments on perception or learning in human subjects take place in a generally neutral or mildly pleasant interpersonal atmosphere. Whether the experimenter realizes it or not, his introduction of the subject to the task at hand and the instructions he gives are efforts to establish a willingness to cooperate with the requirements of the situation. His actions and remarks constitute a remote control of attitudinal conditions that are later presumed to be relatively constant for all subjects.

The remote relation between concept and control may also exist in the situation in which the observation or measurement of dependent variables takes place. Here again, the distinction between direct and remote control is one of intention rather than of environmental conditions, per se. Perhaps an illustration will make the distinction clear. Suppose that a state of frustration has been induced, either directly or remotely, and that the proposition to be tested is that this state produces another state, identified theoretically as hostility. A test of hostility is administered and scored to provide a measure of the dependent variable. The test situation itself exerts control over responses by limiting the variety of relevant behaviors the subject may produce. If this control is considered to bear a *direct* relationship to the concept it represents, the hypothesis must stand or fall on the basis of an analysis of test scores alone; for hostility is specifically and exhaustively identified with behavior in the test situation. If the control is *remotely* related to the concept, then hostility is considered a central condition that may or may not be reflected in scores on the particular test employed.

Dependent variable situations pose greater procedural difficulties than independent variables or research conditions when remote relations between concepts and controls exist. To provide several psychometrically independent measures of a dependent variable (as might be done to check on the adequacy of a remote control of some independent variable or research condition) would merely be to assess additional response processes. That is, in fact, what often happens in studies of personality. Instead of one test of the dependent variable, many tests are employed as multiple indices of a single central process. Sometimes examinations, like the Rorschach, are used instead of tests. Then a variety of specific indices are derived, for example, sum M, sum C, and response time, and are separately related back to the independent variable.

The use of multiple indices is often required in personality research. Serious problems arise, however, when the indices are not carefully identified, in advance of the analysis of data, with the specific aspects of the dependent variable each represents, and when some indices provide results consistent with the hypothesis while others do not. It will often be said throughout this book that there is no substitute in personality research for an investigator's advance commitment to his measures, whatever form they take. Without consent to the proposition that the instruments employed actually assess the psychological events they are said to measure, no research results can be useful to a science of personality.

       Indirect controls. Indirect controls may be exerted through subject selection, through statistical analysis, or through the use of comparison groups.

       Control by subject selection involves choosing subjects for investigation who are presumed to possess a particular psychological characteristic to a known degree, according to some preinvestigative measure. The measure is often, though not necessarily, some standard psychological test. Subject selection is used for controlling independent variables and research conditions. It is the identifying feature of an important and popular method in personality research, the *correlational* method.

       Indirect controls of a *statistical* nature may be exemplified by *covariance analysis, partial correlation,* and *factor analysis.* Statistical controls generally involve the computation and mathematical manipulation of correlation coefficients, or their logical equivalents, to correct or adjust scores on one test for differences that might be accounted for by scores on another. Covariance analysis is a correction for important research conditions that were not controlled in a research, either because it was impractical to do so or because the possibility of their operation was not anticipated in the design. Factor analysis is an extension of the principles of partial correlation and is the identifying feature of a commonly employed method in personality research that is discussed later.

       The third approach to indirect control is through the use of *comparison groups.* The logic of a comparison group is most readily conveyed by referring to the commonly employed, nontreated *control group* in behavioral research. (The expression *comparison group* has a broader implication than the term *control group,* and is probably more useful in the study of personality.) Comparison groups may serve a variety of functions. In general, they represent attempts to provide a null standard against which the effects of given treatments or conditions may be evaluated. They may provide a contemporaneous standard, as when a treated group is shocked but a presumably equivalent untreated group, the null standard, is not. Or, an untreated group may be used to control for the effects of time as well as treatment in a before and after experiment. Comparison groups may be used to evaluate the influence of manipulations of independent variables or the effects of other types of controls exerted on research conditions. For example, one research on the analgesic effects of hypnosis (Barber & Hahn, 1962) included a nonhypnotized group that received the painful stimulus, to provide a null standard for the independent variable, hypnosis, and another nonhypnotized group that received a similar, but nonpainful stimulus, to provide a null standard for evaluating an essential research condition, pain.

Difficulties sometimes arise in selecting comparison groups because it is not always certain what constitutes a genuinely null condition. Consider a research designed to test the effects of positive (coping oriented) versus negative (succumbing oriented) preparation for viewing a presumedly anxiety-provoking film. If subjects are tested for anxiety before and after seeing the film, it may be thought desirable to include a third group that does not see this film, to provide data in which the effects of taking the test twice in a given interval are nullified. But what else, if anything, should the experimenter require of this group? Should it see a different film between testings, or should it not? If it should see a film, what kind of film should it be, a dull or a pleasant one, or a different kind of anxiety provoker? If it should not see a film, what should it do? It could sit quietly or be active in any one of many possible ways.

Perhaps several comparison groups are needed. Perhaps one comparison group should sit and look at a blank screen. Certainly it would be desirable to have a group that receives neutral preparation and then sees the anxiety-provoking film. Perhaps there should also be a group that receives no preparation at all, but that sees the film anyway. To test the effects of preparation alone, it may be necessary to have other groups that are prepared for anxiety, but that are not exposed to the anxiety-provoking film. These questions, and their implied comparison groups, can be extended indefinitely.

Another illustration of the problems that may arise when null standards are sought in personality research is afforded by the work of Lindzey, Lykken, and Winston (1960) on the effects of infantile trauma (the ringing of a doorbell) on the later behavior of mice. In this study the stimulated group of animals was placed in a washtub in which a doorbell was suspended, and the bell was rung for two minutes. The nonstimulated comparison group was also placed in the washtub, but the bell was not sounded while the animals were in the apparatus. Levine (1961) criticized this study because he felt that the stimulation associated with the process of transferring the comparison animals from cage to apparatus and back was sufficiently strong to cast doubt on the validity of the investigation. He argued that the production of a truly nonstimulated (null) condition would require a comparison group that was exposed to neither the doorbell nor the washtub in infancy. Lindzey et al. (1961) replied that the type of comparison group demanded by Levine was not essential to their investigation. They seriously doubted that a completely null condition of stimulation could ever be experimentally achieved. In any case, it seemed clear to them that their procedures had produced a sufficiently large difference in stimulation level between groups to justify the conclusions drawn from the data. They therefore asserted that their research was suited to the problem as they had conceptualized it and that their study was therefore not subject to attack on the grounds of procedural inadequacy.

Since it is evidently possible for reputable scientists of equal skill and devotion to their subject to disagree completely on questions of this sort, it is clear that the problem of the selection of adequate comparison groups is difficult, at best. Rarely can one include all the groups that might seem to be called for, if every possible objection to a design is to be anticipated and dealt with satisfactorily. Problems of comparison group selection as a means for providing indirect controls of research variables are obviously highly important and extremely delicate in personality research. They will be dealt with again in the discussions that follow.

CLASSIFICATION OF RESEARCH METHODS

Research methods are not taxonomically discrete. Obvious or natural demarcations among them are lacking. But it is possible to identify with some certainty extreme types (case studies and direct controls) that are commonly advocated or employed in the study of personality. These types may serve as anchor points; and between them, other methods may be roughly ordered according to the relative similarity of their properties to the ends of the distribution.

Although methodological classes can be identified, it does not follow that every research can be neatly pigeon-holed. Neither does it follow that methodological purity or simplicity is recommended or considered especially meritorious. Methodological mixtures are common, and they are well suited to the investigation of important problems in the study of personality. They are not dealt with at length here primarily because they are too complex for inclusion in a relatively elementary presentation of basic principles.

The identification of methods classes is certainly only an operation of convenience. It provides a useful device for describing methodological characteristics and a handy rationale for discussing them in a particular sequence, but it does not represent or suggest any a priori judgment of the relative value of its constituent classes. If any judgment is to be made, it is perhaps that none of the usually employed methods is fully adequate to all the purposes of personality research. At the same time it must be admitted that no method is wholly without value and that if used properly, each has positive, though sometimes limited, potential for contributing to the development of an improved science of psychology.

In the final analysis the design, execution, and communication of research involves as much art as science. Like the artist the student of personality should make the best possible use of the tools and materials at his command; but he should be a master of his basic craft before he tries new combinations and techniques for accomplishing his purposes. Established, fundamental rules must be understood before they can be varied or combined effectively. The advanced study of the advantages and disadvantages of various methodological combinations poses a challenge, but it is one that cannot be effectively met until more basic needs are satisfied.

Organization of the chapters. Because the problem of greatest significance in personality research, indeed in all science, is measurement, the methodological aspects of this subject are discussed in the next chapter. In succeeding chapters, specific research methods in personality are identified, illustrated, and evaluated. The method which is most descriptive and which is characterized by least complete control, the *case study*, is considered first. Other methods are then taken up in an order that reflects progressively more emphasis on experimentation and on the directness of relationships between constructs and controls. The rest of the methods in order are *actuarialism, factor analysis, correlational method, use of natural processes, remote manipulation,* and *direct control.* Following these chapters, a section is devoted to proposing the method of the representative case, as a possibility for future development in personality research.

Although examples are used freely, the present discussion does not provide a survey of the research literature on the subject of personality. Examples and illustrations of each of the methods were chosen more for their clarity than for their representativeness of past or current research trends. The references also reflect to a large extent the interests and familiarities of the author. Personal bias and preference have unavoidably entered into the selective process, but the emphasis of the text is upon the formal properties of the methods and not often upon the contents of specific papers. It would be a simple matter for the interested reader to construct lists of supplementary or alternative examples that would serve the purposes of this presentation equally well.

In the first chapter, collections of papers edited by Sarason (1962), by Mednick and Mednick (1963), and by Southwell and Merbaum (1964) were cited. These have been extremely useful as sources, and reports that are reprinted in these books are noted in the reference lists at the end of each chapter by appropriate parenthetical identifications.

As indicated previously, treatments of statistical procedures are held to a minimum throughout so that attention will not be diverted from essential purposes. It will aid the reader to know that each method is distinguished by a relatively small number of identifying features. Most of the text is devoted to elaborating the implications of these features as they apply to personality research. Examples are provided to demonstrate these implications concretely. Confusion will be avoided if the basic features of each method are mastered first and if ensuing discussions are frequently related back to the few principles from which they were derived.

References

BARBER, T. X., & HAHN, K. W., JR. Physiological and subjective responses to pain producing stimulation under hypnotically suggested and waking imagined "analgesia." *J. abnorm. soc. Psychol.*, 1962, *65*, 411-418.

KENDLER, H. H. *Basic psychology.* New York: Appleton-Century-Crofts, 1963.

LEVINE, S. Discomforting thoughts on "Infantile trauma, genetic factors, and adult temperament." *J. abnorm. soc. Psychol.*, 1961, *63*, 219-220. (In Mednick & Mednick, pp. 122-124 [see below].)

LINDZEY, G., LYKKEN, D. T., & WINSTON, H. D. Infantile trauma, genetic factors, and adult temperament. *J. abnorm. soc. Psychol.*, 1960, *61*, 7-14. (In Mednick & Mednick, pp. 111-122 [see below].)

LINDZEY, G., LYKKEN, D. T., & WINSTON, H. D. Confusion, conviction, and control groups. *J. abnorm. soc. Psychol.*, 1961, *63*, 221-222. (In Mednick & Mednick, pp. 125-127 [see below].)

MEDNICK, MARTHA T., & MEDNICK, S. A. *Research in personality.* New York: Holt, Rinehart and Winston, 1963.

OSGOOD, C. E., SUCI, G. J., & TANNENBAUM, P. H. *The measurement of meaning.* Urbana: Univer. Ill. Press, 1957.

SARASON, I. G. *Contemporary research in personality.* Princeton, N.J.: Van Nostrand, 1962.

SHONTZ, F. C. Concept of motivation in physical medicine. *Arch. phys. Med. Rehabilit.*, 1957, *38*, 635-639.

SOUTHWELL, E. A., & MERBAUM, M. *Personality: Readings in theory and research.* Belmont, Calif.: Wadsworth, 1964.

STEPHENSON, W. *The study of behavior: Q-technique and its methodology.* Chicago: Univer. Chicago Press, 1953.

STEVENS, S. S. Mathematics, measurement, and psychophysics. In S. S. Stevens (Ed.), *Handbook of experimental psychology.* New York: Wiley, 1951. Pp. 1-49.

WOODWORTH, R. S. *Experimental psychology.* New York: Henry Holt, 1938.

3

Measurement of theoretical constructs

It is self-evident that research involves the collection of data and that if an investigation is to be well regarded by scientists, these data must be explicit. One of the best ways to assure explicitness is to construct and publicly describe a measuring instrument that yields information which can be compared from one investigation to another. Generally this information is expressed in the form of numbers, to which statistical operations may then be applied.

Fiske (1963) observed the weakness of personality research that is evidenced by "its relative lack of adequate measurement operations." It is not a question of quantity, however, for a wide variety of tests and examinations is currently available and their number grows steadily. The difficulty lies in the quality and acceptability of the devices that are currently used to assess personality processes. Fiske rightly pointed out that the essential problem is one of validity, and this matter essentially boils down to the question of whether a given instrument or technique provides a satisfactory index cf the concept it was designed to evaluate.

The validity of a measuring instrument used in personality research cannot be clearly judged unless four conditions are fulfilled. First, the theoretical properties of the concept to be measured must be made known. Second, the characteristics of the proposed instrument, including instructions for its administration and scoring, must be fully described. Third, the relation between concept and instrument must be clearly delineated. Finally, research must be conducted to establish the usefulness of information gathered with the instrument as a measure of the defined concept.

Inductive strategy. The four conditions outlined above specify the requirements that must be fulfilled by an instrument that is developed according to a *deductive* model of the measurement process. There is another general approach to measurement that applies an *inductive* strategy. When proceeding inductively, the investigator begins with a measurement of some unknown psychological function and then conducts research to discover what it is that he is measuring. Goodenough (1949), in her classic work on mental testing, called one form of inductive measurement the method of "signs" (pp. 82-84). She observed that this method is synthetic in character, in that the concept is permitted to grow out of or emerge from experience with the measure itself. She characterized projective devices, not as tests, but as "systems of diagnosis based upon signs rather than samples" of a predefined universe (p. 416).

There is something to be said for instruments that generate carefully developed inductive research. Still, no measuring device is fully adequate to its purpose until its relation to a clearly stated theoretical construct is explicated and its empirical validity is established in conceptually guided research. For this reason the present discussion considers only methodological problems associated with the development of deductive instruments, that is, those designed to assess concepts that are theoretically specifiable in advance.

Concepts

It is helpful at this point to review Underwood's distinctions among concept-types in psychology (1957). Of particular importance are the differences among the first four levels. It will be recalled that at level 1, concepts are identified with specific operations that induce responses from subjects. At level 2, the concepts are identified with observed responses to specified sets of conditions. Level 3 is characterized by the ascription of causal properties to a concept that may yet be defined in purely operational fashion.

Level 4 concepts are postulated processes that incorporate a variety of phenomena into a single, more inclusive unit.

The importance of the differences among possible concept types may be appreciated by considering a hypothetical example. Suppose an investigator wished to assess hostility with a set of personality inventory items. If asked what he means by the term *hostility*, the investigator would reply differently depending upon the type of concept he has proposed. In the most improbable event that hostility were a purely instrumental concept, he would presumedly say, "Hostility is defined by the properties of that scale." He would not necessarily be referring to the content of the items, especially if they were selected actuarially. Neither would he be referring to the score a subject receives when the scale is administered. The stimulus properties and administrative procedures of the instrument itself would exhaust the meaning of the term *hostility* completely.

If hostility were a response-defined concept, the investigator might reply to the same question, "Hostility is the total score a subject gets when he answers the items on that scale according to instructions." Each item might be viewed as producing a specific response that may or may not be described as hostile. A *composite index* (total score) is then taken to represent the number of times hostile phenomena are observed under a variety of related conditions (the items on the scale). Again the concept would be contentless, except insofar as it is a composite of recognizable responses to standard stimuli.

If the concept were at level 3, the theorist would probably say something like, "Hostility is a state of the person that leads him to get a high score when he responds to the various items on that scale." The concept thus becomes a property of the behaver; but it is still identified only in terms of particular measuring instruments.

If hostility were a postulated process (level 4), the investigator might say, "Hostility is a state of the person that may induce him to behave in many apparently different ways. The items on this scale describe some of the ways of behaving that are characteristic of hostile people. If a particular person agrees that he behaves in these ways, he is probably hostile." The investigator might add that the sample of behavior represented by the items on this scale is incomplete, and therefore the scale will not necessarily identify all hostile persons correctly. He might also point out that a personality inventory may be sensitive to only one or a few kinds of hostility. To measure the complete concept accurately would require the inclusion of several additional tests in the battery, including, perhaps, projective devices or observations of the subject in real-life problem-solving or interpersonal situations. These recommendations might be justified on the grounds that hostility is not always a conscious, reportable condition; indeed, the most important hostility may be that of which the subject is not aware. To complicate the issue further, the investigator might point out that hostility could even appear under the guise of love, although it would certainly not be the kind of love most people would care to receive. Last, but by no means least, he might observe that the question of "how much hostility a person has" cannot be meaningfully answered apart from the question of "how it affects him." Moderately high scores on many indices may have an entirely different meaning from a single outstandingly high value on one scale. Is the person who is always irritable or grouchy but who never harms anyone, more or less hostile than the one who is tender and kind 99% of the time but who commits mayhem when he loses his temper? Although both these people are hostile, it can hardly be said that their differences are readily quantified along a single dimension.

It is no wonder that measurement specialists throw up their hands in despair at such difficulties and demand that personologists simplify their concepts to make unidimensional measurement possible, at least in principle. Neither is it surprising that the personality theorist, who is acutely aware of the complexity of his subject, objects to any suggestion that he artificially simplify his concepts by equating them with scores on self-rating scales or other such devices.

If research in personality is to be effective, its concepts must certainly be measurable; but it need not follow that their essential properties must be sacrificed to meet this demand. Although personality constructs are inherently more difficult to assess than some other, more specific variables that interest psychologists, there is nothing in the notion of personality itself that prevents them from being properly measured. It must be admitted that the development of well-delineated theoretical constructs and of instruments that are well suited to the needs of personality research has hardly begun and has too long been avoided; but perhaps an awareness of the issues will facilitate the needed corrective action.

Measurement Operations

It is not feasible to attempt a detailed account of the procedures available to the theorist for expressing his concepts as measures of behavior. The best source for such information is the research literature itself. Measurement operations range from highly structured procedures, like personality inventories, to almost completely unstructured situations, such as projective examinations. Measurements may be *immediate,* in the sense that they consist essentially of factual accounts of directly observed behavior, or they may be *mediated,* as when an inferred process, such as *insight,* is assessed by having judges rate tape recordings of counseling or interview sessions. They may record predominantly physiological functions, like skin conductance; or they may evaluate high level psychological processes, such as the ability to assume the *abstract attitude.* They may bear an obvious relationship to the concept they represent, as items on an attitude scale usually reflect in fairly straightforward fashion the variables they stand for; or they may constitute symbolic manifestations of inferred, underlying states or complexes, as occurs in the expression of personality on word association tests or in drawings of the human figure.

The number and variety of possible instruments is limited only by the ingenuity of the investigator who constructs them. This limitlessness, as much as anything else, compels the student of personality to begin with a clear conception of what he wants to measure and to proceed with the utmost care in developing and establishing the usefulness of the instruments he devises.

Concept-Instrument Relations

Undoubtedly, the relationship between concept and instrument is the most important aspect of measurement construction research planning. It is difficult to overstress the point that an investigator who is testing a theoretical proposition should, ideally, be so committed to his measurements that he is more willing to abandon his hypothesis than to explain away nonsignificant results on the basis of inadequate instrumentation.

An obvious way to achieve the goal of adequate measurement is to simplify concepts to the point where unequivocal, exhaustive operationization becomes possible. But it has already been noted that such concepts do not suit the needs of personality theories, and simplification is not the only possible answer to the problem. There are at least three rather complicated, but more satisfactory alternatives in popular use. When an investigator needs a single measure of a comprehensive concept, he may elect to use a *global index*. When only specific aspects of an inclusive concept are of interest, *partial indices* may be selected for research use. Finally, *multiple indices* are sometimes combined into composite scores in studies of complex or inclusive personality variables.

Global indices. A global index uses a single set of scores or measurement classes to represent a complex concept, without loss of its essential, comprehensive character. If the Kraepelinian scheme for classifying psychological disorders were considered to reflect an internally consistent theory of personality, then psychiatric diagnoses would qualify as a global classification of personality types. School grades are global indices of academic achievement, as are most judgments of success in therapy, level of adjustment, and so forth.

Obviously, global measures involve the integration of many diverse bits of data into a final evaluation that characterizes the whole. They are virtually always mediated, since they can usually be obtained only through the use of trained judges, who apply a more or less standardized and reliable scoring scheme as a guide for drawing complex inferences from data.

Global indices must be distinguished, in principle, from *composite indices,* which are produced by combining more specific measures into a final score, by applying strictly mechanical procedural rules (e.g., adding the scores on separate items of a test to yield a sum). A concrete example of the difference between composite and global indices is to be found in the research by White, Fichtenbaum, and Dollard (1964). The study used, as raw data, transcriptions of initial psychiatric interviews of clients seeking help at an outpatient clinic. The transcriptions were scored according to a standard scheme by which judges assigned plus, minus, or zero values to interview units, as a function of the probable value of each for predicting continuation in treatment. For every interview, sums of unit values were then obtained and compared to produce a prediction of continuation or of dropping out. When the total of the plus ratings exceeded the total of the minus ratings, continuation was predicted; when the minus total exceeded the plus, dropping out was predicted. In short, predictions were derived from a composite index, constructed by adding together measures of the properties of specific transcription units.

The success of the composite index predictor (about 80%) was compared with the success of global indices, obtained from a sample of transcriptions. Global judgments were provided by an experienced psychiatrist and an experienced social worker, who read each transcription and made an overall prediction, without using the scoring scheme. They were about 50% accurate. In this research, both the composite and the global indices involved mediated (or inferential) measurement; but the former was built up by mathematical rules from more specific measures, while the latter was obtained without the use of specific subscores.

Global indices are often more successful than they were in this particular investigation. Nadler, Fink, Shontz, and Brink (1959) studied the ability of occupational therapists and psychologists to make global judgments of Bender-Gestalt reproductions provided by brain-damaged and non-brain-damaged subjects. In this research, global indices were found to be as accurate and reliable as composite scores which were derived from a complex rating system that required intensive training and a good deal of time to apply properly to the data.

Although global indices are generally less explicit than composite scores, they are likely to be more effective in many research situations. It is certainly better to make admittedly global judgments, when necessary, than it is to apply to data a complex quantitative procedure that may suggest a higher degree of methodological sophistication than actually exists. Global indices are most obviously useful when the concept to be measured cannot readily be analyzed into subparts and when the data themselves are qualitative in character (for example, in evaluating the psychodynamic significance of symbolic productions, such as occur in dreams). Properly employed they provide a valuable solution to the problem of assessing complex concepts in personality theory. Carelessly applied, however, they may be worse than useless; for they can convey a false impression of measurement if they do no more than disguise unverifiable impressions in a cloak of apparent objectivity. The fact that an index is global does not exempt it from the necessity of fulfilling the requirements of all good measuring instruments.

Partial indices. If an investigator is interested in only one aspect of a complex construct (e.g., introversion, as reflected in religious values) or if he is unwilling to employ global indices, he may select only one, or perhaps just a few, partial indices and concentrate on these.

For example, stress might be equated only with responses to a self-report inventory or solely with changes in skin conductance. An investigation may then be conducted as if this single indicator were sufficient to the task of measuring the global stress condition. This approach is entirely acceptable if certain conditions are met.

One condition is that the investigator recognize that he is ordinarily measuring only a very limited aspect of the process that concerns him. It is not sufficient merely to assert this recognition; it is required that the measured aspect be explicitly described and that its relation to other aspects of the underlying process also be made known.

A second condition is that there be sound reason to suppose that the particular aspect of the process that is assessed will be related to the behavioral result that is predicted in a hypothesis-testing investigation. It would, for example, be unsuitable to use only a specific index of situational anxiety in a research designed to test the effects of chronic anxiety states on responses of some kind. To do so would be to presume that people who are anxious in one situation also experience anxiety as an enduring condition. The validity of that assertion is as yet far from being established with any degree of certainty. The investigator would therefore be begging a meaningful scientific question, and he would be introducing an unnecessary source of ambiguity into his results. If the reason why a relation should exist between the specific aspect of the concept that is measured and the final behavior that is observed is not evident from existing research, it should certainly be explained on theoretical grounds.

In general, difficulties with the partial index arise from confounding its concrete meaning with the abstract properties of the construct it incompletely represents. Consider, for example, a research by Greenfield and Fellner (1963), in which grade point average in college was taken to be a measure of ego functioning. It was presumed that college grades represent "quality of sustained intellectual performance" and that this constitutes "an aspect of ego function."

It was reasoned that physical disability constitutes a more profound castration experience for males than for females, while obesity carries a greater fear of rejection for females than for males. These experiences and fears would then be expected to affect ego functioning and, hence, grade point averages. A survey of college medical records produced samples of handicapped males and females, obese males and females, and additional comparison groups of nonhandicapped, nonoverweight males and females. Comparisons of grade point averages for these groups were then interpreted as confirming the initial hypothesis.

There are at least two measurement problems in this study. One of these concerns the use of physical states, such as obesity and disability, as indices of certain presumed psychological reactions to these states, that is, castration and rejection experiences. The lack of correspondence between degree or type of disability and degree or type of personality adjustment and organization has been repeatedly demonstrated (Wright, 1960). Thus, existing evidence makes it hard to justify asserting the existence of any particular central psychological state on the basis of a knowledge of somatic conditions alone.

The second problem is the use of grade point average as an index of ego function. Although sustained intellectual effort may be one aspect of a healthy ego, there is certainly reason to doubt that grade point average is an adequate index, even of this aspect of ego functioning. A college grade, as most educators know, is determined by a variety of factors besides ego strength; and it is obvious that a dull student may put forth as much sustained intellectual effort as a bright one and still do less well in the long run. In this study specifically, there are several additional objections that cast doubt on the validity of grade point average as a partial index of ego functioning. One does not know, for instance, whether males with physical disabilities tend to take more technical courses than females with disabilities and therefore experience greater difficulty in completing assignments (e.g., in the laboratory). It is also not known whether obese women and men with disabilities tend to cheat less than others on examinations or to take more difficult courses or whether, perhaps, they come from particularly deprived backgrounds that fit them less well for college activities. It is certainly not unlikely that instructors, because of their own attitudes toward atypical persons, give lower grades to disabled males and obese females than to other groups. There are a host of determinants, other than the ego functioning of the student, that profoundly influence grade point averages. There are, indeed, so many possibilities that it is difficult to see how this index can be used as anything other than what it is: an average rating of success in college class work.

Another example of the problems that can arise in the use of partial indices is afforded by the confusion that has resulted from the attempt to measure the global concept, anxiety, with single scores derived from personality inventory items. Janet Taylor (1953) utilized clinicians' judgments of the contents of MMPI statements to construct a well-known scale for measuring "manifest anxiety," a concept thought to be useful as an index of drive level in human subjects. Anxiety is, of course, a subject of particular interest to personality theorists; and criticisms of the Manifest Anxiety Scale were soon forthcoming from a variety of sources. A major question was whether this scale proposed to reduce the idea of anxiety to merely another form of drive, like hunger and thirst. The answer to this question requires careful explication of the theory behind the original selection of items for the Manifest Anxiety Scale. Taylor (1956) responded by noting that the scale was intended to be a measure of "general drive level," but that its popular title was not inappropriate, considering the way in which the scale was devised. In any case, she argued, manifest anxiety is operationally defined by the numerical value a subject obtains on the test. These statements hardly seem designed to resolve the issue; but Spence, Farber, and McFann (1956) conceded that the name assigned to this scale was "unfortunate," since it was not intended to provide an index of anxiety, as that phenomenon is observed or explained by the personality theorist. It was constructed merely to provide an index of *drive*, as the term is used in learning theory;

and it should never have been construed to do more. That would seem sufficient to establish that the test is irrelevant to the study of personality. Unfortunately, however, the Manifest Anxiety Scale continued to be used as a measure of anxiety; and it was again referred to as a "personality test" in later publications by its originator (Janet Taylor Spence, 1963, p. 22; Spence & Spence, 1964).

While arguments over the nature and measurement of anxiety developed, a vast array of research studies was published that contributed little but confusion for learning theorist and personologist alike. Some of these are reviewed by Sarason (1960); see also Jessor and Hammond (1957) and Kausler and Trapp (1959). Meanwhile, the concept of drive, as applied to human subjects by learning theorists, lost the clarity of its reference; and the term *anxiety* all but lost its usefulness as a concept in legitimate theories of personality.

Partial indices, such as those derived from the Manifest Anxiety Scale, can be extremely useful; but their use must be based on a clear understanding of their specific properties. This understanding must begin with a clear statement, in conceptual terms, of the nature of the more comprehensive concept to be evaluated. There must follow a delimiting of the concept that clarifies which aspects or specific manifestations of its presence are of immediate concern. These must then be expressed in rules of correspondence that leave no uncertainty about the degree to which instrument and concept may be equated. The process is plainly deductive in character, and its steps must be explicit (see especially Jessor & Hammond, 1957). It is to be expected that the conduct of validating research will then lead to subsequent refinement of both concept and measure.

Multiple indices. Still another approach to the measurement of complex constructs utilizes many measures, each designed to tap an important aspect of the concept of interest. Cowen (1960) recommended this approach to the study of stress, as an internal state that is aroused when certain kinds of environmental situations occur in the context of particular mediating organismic conditions. The proper measurement of stress requires that many indicators of its presence be available. Cowen proposed that these are of four types: *affective,* that is, expressions of stress, as evaluated by self-report or by ratings of behavior; *motoric,* as measured by behavior ratings, electromyographic recordings, etc.; *physiological,* as measured presumedly by usual polygraphic devices; and *hormonal,* for example, the assessment of thyroid and adrenal action through evidence provided by measurements of plasma hydrocortisone, serum-bound protein iodine, and urinary hydroxycorticoids.

An investigator who wished to determine the effects of stress (for example, on the performance of a complex behavior, such as might be involved in taking a final examination in a college course) would be able to determine completely the degree or type of stress in his subjects only by obtaining measurements of all four of the above types. Once obtained, he would then have to decide how to combine all available indices into a composite judgment for each subject. He could then correlate stress, as measured in this multiple way, with whatever aspects of final examination performance his theory indicates are likely to be affected by the stress condition. If he decides that there are several types of stress, depending upon individual patternings of stress measures, and that each type produces a different kind of response to final examinations, he might wish to make appropriate predictions and test hypotheses of this type as well.

In this example, it almost goes without saying that the measures of final examination performance should not be the same as those used to assess the central stress state. Evaluation of the student's writing for signs of tremor, for example, might be acceptable as a stress indicator, but not as a measure of the effects of stress on other behaviors. It would simply constitute an index of the motoric aspects of stress itself. Examination grades, verbal output, time spent on each question, and early or late appearance for the examination are measures that would be less subject to such criticism.

The multifaceted approach to the assessment of central states has much to recommend it. It does not oversimplify the processes it evaluates, yet it makes explicit the way in which the operation of those processes is inferred. It has practical drawbacks however. It is not usually easy or feasible for a single investigator to make all the required measurements, particularly when highly specialized assessments are involved. Even when all the necessary scores can be obtained, the task of integrating them into composite indices cannot usually be accomplished in a standard fashion that is universally acceptable. Finally, there is the difficulty that in many researches of this type the process of measurement itself may interfere with the operation of the variable of interest. If multiple measures are taken during the evaluation of dependent behavioral effects, the process of measurement may interfere (if only mechanically) with responses. For example, a student cannot very well write a final examination with GSR electrodes fastened to one hand and a tremorpedal under the other.

Many of the difficulties associated with multiple indices will doubtless be resolved as improvements in technology become available. For the present, however, the proper use of multiple indices seems to demand a higher level of instrumental and mathematical sophistication than exists in the study of personality. A multifaceted relationship between concept and measurement is probably ideal; but it seems likely that personality research will have to content itself with global and partial indices for some time to come. Carefully developed and employed, these should be quite adequate to challenge the skill of most investigators.

VALIDATION

Cronbach and Meehl (1955) are to be given credit for outlining the several ways by which validation may be accomplished. They spoke of four types of validity: *predictive, concurrent, content,* and *construct* (see also Cronbach, 1960, pp. 103-123). Of these, the last two are probably the most important to the personologist; but each will be discussed in the sections to follow.

Predictive and Concurrent Validity

Predictive and *concurrent* validity are referred to as *criterion-oriented* procedures because a score can be obtained or already exists that provides an acceptably accurate measure of the characteristic or behavior the new instrument was designed to evaluate. A study by Briggs, Wirt, and Johnson (1961), which is discussed again in a later chapter of this book (chapter 5), provides an example of an attempt to establish the predictive validity of a measurement based, in part, on MMPI data. In this research, the later occurrence of juvenile delinquency was predicted for boys who showed specific test signs. A follow-up study was conducted to determine the actual accuracy of these predictions, as a means for judging the predictive validity of the test signs themselves.

Concurrent validity is usually involved when one instrument is designed to replace another. For example, short forms of intelligence tests are often validated by demonstrating the existence of a high correlation between scores on the briefer version and scores derived from the complete examination (e.g., Satz & Mogel, 1962; Estes, 1963; Karras, 1963; Pauker, 1963). The scores on the complete examination are the criteria in this case.

When it is possible to discover an acceptable criterion, it is well to establish the concurrent or predictive validity of a new instrument. Unfortunately, criteria appropriate for assessing the validity of personality measures are not easily obtained. In some cases, judges' ratings, or similar estimates, may be used as criteria, for example, in the assessment of therapy outcomes; but the problem of establishing the validity and reliability of the ratings themselves must then be faced. Furthermore, it is generally thought that the criterion ought to be a better measure of the concept than the test; and it is not uncommon in these situations for the researcher to feel that when rater and measurement disagree, the latter is more likely to be correct than the former.

By the method of successive approximation, in which new and presumably better measures are validated against poorer existing instruments, it is sometimes possible to improve measures considerably. Intelligence testing is a case in point. The original Binet scale was validated against school performance (essentially as rated by teachers). Later tests of intelligence were then validated against revisions of the Binet test, which had become more acceptable than the original criteria through continued successful use. Wechsler (1958, p. 108) noted this turn of events in his analysis of the validity of the Wechsler Adult Intelligence Scale. He had, himself, correlated his original scale, the Wechsler-Bellevue, against the Stanford-Binet, reporting a high correlation between IQ's derived from both scales on a group of 75 subjects, 14 to 16 years of age (Wechsler, 1944, p. 129). Wechsler's scales, in turn, have since become the criteria for numerous assessments of the concurrent validity of new intelligence tests.

It is possible that such "bootstrap" methods will bring about a similar course of evolution in the development of important measures of personality functions or organizations. However, the present state of the art and the complexity of the problem make it seem unlikely in the near future.

Content Validity

An important feature of the procedures just discussed is that they are essentially quantitative in character. In predictive and concurrent validity studies, the matters of major importance are the magnitude and statistical significance of test-criterion correlation values. Neither procedure requires explication of the logical relationship between the concept measured and the content of the test instrument.

By contrast, the essence of *content* validity is its stress upon the qualitative features of measuring devices. To possess content validity, the items of a test must fairly sample or represent the defining properties of a proposed construct. Much discussion in this chapter has already been devoted to explaining the need for content validity in the construction of partial indices of personality variables or characteristics. Content validity is, of course, required in all deductive measures. Its importance may be most fully realized if one considers that in principle it is the only type of validity that can be absolutely demanded from a measurement of a theoretically defined characteristic. If an investigator designs his measurement procedure to reflect his concept faithfully and if the resulting instrument evidences satisfactory reliability (a characteristic that is discussed later), he may then claim that his test is complete and valid. As long as he is willing to equate measure with concept, he may proceed to use the instrument in research. Of course, he will not have established the value of the concept itself by this procedure. That can only be demonstrated by showing that the instrument enables the investigator to make meaningful predictions about behavior.

A test of creativity. It might be well to examine a research in which the relationship between theory and instrument is particularly explicit. Such a study is the one by Mednick (1962), describing the development and preliminary validation of a measure of creativity, the Remote Associations Test.

Creativity was defined by Mednick as the "forming of associative elements into new combinations which either meet specified requirements or are in some way useful." These new combinations may be formed when the environment fortuitously presents contiguous stimuli that evoke associative elements never before connected in thought (serendipity). New combinations may also be formed on the basis of similarities among associative elements aroused by processes such as stimulus generalization. Finally, common elements may mediate associations that might not otherwise have appeared; for example, a theoretical construct like *reaction formation* may mediate the association by similarity of behaviors that appear superficially to be quite different (euphoria and pessimism, for instance). Individual differences in creativity may be accounted for in terms of the availability to the person of materials or stimuli that promote creative association, the type and strength of associative organization that characterizes particular subjects (e.g., the stronger the existing associative bonds, the less probable a creative solution), the number of associative possibilities open to the person, and the cognitive style that is typical of his thought processes.

As the author himself put it, this definition of creativity "dictates the structure of the test." Each test item therefore consists of three words "drawn from mutually remote associative clusters" (i.e., that do not appear to be related at first sight). The subject is then required to find an associative (not a logical or conceptual) link that connects all three words. For example, if the stimuli were "rat, blue, cottage," the correct answer would be "cheese." The test consists of thirty items, and the subject is allowed forty minutes to complete it. The score is the number right.

Mednick's theory suggests predictions about individual differences in test performance that may be tested for confirmation of the usefulness of the instrument. Some of the methods employed for establishing the construct validity of the Remote Associations Test are considered in the next section.

Construct Validity

Since few concepts that are of interest to personality theorists can be satisfactorily evaluated against acceptable criteria, it is not usually possible to establish the validity of a personality measure in a single research that merely correlates one set of test scores with another. It is often possible, however, to show that predictions de-

rived from the broad theory of which the measured concept is a part
are confirmed when subjected to empirical test. Thus, for example,
there may be no satisfactory criterion measure of a complex variable
like anxiety. Nonetheless, the construct validity of a test designed to
measure one aspect of it (perhaps "susceptibility to situational anxiety") may be established in part, if it can be shown that high
scorers display more physiological signs of tension than low scorers
when exposed to a supposedly anxiety-producing situation. The
validity of this measure might be further demonstrated if it were
also shown that scores on the test correlated significantly, though
not necessarily at high levels, with scores on tests designed to measure other aspects of anxiety, but did not correlate significantly with
tests designed to measure theoretically unrelated concepts, such as
intelligence.

It should be apparent that construct validation is a general
approach rather than a specific type of research design. It would be
rare, indeed, for construct validity to be established in one research
project. The focus of construct validation research is on the empirical utility of the concept, as it is measured by the proposed instrument. It follows that research findings may be "fed back" to the
concept itself as well as to the features of the instrument. Both may
be modified, improved, and made more explicit as results suggest
appropriate changes.

Several types of research have been suggested as being suitable
for purposes of construct validation. Groups may be selected that
are expected to be different, on the basis of theoretical properties
ascribed to the concept. Confirmation of these differences on the
proposed measure tends to support the validity of the instrument.
Correlational methods, including factor analysis, may also be employed, provided that the nature of the concept permits prediction
of resulting factor structures with adequate univocality. Analyses of
correlations among specific test items or of correlations between
responses to specific items and the total score may be used in similar
fashion. The conditions under which measurements are taken may
be systematically varied, as in classical experimentation, to produce
predicted changes in measurement values. Another possibility is to
observe and analyze the test-taking process itself. Careful observation and analysis of subjects' behaviors while they are providing the
required responses sometimes suggest improvements in the concept
or the instrument. Introspective reports, obtained from the subject

while responding or following administration of the instrument, could prove helpful in much the same way.

Consider again the example of the Remote Associations Test (RAT). Scores on this test were correlated with faculty ratings of student performance in a school of architecture. They were also compared with faculty ratings of the research creativity of first year graduate students in psychology. In both situations the results were judged to be consistent with the proposition that the test measures creative abilities. RAT scores were found to correlate slightly negatively with grade point averages of undergraduate college students; but high scorers were found to receive higher grades from teachers who were considered to be less dogmatic while low scorers received higher grades from more dogmatic teachers. Other researches established a positive relationship between RAT scores and liberality of attitudes toward sexual morality and between RAT scores and vocational interest patterns, the higher scorers tending to show greater commonality of interests with members of creative professions, such as art, psychology, and medicine. These differences were independent of variations in intellectual ability. RAT scores were also found to correlate positively, but not at a high level, with a questionnaire index of originality and to correlate negatively with a measure of conformity.

In other studies RAT scores were correlated with performance on different measures of associative behavior. For example, subjects were asked to produce as many associations as possible to stimulus words or to produce anagrams based on the letters in a given stimulus word. Again comparison of results indicated that individuals tended to score consistently on the two types of measures of associative behavior.

Finally, high and low scoring groups were compared in an experimental situation designed to test the hypothesis that creativity serves to satisfy a need for improbable associative stimulation. The stimuli in this experiment were word pairs, presented on 3 x 5 cards. Each pair consisted of a noun and a non-noun (e.g., verb, adjective, adverb). The subjects were to respond to these stimuli by choosing one or the other of the two words. In the experimental group, consisting of both high and low RAT scorers, noun choices were selectively reinforced: the examiner provided an improbable association only when the subject read a noun. Probable (i.e., presumedly nonreinforcing) associations were provided for other choices. In the control group, which also consisted of high and low RAT scorers, probable associations were provided to all responses. These were not expected to be selectively reinforcing to any subjects. It was supposed that if the provision of remote associations were, in fact, selectively reinforcing, the high RAT scorers in the experimental group should show an increase in their choice of nouns over the 160 trials involved in the investigation. The comparison groups should show no change. Since the results were in line with predictions (the low scoring experimental group even showed a decrease in noun selection), it was concluded that creative association satisfies a need in highly creative subjects.

Our concern is not with the tenability of the theory involved in Mednick's approach to the problem of creativity or even with the question of whether the RAT is valid, but with the variety of methods employed to establish the validity of the Remote Associations Test. The example these investigations provide is a convincing demonstration that there is no single measure of the validity of a measuring instrument. Correlations with criteria, demonstrations of predictable correlations with instruments measuring related functions, confirmation of hypotheses derived from the theory, of which the instrument is, itself, an expression—all of these provide evidence which is relevant to the judgment of the validity of the instrument itself. None is sufficient in isolation.

So varied are the possibilities for construct validation research that Cronbach and Meehl maintained that the determination of validity in this way "is not essentially different from the general scientific procedures for developing and confirming theories" (1955, p. 300). This does not necessarily imply that the study of personality is nothing but a process of construct validation, but it may suggest that the problem of validity is one that must be taken very seriously if progress is to be made in personality research.

RELIABILITY

Psychometricians often distinguish between the validity and the reliability of a measurement. Validity, as has been shown, is a judgment, based on content analysis and upon accumulated research evidence, of the usefulness of a particular instrument as a measure of the concept it was intended to represent.

Reliability also involves judgment, since it may be evaluated in several ways. (See Guilford [1954, pp. 373-398] and Anastasi [1954, pp. 94-119] for discussions of some specific procedures for determining reliability.) One general form of reliability is judged by the ability of the instrument to differentiate among individuals when the test is administered once to a large number of subjects. This type of reliability provides an estimate of the *sensitivity* of a measure. Its basic premise is readily understood if one realizes that a ruler calibrated in eighths of an inch is more sensitive to differences in length than a ruler that measures only to the nearest half inch. It follows, then, that a psychological test which spreads subjects out along a finely divided continuum is more sensitive than one that bunches them up all in one place.

A second form of reliability is involved when more than one measure is used to assess the same variable (as when multiple raters judge behavior). This form of reliability requires consensus among measures (raters). It provides an estimate of *reliability of agreement*. Procedures that utilize equivalent forms of the same test or that involve correlating subjects' scores on one half of the items of a test with their scores on the other half may also be considered forms of agreement reliability.

Yet a third form of reliability requires the measure to make consistent discriminations among subjects when the instrument is administered on more than one occasion. This type of reliability provides an estimate of the *temporal*, or *situational, stability* of the measure.

Not all forms of reliability are equally demanded by measures of psychological functions, particularly those of interest to the personologist. High sensitivity may be a desirable, though not universally attainable, characteristic for all measures; and maximal agreement reliability is certainly needed where multiple estimates are obtained. Temporal stability, however, is required only when the concept is theoretically characterized as one that is expected to remain constant over a period of time. If experimental manipulation is introduced between test and retest, it is possible that high temporal stability would be considered undesirable.

Suppose that a group were divided into high and low scorers on a measure of aggressiveness and that the high scorers were subjected to a treatment designed to reduce aggressiveness, while the low scorers were subjected to a treatment designed to increase it. If the treatments were successful and a retest showed appropriate changes in mean aggression scores, the overall correlation between test and retest would be low, perhaps even negative. This would occur because individuals will have shifted their positions relative to each other in the total group; and it is this type of shift to which the usual indices of temporal reliability are highly sensitive. Under these conditions the careless investigator might find himself in the difficult position of having to assert that the test is valid because it is unreliable.

Temporal stability of some characteristics may be extremely important. A measure of a more or less permanent characteristic, such as life style or ego strength, would be expected to remain consistent over at least a period of several weeks, if the subjects were not in some form of psychological treatment. The nature of these variables is such that no instruments designed to assess them could be considered satisfactory unless it were shown that the scores they produce are as stable as the concept they represent. Here is a situation in which an investigator might be willing to sacrifice even considerable sensitivity to achieve a sufficiently stable measure of these complex but most important theoretical concepts. Even if he were able to accomplish only a crude dichotomous ordering of subjects into high and low groups, he might feel his effort to be worthwhile, provided the temporal consistency of the grouping is maximal. Similarly, in some instances, agreement reliability may be more valued than other forms. Mediated ratings of observed behavior must always be substantiated by evidence of satisfactory interjudge reliability; and an increase in level of agreement among judges may well be worth some sacrifice of sensitivity, if a choice must be made.

The same principles apply to the assessment of reliability as to the judgment of validity. There is no single approach that is to be universally recommended. The type and degree of reliability required in a measuring instrument is a function of the nature of the concept being evaluated and of the uses to which the instrument will be put.

COMMENTS AND CONCLUSIONS

In constructing and validating measures of the variables which interest him, the personality theorist is confronted with, and must resolve, all the key questions that face any scientific investigator. First, he must define the theoretical entity that concerns him. To accomplish this successfully, it is necessary not only to state a formal definition of the concept itself but to express with clarity its relationship with other concepts in the overall theoretical structure. This, in turn, requires that other variables be identified and defined with clarity. Next, that concept must be tied to measurement operations by specifying appropriate rules of correspondence. The investigator must decide whether a single global measure is sufficient to carry all the weight of the meaning that theory ascribes to the concept or whether partial or multiple indices are required. If multiple indices seem to be called for, he must consider how they are to be combined for research purposes. He must decide whether his measure is to be immediate or mediated, that is, whether his instruments are to yield indices that may be directly identified with the concept or whether the type of information he gathers from his subjects is then to be interpreted by expert judges, trained to draw reliable inferences from the data. He must then devise an instrument, the content of which clearly represents the concept he intends to measure; and he must be prepared to spell out, in considerable detail if necessary, the relationship between theory and test items or measurement procedures. Finally, he must undertake research to establish that the concept, as measured by his instrument, leads to meaningful predictions of correlations with other measures or to the experimental confirmation of hypotheses derived from the theory of which the concept is, itself, a part. He must establish that his measures are stable and consistent when theory dictates that they should be stable and consistent, and that they change appropriately when theory dictates that they should do so.

These requirements provide a guide to scientific thought that enables the investigator to proceed intelligently in the conduct of his research. They also provide a set of criteria by which published reports of research may be evaluated. Almost every systematic investigation involves some form of measurement; and every measurement should be able to withstand the scrutiny of careful logical and empirical analysis. To argue that careful measurement is undesirable is to argue against the methods of science itself.

Groups and Individuals

It is strange that the worth of an instrument designed to evaluate particular individuals can be assessed to the modern psychologist's satisfaction only by the conduct of investigations that involve large groups of subjects. To the unsophisticated it would seem obvious that a personality measure that is to be used for the description of single individuals ought to establish its utility through research that involves single individuals. Strictly speaking, the fact that a group mean or average on a test changes predictably rarely implies that individual scores will do so as well. Even a high correlation leaves a good deal of individual variance unaccounted for.

A case in point is the research by Mumpower (1964). This investigation dealt with intelligence testing, but its implications for personality measurement are obvious. Mumpower noted the tendency among practicing psychologists to substitute short forms of the Wechsler Intelligence Scale for Children (WISC) for the full examination procedure. These short forms have, in the past, been demonstrated to possess remarkably high concurrent validity. Correlations with full scale IQ's have generally run from .87 to .95, values which ordinarily "would be welcomed with open arms." To establish the utility of such values for individual cases, Mumpower selected 50 case studies of exceptional children, all of whom had been administered the WISC. The Block Design and Vocabulary subtest scale scores were used as a short form, and full scale IQ's were estimated from these two subtests. The correlation between long-form and short-form IQ's was .95. There was no significant difference between the mean IQ values obtained from the two forms. (Correlations are not sensitive to differences between means, so a separate evaluation had to be made.)

Mumpower then established a general classification scheme, such as is commonly used in clinical and research practice, by which his cases were subdivided into ten groups, from "exceptionally able" to "retarded custodial." The cases were subdivided twice: once on the basis of fullscale IQ, once on the basis of short-form IQ. Of the 50 double classifications, 39 were found to agree. In the other 11 cases the classifications differed, and the average IQ discrepancy was found to be 9.5 points. A second study used two other tests as estimates of overall IQ (Bender-Gestalt and Full-Range Picture Vocabulary). Again, although the correlation between the two sets of IQ's was .92, twelve of fifty subjects were misclassified by the briefer tests. For these twelve cases, the average IQ discrepancy between tests was 15.4 points.

Mumpower correctly pointed out the importance of clinical decisions in the individual case and raised the question of whether psychologists should be willing to accept a measurement that "is likely to be wrong in one out of every four or five cases." The implied answer to this question is, of course, "no" as long as better measures are available.

The question for research in personality is much the same as that raised by Mumpower for the practicing clinician; but the issue in personality is less clear-cut. For the current choice is usually not between an instrument that makes many errors and one that makes a few, but between instruments that do a poor job and instruments that do not do the job at all. The goal of being able to measure accurately the behavior of every subject in the sample is a long way off, but it must be more closely approximated than is currently the case if personality research is to make significant progress.

The measurement situation in personality research would be considerably improved if tests and examinations were validated not only through group research, but also through the intensive study of series of individual subjects, each of whom provides an independent basis for judging the validity of the instrument. One way to accomplish this would be to select particular persons who respond in known ways to the new measurement and to expose each subject to sets of systematically varying conditions that are tailor-made to elicit responses predicted to occur by the theory from which the new instrument was devised. Extensive experimentation with individuals, combined with the collection of introspective data and the careful observation of both test-taking and experimental behavior, might then be employed to evaluate the construct validity of the instrument.

Another possibility would be to have each subject's perform-ances on a variety of nonexperimental tasks observed and rated for more naturally occurring manifestations of the processes supposedly measured by the instrument. Concretely, if the measure character-ized a given subject as an extravert, data might be obtained from his associates regarding his daily activities or he might be followed about and observed by a trained rater, during his normal daily routine, for evidence of extraversion.

Still another possibility would be to select, in advance, a spe-cific subject who simply must score in certain ways on the instru-ment if anyone is to accept it as valid. If a test is intended to measure religiosity, it might be a good idea to find the most reli-gious person in town and have him take the test. If that person does not achieve a high score, the instrument must certainly be useless.

There is actually nothing radical about these proposals. One of the original purposes of the statistics that are commonly employed in group research was to summarize, condense, and simplify data obtained from the study of individual cases. The present source of difficulty is the fact that psychologists often seem to be more con-cerned with summarizations than with the individual cases these summarizations represent. They all too willingly label as error those data that are inconvenient to their general purposes, and they are prone to ignore the fact that important phenomena in particular cases are often concealed in massed data. A too narrow concern for central tendency differences can easily lead the investigator away from findings that may have significant implications for the study of personality.

Consider the situation in which groups of subjects are meas-ured with the same instrument and in which significant differences are found between indices of variability within groups. Heteroge-neity of variance sometimes occurs when a given condition (a drug, an illness or a disability, an experimental situation) influences some subjects strongly but leaves others relatively unaffected. For ex-ample, the ingestion of alcohol may lower the inhibitions of some subjects but not others. When this happens, the investigator who seeks only significant group differences is likely to think only that a large component of error has somehow entered his data. He will then search out a way to eliminate or adjust for this error so that a purer test of the general influence of the independent variable may be achieved.

Most such investigators have been given the impression in statistics courses that heterogeneity of variance is to be considered, at the very least, an inconvenience that introduces annoying complications into the use of conventional, parametric tests of statistical significance. To the psychologist who is truly interested in individual responses, however, these same findings would not necessarily suggest that the research is faulty. They would, rather, point up worthwhile research problems that should be pursued further. Such an investigator would certainly want to know the nature of the subject differences that account for differential reactivity to the independent variable. Indeed, that could well become his most important concern; for if he could solve this problem, he would be in a position to produce or describe on demand groups of persons or individual subjects who will respond in predictable ways to the condition of interest.

All in all, it has probably become too easy for psychologists to write off measurement problems as exceptions to the overall tendencies of groups. But the personality theorist who wishes to measure an important theoretical variable should, in principle, be so concerned with the accuracy of his conceptualization and his measurement procedures that he allows no exception to escape his careful attention. The subject who, by all other available criteria, is obviously a person with a strong ego, but who scores at a low level on a proposed measure of ego strength, is the very person from whom a great deal can be learned about the nature and measurement of ego strength. To ignore him or to submerge him in a larger group, so that his individuality becomes obscured in a mean, standard deviation, or correlation coefficient, is to throw away valuable information that could lead to significant advances in measurement construction and validity.

References

ANASTASI, ANNE. *Psychological testing.* New York: Macmillan, 1954.
BRIGGS, P. F., WIRT, R. D., & JOHNSON, ROCHELLE. An application of predictive tables to the study of delinquency. *J. consult. Psychol.,* 1961, 25, 46-50.
COWEN, E. L. Personality, motivation and clinical phenomena. In L. H. Lofquist (Ed.), *Psychological research and rehabilitation.* Washington, D.C.: American Psychological Association, 1960. Pp. 112-171.

CRONBACH, L. J. *Essentials of psychological testing.* (2nd ed.) New York: Harper & Row, 1960.

CRONBACH, L. J., & MEEHL, P. E. Construct validity in psychological tests. *Psychol. Bull.,* 1955, *52,* 281-302.

ESTES, BETSY W. A note on the Satz-Mogel abbreviation of the WAIS. *J. clin. Psychol.,* 1963, *19,* 103.

FISKE, D. W. Problems in measuring personality. In J. M. Wepman & R. W. Heine (Eds.), *Concepts of personality.* Chicago: Aldine, 1963. Pp. 449-473.

GOODENOUGH, FLORENCE L. *Mental testing.* New York: Holt, Rinehart and Winston, 1949.

GREENFIELD, N. S., & FELLNER, C. H. Differential correlates of physical handicap and obesity with grade point averages in college males and females. *J. clin. Psychol.,* 1963, *19,* 263.

GUILFORD, J. P. *Psychometric methods.* (2nd ed.) New York: McGraw-Hill, 1954.

JESSOR, R., & HAMMOND, K. R. Construct validity and the Taylor anxiety scale. *Psychol. Bull.,* 1957, *54,* 161-170. (In Mednick & Mednick, pp. 245-254 [see References, chapter 1, above].)

KARRAS, A. Predicting full-scale WAIS I.Q.'s from WAIS subtests for a psychiatric population. *J. clin. Psychol.,* 1963, *19,* 100.

KAUSLER, D. H., & TRAPP, E. P. Methodological considerations in the construct validation of drive-oriented scales. *Psychol. Bull.,* 1959, *56,* 152-157. (In Mednick & Mednick, pp. 255-260 [see References, chapter 1, above].)

MEDNICK, S. A. The associative basis of the creative process. *Psychol. Rev.,* 1962, *69,* 220-232. (In Mednick & Mednick, pp. 583-596 [see References, chapter 1, above].)

MUMPOWER, D. L. The fallacy of the short form. *J. clin. Psychol.,* 1964, *20,* 111-113.

NADLER, E. B., FINK, S. L., SHONTZ, F. C., & BRINK, R. W. Objective scoring *vs.* clinical evaluation of the Bender-Gestalt. *J. clin. Psychol.,* 1959, *15,* 39-41.

PAUKER, J. D. A split-half abbreviation of the WAIS. *J. clin. Psychol.,* 1963, *19,* 98-100.

SARASON, I. G. Empirical findings and theoretical problems in the use of anxiety scales. *Psychol. Bull.,* 1960, *57,* 403-415. (In Sarason, pp. 23-33 [see References, chapter 1, above].)

SATZ, P., & MOGEL, S. An abbreviation of the WAIS for clinical use. *J. clin. Psychol.,* 1962, *18,* 77-79.

SPENCE, JANET TAYLOR. Learning theory and personality. In J. M. Wepman & R. W. Heine (Eds.), *Concepts of personality.* Chicago: Aldine, 1963. Pp. 3-30.

SPENCE, K. W., FARBER, I. E., & McFANN, H. H. The relation of anxiety (drive) level to performance in competitional and noncompetitional paired-associates learning. *J. exp. Psychol.,* 1956, *52,* 296-305. (In Mednick & Mednick, pp. 232-242 [see References, chapter 1, above].)

SPENCE, K. W., & SPENCE, JANET T. Relation of conditioning to manifest anxiety, extraversion, and rigidity. *J. abnorm. soc. Psychol.,* 1964, *68,* 144-149.

TAYLOR, JANET A. A personality scale of manifest anxiety. *J. abnorm. soc. Psychol.,* 1953, *48,* 285-290.

TAYLOR, JANET A. Drive theory and manifest anxiety. *Psychol. Bull.,* 1956, *53,* 303-320. (In Mednick & Mednick, pp. 205-222 [see References, chapter 1, above].)

UNDERWOOD, B. J. *Psychological research.* New York: Appleton-Century-Crofts, 1957.

WECHSLER, D. *The measurement of adult intelligence.* (3rd ed.) Baltimore: Williams & Wilkins, 1944.

WECHSLER, D. *The measurement and appraisal of adult intelligence.* (4th ed.) Baltimore: Williams & Wilkins, 1958.

WHITE, ALICE M., FICHTENBAUM, L., & DOLLARD, J. Measure for predicting dropping out of psychotherapy. *J. consult. Psychol.,* 1964, *28,* 326-332.

WRIGHT, BEATRICE A. *Physical disability—a psychological approach.* New York: Harper & Row, 1960.

4

Case studies

The psychologist who wishes to study the complex psychological organization of an individual human being often employs a method that is essentially descriptive, the *case study*. Case studies are familiar tools in many professions. The fields of social work, psychiatry, and clinical psychology rely heavily upon case reports for recording and communicating descriptions of individual patients. Physicians also often publish detailed reports of patients with particularly interesting or informative physical pathologies.

Case studies are not restricted in principle to the description of a single individual. Sociologists and anthropologists have long employed the method for dealing with the behaviors and organizations of groups of people in social units. Reports of this nature frequently possess considerable interest for personality theory, since they sometimes bear directly upon hypotheses regarding the development of personal psychological organization. A classic example of the use of group-oriented case studies in the field of personality is Kardiner's theoretical analysis of anthropological information on the Marquesan and the Tanala and Betsileo cultures (1939). Using as basic data descriptive material collected by Linton, Kardiner raised questions about the validity of certain tenets of psychoanalytic theory. He attempted to show that in Marquesan culture hunger drives and sexual motives play entirely different roles in personality structure than they do in our society. He also attempted to demonstrate that the economic conversion from dry to wet rice cultivation, which changed the overall society of the Tanala of Madagascar into a new form (Betsileo), accounted for significant differences in basic personality structure through its influence on family patterns, social values, and interpersonal behaviors. Kardiner felt that the study of these cultures indicated that economic and social factors are more important in determining personality than is suggested by an almost exclusively instinctual, libido-oriented theory, such as orthodox psychoanalysis.

As useful as ethnographic reports are to psychology, they do not constitute the stock-in-trade of the student of personality. Although he may analyze and relate sociological and anthropological materials to subjects of his own interest, the personality theorist does not ordinarily collect such data himself; and he is not usually qualified to do so in systematic fashion. The present focus is therefore primarily on case studies of individuals rather than of groups. The basic characteristics of the case-study method probably do not differ greatly in the two situations.

Controls

The case study may be characterized in a negative way by its lack of control over the variables operating in the data collection situation. Next to a purely anecdotal strategy, which does not qualify as a research method, it is the least systematic of all approaches to the study of personality. In its simplest form it consists merely of reports of experiences gained through such activities as diagnosing, treating, living with, and talking to individual persons. Sometimes its most crucial data consist primarily of impressions. Frequently the case that is presented was not even sought out in advance.

It often happens that an interesting or unusual person appears fortuitously, say in clinical practice, and the researcher decides that the case merits being reported in the scientific literature. Or it may be that a psychologist crystallizes a theoretical idea that he thinks would be well exemplified by cases he had dealt with in the past. Under these circumstances, he may turn to his files, or simply to his memory, for specific instances that bear out his new conception. He may organize these instances into a formal presentation for communication to his colleagues in the form of a case study.

In many such instances the purposes for which the initial data were collected are not specifically those to which the data are eventually applied. Information from routine psychological examinations, administered primarily to establish diagnostic and treatment recommendations, are often employed. Routinely collected transcriptions of therapy sessions are also common sources of case study data.

It is almost too easy to view the lack of systematic control exerted in case studies as a weakness, perhaps a fatal one, in the method itself. In the study of personality, however, this apparent defect actually identifies the method's most useful features. Case studies have two distinct advantages. First, they are well suited to research on the subject that is of universal interest to personologists, the particular individual. Second, they have the potential for presenting that individual in his full complexity; they do not require that the contextual and organizational properties of human behavior and experience be ignored or artificially eliminated. They are capable of yielding an overall picture of the naturally functioning person that can scarcely be obtained in any other way.

Usually case studies are also rich in speculative possibilities. They suggest new ideas and challenge old ones; they offer opportunities for insights that other methods ignore or eliminate in their approaches. Because they often deal with qualitative materials, the observational and intellectual scope of the researcher remains unimpeded. They give both the observer and the subject a maximum of flexibility of approach and expression; and they usually interfere minimally with the natural situation. In this way, case studies often provide a kind of information that is not obtainable under highly controlled conditions.

These advantages are not to be despised, for it is precisely the particularity of the organized individual that is the subject matter of personality theory. Neither are they to be greatly exaggerated, for certain weaknesses of the method cannot be ignored. Case studies rarely provide conclusive evidence for or against a point of view, even when they are well executed. Their lack of control usually leaves room for many questions about and diverse explanations of their data; and it is virtually impossible to establish convincingly in a single case report that the author's opinions are the only acceptable alternatives under the circumstances. There are legitimate purposes that are unquestionably better served by the case-study method than by any other. Although hypothesis testing is not one of them, the rest are legitimate and important. The various possibilities are examined briefly in the following sections.

USES

Case studies most commonly serve more than one purpose, but it is convenient and useful to distinguish among seven broad possibilities that are commonly represented in the literature. The purpose of a given case study is not always stated clearly by its author, and the reader is frequently left to infer it from the study itself. Even when a purpose is explicitly stated in an introductory paragraph, it is often supplemented, and sometimes contradicted, by material that comes later. The key to the identification of purposes is usually to be found in the discussion or conclusions section of the report.

The Remarkable Case

A case may be written up and published simply because the author has had an unusual opportunity to observe a particularly interesting phenomenon. A patient in therapy, for example, may demonstrate the characteristics of a certain diagnostic group with uncommon clarity, or he may display a type of personality structure that has rarely been carefully observed by others.

This use of the case study is more familiar in medicine than in psychology. Physicians are aware of the value of the atypical or remarkable case, and it is not uncommon for them to present in minute detail the full range of clinical data available on a patient with a rare or unique somatic condition. Psychiatry also employs the case-study method to advantage; and much of the psychoanalytic literature is devoted to the purpose of communicating descriptions of particularly intriguing cases in therapy.

One of the most striking examples of a remarkable case is afforded by the report of detailed clinical material obtained from a woman with a multiple personality (Thigpen & Cleckley, 1954). Despite ubiquitous interest in multiple personalities, it is, in fact, rare for any clinician to deal with this condition directly or to collect any sizable amount of data on the subject. Persons presenting clear-cut evidence of nearly complete splits in personality organization are simply not met with frequently. The case of Eve White, of course, became famous among behavioral scientists; and her unusual, tripartite personality intrigued movie makers and publishers of popular books as well. Popularity aside, however, the careful description of this woman's behavior revealed at least as much about the general nature of multiple personality and related conditions (e.g., fugue states and amnesia) as might have been accomplished by any number of carefully controlled laboratory studies or by even a substantial mass of anecdotal accounts.

Another example may be drawn from the report of the case of Oleg (Beier & Bauer, 1955), a defector who crossed the Berlin border from East into West Germany. This case is particularly interesting because it makes publicly available psychological information which cannot be otherwise obtained by the vast majority of interested behavioral scientists.

Some other especially interesting examples of this use of case material are afforded by Plank and Horwood's description (1961) of the psychological reactions of a four-year-old girl to the amputation of her leg and by Joseph and Tabor's report (1961) of the simultaneous psychoanalysis of a pair of young adult male twins with markedly different types of adjustment problems. The latter paper is immediately followed, in the same volume, by a theoretical discussion of the problem of identification in twins (Leonard, 1961). In this paper, Leonard uses case materials in an essentially illustrative way, which characterizes another important purpose of the case study.

Exemplifying or Illustrating A Point of View

Exemplifying or illustrating a point of view is perhaps the most obvious use to which case material may be put, in psychology and in related professions. It frequently happens that a complex, abstract theoretical idea cannot be adequately conveyed in conceptual terms alone. To make such an idea clear requires that it be concretized by specific example or illustration; the case study is the choice method for such a purpose.

Shontz (1962) used the case study for illustrative purposes in his exposition of the problems of psychological adjustment to severe chronic illness. In this paper, material from a book by Roy Campanella was quoted to illustrate and make meaningful the concepts of *threat, neutralization,* and *positive motivation.*

In two familiar works, White has made excellent use of selected case material to facilitate his presentation of the subject matter of abnormal psychology (1956) and personality (1952). White is particularly sensitive to the fact that science has sorely neglected the study of ordinary people as they conduct the affairs of daily life, and he feels that this neglect has produced a partial view of human nature that fails to portray it accurately. To demonstrate the usefulness of the case study approach, White (1952) presented detailed material on three persons: Hartley Hale, physician and scientist; Joseph Kidd, business assistant; Joyce Kingsley, housewife and social worker. The interview was his basic tool for data collection, although psychological tests and examinations were also employed. Each case was described separately, and the three descriptions were related to each other to produce a picture of psychological growth that the author felt was capable of doing justice to the three deterministic views of man (the social, the biological, and the psychodynamic) without reducing him to a passive reactor to forces beyond his own creative control.

Demonstration of Technique

Case materials are almost universally used to demonstrate how particular examination or therapeutic procedures are employed. Roger's use of transcriptions of nondirective counseling sessions served this purpose, at least in part. Publishers of tests commonly use case studies for demonstration purposes. Klopfer and Davidson (1962) used detailed case studies to demonstrate Rorschach scoring procedures; Holtzman, Thorpe, Swartz, and Herron (1961, pp. 222-249) utilized a similar device to describe and explain their own inkblot test.

An ingenious use of case material for demonstrating techniques is shown in one of Beck's books (1960) about the Rorschach. Beck's intention in this particular volume was not to teach Rorschach administration or to test specific propositions derived from personality theory. He described his objective as being "to demonstrate the processes entering into the interpretation of a Rorschach test protocol" (p. vi). To accomplish this purpose he presented the complete examination records of ten patients in serious psychological trouble. He then attempted to record in detail the process of inference he followed in arriving at personality descriptions of each patient, on the basis of these records alone.

It need be of no great concern that Beck referred to the Rorschach as a "test" or that his book is titled *The Rorschach Experiment,* for it is clear from his first chapter that his use of terms differs somewhat from that advocated here. The unique opportunity the reader has to look into the operations of the mind of a respected and admired diagnostician is more than worth a little semantic ambiguity.

Surveys

Collections of case study materials are often used for discovering or describing general trends in large groups of subjects. Large numbers of detailed case studies may be accumulated in research designed to examine, on an exploratory basis, aspects of behavior that have never been intensively studied before. The original data, collected by Escalona and Heider (1959) for a study that is also cited in the following section, was intended to serve such a purpose.

In more familiar types of survey research, the focus of investigation is usually fairly specific at the outset; and the data are therefore limited in scope. The better-known public-opinion surveys and television rating services provide good examples of such limited-goal, descriptive case-study research.

Of particular interest to the student of personality is the procedure, called the *critical incident technique,* devised by Flanagan (1954). The critical incident technique comprises the collection and classification of reports of particularly meaningful experiences from a large number of individuals. It is essentially a survey device, and its data are case study descriptions of occurrences that have had an important effect on some predesignated aspect of subjects' lives. Though originally designed for use in industrial settings (for discovering criteria for predicting or evaluating the performances of foremen, aircraft pilots, and mechanics, etc.), the technique is highly flexible and holds great promise for broader application. For example, it has been used in a hospital for the chronic physically ill to examine how hospital procedures satisfy and frustrate patients' psychological needs of various types (Fantz, 1961).

Establishing a Data Pool

It sometimes happens that case material is collected for purposes that cannot be particularized in advance. Investigators with an interest in special phenomena may exert efforts to collect case study information for later analysis, but they may not have in mind the exact approach that will be taken to their data once the data become available. They simply accumulate a type of information that their professional judgment suggests will be useful and valuable to themselves or others when a sufficient amount of it has been obtained.

An example of a study conducted from records available in the published literature is the work by Barry, Bacon, and Child (1957) on the influence of culture on sex differences in behavior. Barry and his colleagues analyzed ethnographic descriptions (i.e., case material) of 110 cultures. These descriptions were rated on a number of variables relating to economic conditions and to social and personal behaviors. Correlations among rated variables were then employed to test relevant hypotheses (most of them implicit); and it was concluded that sex differences in behavior are culturally, rather than biologically, determined.

Another example of such a study is the previously mentioned work by Escalona and Heider (1959). In this investigation, data from two descriptive surveys of the same group of children were utilized to test the usefulness of information obtained from infants, from four to thirty-two weeks of age, for predicting the behavior of the same subjects two to five years later. Detailed case study records taken during the first descriptive study served as the basis for prediction. Similar records from the second study provided the criteria. The important feature of this work is that it was not planned as a predictive study from the start, although the extensive case materials available made such a study possible. Both descriptive studies constituted collections of data, about which no specific hypotheses were made. The test of prediction constituted a later addition to the original purposes of these exploratory investigations.

The outstanding feature of this way of using case study information is that the data themselves are collected without prior commitment to their use in the specific manner that is finally employed.

The same descriptive reports may often be used in a variety of ways to test a variety of hypotheses.

A pertinent development in psychology has been the interest in collecting "specimen records" of behavior (Barker & Wright, 1954). As it is used with children, a specimen record is a "detailed, sequential narrative of a long segment of a child's behavior and situation." Specimen records are obtained by having a trained person observe one subject for thirty minutes or less. The observer makes notes about all features of the subject and environment that are important in the total situation. Newer techniques, in which the observer wears a face-mask microphone and carries a portable tape recorder, make the note-taking process even more elaborate and complete. The notes are later converted into a "detailed minute-by-minute description" of all that took place during the observation period (Schoggen, 1963). Specimen records can, and often do, provide a valuable source of data for later studies.

Challenging Existing Modes of Thought

The purpose of challenging existing modes of thought is commonly combined with the purpose of presenting evidence for, or illustrations of, alternative theoretical positions. Usually the strategy employed is to present a *negative instance,* that is, a case that cannot be explained satisfactorily by the challenged theory.

Scientists are generally reluctant to accept exclusively negative evidence unless alternatives are also offered that explain the case more readily or more completely. They are unlikely to see much merit in destroying a theory of limited value unless it is replaced by another that is better, or at least just as good. It follows that an investigator is usually under some obligation to show that what constitutes a negative instance for one mode of thought is, in reality, a positive or confirming instance for another, namely, his own. The work by Kardiner (1939), cited at the beginning of this chapter, exemplifies the use of case studies in this way.

A case study that approaches fairly closely the purely negative function is one by Lenneberg (1962) describing an eight-year-old boy who had "a congenital disability for the acquisition of motor speech skills" (i.e., who was unable to talk) but who had unimpaired ability to learn to understand language. Lenneberg provided medical and family history information and summarized the results of physical and psychological examinations on his subject. This material was then brought to bear on the hypothesis that hearing oneself speak is essential to the learning of language skills. It was concluded that the hypothesis inadequately explained how this child and others like him are able to learn to understand language without the ability to speak. Lenneberg briefly suggested that central processes are responsible for the learning of both receptive and expressive language, so his study is not entirely negatively oriented. Nevertheless, since he did not elaborate his alternative, it is reasonable to conclude that the burden of his paper was primarily to challenge an accepted point of view.

The case studies presented in May, Angel, and Ellenberger (1958) are also somewhat representative of the use of this method to challenge the adequacy of existing theories and to present more satisfactory alternatives. The discussion of the case of Ellen West, for example, was clearly designed to show that, while a psychoanalytic approach would not be called incorrect in describing her, a more suitable vehicle for understanding the complexities of this woman's life would be existential analysis, due to its greater breadth and scope. Ellen West was perhaps presented as a *critical,* rather than as a negative, instance, because it was not maintained that her personality was psychoanalytically inexplicable. The more basic question was the value of theoretical explanation alone as a technique for completely understanding any person.

Confirming Theories and Hypotheses

It is sometimes argued that one case proves nothing, but many prove a great deal. Sheer weight of confirming case study material is occasionally called upon to bear testimony to the truth of an hypothesis. This argument has only limited value, for the quality of the material is at least as important as the amount. The demonstration of the dangers inherent in this strategy is easy. One of the most disastrous treatises ever to appear in Western civilization was based almost entirely upon case-history methods. The infamous *Malleus Maleficarum,* originally published in the late fifteenth century, not only described how to identify, interrogate, torture, and punish witches, but also analyzed in scholarly tones their nature, their behavior, and their influence on others (translated by Summers, 1928). Relying entirely on anecdotal and case-study methods, its original authors, Henry Kramer and James Sprenger, whose eminent qualifications for their job could not be denied, established the validity of their propositions almost beyond question through sheer mass of evidence and authoritative opinion. Beginning with a basic premise that was fostered and encouraged by the society in which they lived, they accumulated proofs that seemed undeniable to those who already believed in the reality of witches. Though inspired by most admirable religious motives, Kramer and Sprenger's writings were responsible for the death of thousands of innocent people.

As a more fairly appraised and more directly scientific example of the modern use of the case-study method to prove a theory, one finds in Freud's famous report on Little Hans (1962, orig. pub. 1905) a good illustration of the use of an intensive case analysis to establish the validity of a particular theoretical point of view. Little Hans was a five-year-old boy who suffered a phobia of horses. His father, a disciple of Freud, treated Hans by psychoanalytic methods; and with Freud's help, the child was eventually relieved of his disturbing condition. There can be little doubt that Freud considered this case a strong argument in favor of his theory of infantile sexuality.

Many years later, Wolpe and Rachman (1960) attacked the evidential basis for Freud's conclusions. They pointed out, for example, that Hans often spontaneously rejected interpretations of his behavior, offered by his father. Frequently the boy himself suggested interpretations, which the father then totally ignored. When Hans finally did accede to the explanations provided by others, it often appeared that he did so only superficially and halfheartedly, rather than with genuine insight as Freud supposed. Further, there seemed to be no basis for concluding that teaching Hans what to believe about his symptoms bore any necessary relationship to his final cure.

Wolpe and Rachman offered an alternative view of Hans' problems and treatment, which explained the onset and cure of the phobia in terms of the principles of conditioning, as expressed in Hullian learning theory. The cautious reader would, of course, take this theoretical alternative for no more than what it is—a demonstration that other explanations of the case of Hans are possible. The fact that alternatives exist or can be devised, obviously proves nothing about the validity of those alternatives themselves.

EXPLICITNESS

The term *explicitness* has already been defined in chapter 2, but it must be considered once again, for the degree and type of explicitness of a given case study may be an important indicator of its value to the study of personality.

Explicitness of Data

Clearly, a set of clinical impressions does not provide highly explicit data. The same must be said of reconstructions from memory of experiences with interesting clients or subjects. Explicit case-study data possess three essential properties: detail, immediacy, and objectivity.

A perfect case study would presumedly record and report, in completely objective fashion, everything the subject does. If that could always be done, there would be few arguments about the accuracy of the information collected. Indeed most of the improvements that have taken place in this method over the past several decades have been in the direction of maximizing the detail, immediacy, and objectivity of the case-study worker's observations. Writing down the significant events of a therapy session immediately after the patient leaves is more objective than waiting an hour, a day, or a week to do so. Writing down the events while they are actually taking place is even better. Verbatim notes, insofar as it is possible to take them, are an improvement over interpretive comments. Tape recordings are more detailed and immediate than any notes a therapist might take; and, of course, sound movies or television tapes, though not perfect, are more revealing and explicit than tape recordings.

It might appear, without further consideration, that the best case study is always the one in which detail, immediacy, and objectivity are maximized. A review of the purposes that are served effectively by the case-study method raises some doubt about this argument.

Case studies that serve purely as illustrations or examples sometimes accomplish their purpose best if they are not too detailed. Immediacy and precise objectivity are also relatively unessential in this situation, even though one must rely upon the writer's unspecified judgments in selecting examples that will be most clear and to the point. Similarly, the unusual or remarkable case does not necessarily demand much extraneous detail to be of interest to its reader.

The need for maximum explicitness enters when the validity of a theory or hypothesis is at stake and when the data are used in surveys or to establish a pool of information from which later studies or surveys may be derived. In these situations it can be safely presumed that the greater the detail, immediacy, and objectivity of the data, the better they will be.

Explicitness of Selective Criteria

Case materials often cover a relatively broad spectrum of observations, many of which are not pointedly relevant to the investigator's immediate purposes. When the mass or breadth of available material is very great, selection must take place so that the information is reduced to manageable proportions.

On the basis of practical considerations alone, it is obvious that it is impossible to observe and communicate absolutely everything that happens in the kinds of natural or quasi-natural settings that are usually employed in case studies. It is also apparent that the choice of one case logically demands the exclusion of others, and this too constitutes a type of selection that cannot be avoided. The problem, therefore, is not whether case study data are selective, but how much selection exists and what the criteria are by which it takes place.

Problems of selection are sometimes built directly into the data collection phase of a case study investigation. While taking handwritten notes on an interview, for instance, a human recorder may on one occasion deem it sufficient to observe that the subject lights a cigarette. Which brand of cigarette, from which pocket it was taken, whether it was lit with a match or a lighter, may not be considered relevant and, for that reason, might not be entered into the data. If, however, the subject should fumble about, experience difficulty in lighting his cigarette, ask the interviewer for a light, or make some comment about the significance of smoking, the recorder might decide to include these facts in his transcription; that is, he would engage in a different process of selection than he would have otherwise.

As suggested in the previous section, these difficulties may be overcome by using less personal and more complete data-recording devices, such as tape recorders and movie cameras. But increased detail of case study materials does not bring unmixed blessings, for any improvement in the completeness of data recording carries with it other problems of selection that assume greater magnitude and significance as the sheer bulk of data grows. As convincing as sound movies or tape recordings may be, they are not readily publishable as such. Communication of findings must be maximally efficient, and the printed word seems best suited to the purposes of research publication in most cases. No one has yet found a way to escape the difficulties that arise from the fact that it takes the same amount of time to view or listen to a complete behavior sample as it took to film or record it originally. Even if this problem were solved, there would still remain the economic consequences of the relative inefficiency of mass reproduction of taped or filmed materials.

At the very least, the investigator with such data at his command must be resigned to the condensation of his data into a form that is suitable for relatively rapid communication to others. If the original medium is to be retained, this often demands a good deal of cutting and splicing. If another medium is preferred, it also implies the necessity for transcription and unavoidable loss. However accomplished, some information will be retained and some (often a very large proportion of the total) rejected. Aside from gaps that are simply a mechanical consequence of particular cutting techniques, the criteria by which such selections are made are based on and reflect the relevance of the various bits of information to the initial purposes of the study.

Criteria for selection to maximize relevance may be *implicit* or *explicit*. Implicit criteria are not stated or specified in describing the procedures of the study; frequently the investigator is not fully aware of them himself. Explicit criteria reflect a systematic effort to summarize or cull irrelevancies from the available observations. For example, trained observers may be asked to describe or rate case study information, according to standardized instructions that employ carefully defined terms.

In general, explicit criteria are preferable to implicit criteria; however, the judgment of adequacy in any given study is always a function of the purposes of the study. It would be unnecessary and inefficient to demand complete explicitness of selective criteria in an investigation that is purely demonstrative or illustrative and that involves no serious matters of theory or principle.

Tests and Examinations as Data Sources

The essential merit of most formal psychological examinations and tests stems from their generally high level of explicitness. A projective examination usually provides more objective information than a clinical judgment without the benefit of formal procedures. A standard test of intelligence is more objective than an employer's or counselor's rough estimate of a client's intellectual level. The reason is simple. Trained examiners and testers generally behave toward their subjects in highly reliable fashion and record relevant material with acceptable accuracy. Even their condensation of data that result in the report of an IQ or an *Erlebnistypus* is sufficiently standardized to be acceptable to most readers of case reports. Examinations and tests have an additional advantage because their selection of particular kinds of information for intensive investigation has been publicly explained in previous reports of highly controlled research. The competent reader of a case report based on these data is therefore already familiar with many of the researcher's procedures and decisions. Examinations and tests do not necessarily gain their explicitness from the amount of detailed factual information they yield; but they do fulfill the criteria of immediacy and objectivity; and they are particularly clear about selective criteria.

EVALUATION

Case studies are often thought of as being merely good preliminary devices. They are characterized as "hypothesis generating" or "inductive" in nature, as opposed to other researches which are "hypothesis testing" or "deductive" in approach. Like most dichotomies, this distinction grossly oversimplifies the issue. Worse, it tends to promote a condescending attitude toward the case-study method. The student is frequently reminded that experimental tests must follow such subjective reporting and speculative hypothesizing as are found in published case studies. Case studies, he is told, are descriptive and suggestive; but they never prove anything. Therefore they are of less use to science than more controlled methods.

As inefficient as case studies may appear to be, the legitimate scientific purposes they can serve should not be depreciated. The use of the method in surveys or for reporting remarkable cases is important if for no other reason than that it arouses interest in phenomena that are not often intensively or objectively observed. The remarkable case frequently provides a valuable demonstration of the application of existing theory to the explanation of phenomena not anticipated (perhaps never even observed) by the theory builder himself. Sometimes cases which are initially thought to be remarkable turn out to be rather common, once the attention of other observers has been drawn to them. Rare and unusual cases also may provide crucial information that cannot be otherwise obtained. Money's interviews of persons who suffered malformation or destruction of genital tissues, for example, makes a significant contribution to our understanding of the importance (or better, the unimportance) of genital sensation in the experience of sexual orgasm (1961). Work of this type frequently raises more questions than it answers; but that is true of all worthwhile scientific pursuits in psychology, even of the most highly controlled experiments.

As a didactic device in illustrating, exemplifying, or demonstrating complex theories or practices, the case study is obviously unexcelled and will not soon be replaced by any other approach. It can be extremely useful when used for the establishment of a **data** pool, upon which others may draw as the need arises. As has already been suggested, the latter use requires a maximum of detail, immediacy, and objectivity, for the usefulness of the pool will be entirely a function of the comprehensiveness of the information it contains.

The use of the case study in providing negative instances to challenge the validity of existing theories is defensible under two main conditions. The first is when the nature of the theory **in** question is such that invalidation cannot be accomplished in any other way. This might be true with respect to such complex points of view as psychoanalysis. The other condition is the rare circumstance in which the theory that is attacked has been proposed as a device for explaining all persons and situations without exception. Few psychological theories, especially theories of personality, are this well structured; and for all practical purposes this condition may be discounted as a currently real basis for reporting a negative instance.

Negative instances must obviously be highly explicit to be of maximum value, particularly so far as the objectivity and the relevance of the data are concerned. A negative instance based on impressionistic data handled in highly speculative fashion can scarcely carry much weight in judging the merit of the point of view it attacks.

Much has already been said about the danger of using case studies as hypothesis-testing devices. Little needs to be added to the previous discussion except that their use in this fashion seems justifiable only when it can be clearly established that no other approach to the problem is possible.

The argument may be made that case studies are inevitably biased, no matter how explicit they may be. Bias is bound to enter, if not into the collection, condensation, and interpretation of data, then into the choice of one particular case rather than another. Granted that this characterization is at least partially valid, it need not be taken as a condemnation of the case-study method as a whole. Bias is not invariably detrimental. As with other methods, the critical question is whether case studies are employed appropriately in specific instances to the accomplishment of purposes they serve best.

In summary, the case study method is much maligned and often misused. Applied properly, however, it is an invaluable aid to scientific communication, an irreplaceable teaching and illustrative device, and a source of new ideas. It provides a means for challenging existing points of view and a type of evidence that may be the last resort in evaluating the merits of hypotheses which would otherwise be untestable.

References

BARKER, R. G., & WRIGHT, H. F. *Midwest and its children.* New York: Harper & Row, 1954.

BARRY, H., BACON, MARGARET K., & CHILD, I. L. A cross-cultural survey of some sex differences in socialization. *J. abnorm. soc. Psychol.,* 1957, *55,* 327-332. (In Mednick & Mednick, pp. 599-607 [see References, chapter 1, above].)

BECK, S. J. *The Rorschach experiment: Ventures in blind diagnosis.* New York: Grune & Stratton, 1960.

BEIER, H., & BAUER, R. A. Oleg: a member of the Soviet "Golden Youth." *J. abnorm. soc. Psychol.,* 1955, *51,* 139-145. (In Mednick & Mednick, pp. 607-616 [see References, chapter 1, above].)

ESCALONA, SYBILLE, & HEIDER, GRACE M. *Prediction and outcome: A study in child development.* New York: Basic Books, 1959.

FANTZ, RAINETTE. Motivational factors in rehabilitation. Unpublished doctoral dissertation, Western Reserve Univer., 1961.

FLANAGAN, J. C. The critical incident technique. *Psychol. Bull.,* 1954, *51,* 327-358.

FREUD, S. Analysis of a phobia in a five-year-old boy. In *Collected papers.* Vol. 3. New York: Basic Books, 1953. Pp. 243-287. Also in *Complete psychological works.* Vol. 10. London: Hogarth, 1962. Pp. 101-147. (In Southwell & Merbaum, pp. 3-32, abridged form [see References, chapter 1, above].)

HOLTZMAN, W. H., THORPE, J. S., SWARTZ, J. D., & HERRON, E. W. *Inkblot perception and personality.* Austin: Univer. Texas Press, 1961.

JOSEPH, E. D., & TABOR, J. H. The simultaneous analysis of a pair of identical twins and the twinning reaction. In Ruth S. Eissler et al. (Eds.), *Psychoanalytic study of the child.* Vol. XVI. New York: Internat. Univer. Press, 1961. Pp. 275-299.

KARDINER, A. *The individual and his society.* New York: Columbia Univer. Press, 1939.

KLOPFER, B., & DAVIDSON, HELEN H. *The Rorschach technique: An introductory manual.* New York: Harcourt, Brace & World, 1962.

LENNEBERG, E. H. Understanding language without ability to speak: A case report. *J. abnorm. soc. Psychol.,* 1962, *65,* 419-425.

LEONARD, MARJORIE R. Problems in identification and ego development in twins. In Ruth S. Eissler et al. (Eds.), *Psychoanalytic study of the child.* Vol. XVI. New York: Internat. Univer. Press, 1961. Pp. 300-320.

MAY, R., ANGEL, E., & ELLENBERGER, H. F. (Eds.) *Existence.* New York: Basic Books, 1958.

MONEY, J. Components of eroticism in man: II. The orgasm and genital somesthesis. *J. nerv. ment. Dis.,* 1961, *132,* 289-297.

PLANK, EMMA N., & HORWOOD, CARLA. Leg amputation in a four year old: Reactions of the child, her family, and the staff. In Ruth S. Eissler et al. (Eds.), *Psychoanalytic study of the child.* Vol. XVI. New York: Internat. Univer. Press, 1961. Pp. 405-422.

SCHOGGEN, P. Environmental forces in the lives of children with and without physical disability. Paper presented at Amer. Psychol. Ass., Philadelphia, August, 1963.

SHONTZ, F. C. Severe chronic illness. In J. F. Garrett & E. S. Levine (Eds.), *Psychological practices with the physically disabled.* New York: Columbia Univer. Press, 1962. Pp. 410-445.

SUMMERS, M. (Trans.) *Malleus Maleficarum.* London: Pushkin Press, 1928.

THIGPEN, C. H., & CLECKLEY, H. A case of multiple personality. *J. abnorm. soc. Psychol.*, 1954, *49*, 135-151. (In Sarason, pp. 367-383 [see References, chapter 1, above].)

WHITE, R. W. *Lives in progress.* New York: Holt, Rinehart & Winston, 1952.

WHITE, R. W. *The abnormal personality.* (2nd ed.) New York: Ronald, 1956.

WOLPE, J., & RACHMAN, S. Psychoanalytic "evidence": A critique based on Freud's Case of Little Hans. *J. nerv. ment. Dis.*, 1960, *130*, 135-148. (In Southwell & Merbaum, pp. 44-61, under the title: A critique of Freud's Case of Little Hans [see References, chapter 1, above].)

5

Actuarialism

Actuarialism is a method designed for solving practical problems of the type commonly encountered by counselors and clinicians in applied situations. In some ways it constitutes a logical extension and quantification of the case study approach. The most essential similarities between the two methods are that both are naturalistic and nonexperimental. They make no attempt to reduce the complexity of the natural, behavior-determining processes that operate in a subject's day-to-day life; and they do not undertake to manipulate independent variables in systematic fashion. Both face the problem of condensing large amounts of available information into convenient and useful forms.

One essential difference between the methods is that actuarial investigations invariably deal with large numbers of subjects. These studies always begin with the discovery and description of general trends or relationships in masses of data, collected from samples with known characteristics. Their ultimate purpose is to develop purely mechanical procedures for arriving at highly specific judgments in similar future cases. This development takes place only after extensive information on preliminary samples has been reduced to statistical summarizations and cross-validated on new groups of subjects.

Another difference between the methods is that the data of actuarial studies must all be reduced to numerical expressions and made amenable to statistical analysis. The techniques by which this is accomplished are usually such as to give assurance that the information used is reasonably objective and that it is selected and condensed by explicit procedural rules.

A third difference is the importance to actuarialism of the *criterion*: a final measure, judgment, or decision to which all other available data are related. Criteria usually reflect the practical and clinical sources of the method itself. They generally consist of such indices as psychiatric diagnosis, number of arrests or police contacts, *Q*-sort arrangements, rated success in psychotherapy, measured IQ, conviction for sexual offense, and recidivism. Investigations using this method are deemed successful if they demonstrate reliable contingencies between sets of quantitative (or quantified) case data and some useful criterion. These contingencies then serve as the basis for making predictions about criterion values in future cases drawn from the same population.

Atheoreticism and Empiricism

The actuarial approach is often thought of as a concrete expression of certain assumptions about the purposes of research and the criteria by which investigations should be evaluated. These assumptions are (a) that research must solve practical problems and (b) that the most efficient (i.e., economical) solutions to these problems are best. The term *actuarial* conveys the purely statistical concerns of the investigator who uses the method (an actuary is a clerk or a calculator of probabilities and risks). If the principles and implications of this method are relentlessly applied, the result is the production of research that is without theoretical content and that deals exclusively with data contingencies. The first of these characteristics may be called *atheoreticism*, the second, *empiricism*.

Atheoreticism may imply either of two judgments about the legitimate purposes of research. It may either reflect the belief that psychological theory is a waste of time and effort which is best abandoned altogether, or it may imply the more moderate notion that the results of empirical investigations should be considered theoretically neutral, since they are useful to psychologists of all persuasions. The first belief is, of course, antitheoretical rather than atheoretical. The second belief does not deny the place of theory in science; it simply removes from the investigator any personal responsibility for theoretical development.

Empiricism, in this context, may also have more than one meaning. On the one hand, it may convey the investigator's preference for "shotgun" or "cut-and-try" techniques. In seeking correlations between predictive measures and a criterion, the shotgun technique involves collecting masses of heterogeneous data in the hope that some of them will accomplish appropriate research purposes and in the knowledge that most will be thrown away as useless. The cut-and-try technique involves the use of a crude predictive formula, despite its known inadequacy, in the hope that subsequent observations of its failures may be employed to suggest improvements in the formula itself.

On the other hand, empiricism may simply mean reliance upon observation, as opposed to dependence upon interpretation, speculation, and subjective judgment. This is probably the meaning that most users of the actuarial method would be willing to underwrite.

A Hypothetical Example

An actuarial study begins with some practical problem that in the investigator's opinion is poorly or inefficiently solved by existing methods. Consider the situation in which a clinical psychologist is called upon to evaluate patients' potential to benefit from psychotherapy or other forms of treatment. Existing practice is usually to make predictions of this type impressionistically. That is, the psychologist gathers together the available information on each patient and formulates an opinion. His opinion is then developed into a prediction, on the basis of which important clinical decisions are made. But the processes of data integration by which this development takes place remain implicit, and the prediction itself is rarely checked for accuracy by empirical methods.

Dissatisfaction with such procedures might lead an actuarial investigator to question whether a better (quicker, more public, more accurate, less expensive) technique for predicting therapeutic outcomes might be devised. He would reason that all judgments of potential therapeutic benefit are based upon past observance of relationships between information available at the time the predictions were made and later judgments of treatment outcome. He would also argue that converting these relationships into mathematical formulas makes them more explicit and, hence, more amenable to objective evaluation. Furthermore, the relative ease with which mathematical procedures can be executed by clerical personnel would make it possible for the busy clinician to turn this job over to others, thereby eliminating much of the tedium from his work and enabling him to direct his intellectual efforts to the solution of other more challenging problems.

As he approached his research, the methodologically consistent actuarial investigator would tend to distrust the use of theory as a guide for selecting measures, partly because he would feel that the theories usually employed by clinicians are too speculative to be useful and partly because he would feel that commitment to a theory is likely to blind an observer to relationships that are empirically real. Theory, he believes, induces an observer bias that is best eliminated from empirical research. To avoid this danger he would adopt the attitude that all possible data are relevant and should be considered without prejudice.

His work from this point on demands a very considerable expenditure of time and energy and is likely to involve extremely complex and sophisticated statistical operations. But, basically, his task is straightforward. First, he must develop a measurement of treatment outcome (a criterion) that meets psychometric requirements. Next, he must collect a wide range of data on the population of candidates for therapy. These data are not restricted, in principle, to those that would ordinarily be called psychological. They might include information gleaned from social workers' reports, from medical records, from public documents, and from the patients' answers to questionnaires, application blanks, or projective examinations. In the strictest use of the method, all possible facts would be grist for the actuary's statistical mill; there is no purely methodological reason why a patient's auto license or his social security number or a count of the windows in his house could not be included in the data.

The next step is to correlate all this available information with the criterion to determine which measures discriminate those patients who eventually benefit from therapy from those who do not. On the basis of these correlations, a battery of minimally redundant predictive measures is then constructed and *cross-validated*. Cross validation requires the examination of a new sample of therapy candidates. Initially observed correlations that are substantiated by examination of data from a cross-validation study are usually considered sufficiently stable to justify their incorporation into the final version of the predictive formula.

The formula is then ready to be tested against existing methods, in this case clinician's predictions of therapeutic success. If it is found to predict judged therapeutic outcome more accurately than the clinician, it follows that the formula is to be preferred in future clinical work. Even if it predicts only as well as, but not better than, the clinician, the greater economy of the quantitative approach may be sufficient to warrant substituting it for previous techniques.

Once the formula has been prepared, cross-validated, and has proven its superiority to clinical judgment (which is likely to be a matter of some years, in this study), it remains applicable to new clients as long as all the conditions under which the initial study was conducted prevail. If therapeutic methods change, if the criteria by which therapeutic success is judged are altered, or if the nature of the candidates for treatment eventually becomes different from what it was when the predictive formula was developed, doubt is *ipso facto* cast upon the validity of the formula itself. Another investigation must then be conducted to determine whether revision or replacement of the predictive device is required by the altered circumstances.

The results of this study could not be applied automatically to settings other than the one in which the initial predictive formula was derived. Any essential dissimilarity of conditions between settings would have an unknown effect on correlation values, and failure to take these into account would result in improper use of predictive formulas.

APPLICATIONS OF THE METHOD

Vocational Interest Blank

Despite the high level of current interest in actuarial research, the principles behind the method are not new. One of the most successful of the relatively early instruments devised by this method was Strong's *Vocational Interest Blank* (1943). According to

Anastasi (1954, pp. 565-571), the basic strategy by which this test was constructed was formulated as early as 1919 in a graduate seminar at the Carnegie Institute of Technology.

The items of the Vocational Interest Blank require the subject to express a variety of personal preferences, either absolutely (by signifying whether he likes, dislikes, or is indifferent to the content of the item) or relatively (by ranking items within lists). Preferences are expressed not only for obviously vocationally relevant items, but for contents having to do with recreational activities, reactions to peculiarities of others, assessment of one's personal characteristics, and so forth. Of particular interest is the fact that item content, per se, is totally irrelevant to the scoring of the test.

The Vocational Interest Blank was standardized by administering it to samples of persons engaged in a variety of occupations, generally at the professional or semiprofessional levels (e.g., physician, architect, salesman, psychologist). Responses of persons in each occupation were then statistically compared with the responses of a general reference group of professional and business men. On the basis of this comparison, particular groups of items were selected and "keyed" for specific occupational groups. These items, regardless of content, were identified by the fact that the responses of members of the relevant occupational group differed statistically from the responses of the nonspecific reference sample.

When a client seeking vocational guidance now takes the Vocational Interest Blank, his answers to the four hundred miscellaneous items are scored with templates developed to reflect the response characteristics of persons in the various occupations for which norms were previously established. The scorer rarely knows or cares what the content of the items may be; his concern is solely with response similarity. Other things being equal, the more similar the subject's responses are to those characteristically provided by a given occupational group, the more strongly the counselor is convinced that success for his client is possible in that particular line of work.

The Vocational Interest Blank is of some interest to students of personality, because this inventory probably gains its value not so much from the fact that it is actuarial in character as from the fact that its success demonstrates the stability of those behavior organizations with which the concept of personality is identified. Unfortunately the items of this inventory do not possess a theoretical structure by which hypotheses about personality differences among vocational groups may be tested, and serious attempts to determine the psychological significance of discriminating items are few and far between (but, see Tyler [1959] for an interesting exception).

MMPI

The well-known psychometric instrument, the *Minnesota Multiphasic Personality Inventory* (MMPI), is more obviously tied to the interests of the personologist than is the Vocational Interest Blank. This test made its first appearance on the professional scene in 1940, and the official manual for the MMPI (Hathaway & McKinley) was published in 1943. It was, therefore, a contemporary of Strong's Vocational Interest Blank and was constructed according to similar principles.

The MMPI consists of 550 miscellaneous statements, many of which are of the usual personality inventory type. They represent a variety of symptoms, traits, and personal characteristics, both physical and psychological. The subject is instructed to describe himself with these items, classifying each as *true, false,* or *cannot say.* Because the method is actuarial, the examiner is uninterested in the content of the items classified in a particular way by the subject or in the content of the subject's self-description. What does concern him is the degree of correspondence between the responses of a given subject and the characteristic responses of a variety of psychiatrically defined groups.

Preliminary studies on the MMPI utilized responses from about seven hundred nonclinical subjects for standardization purposes. Additional samples of patients with specific psychiatric diagnoses (e.g., hysteria, hypochondriasis, depression, paranoia) served as *criterion groups.* The responses given by each criterion group were then analyzed to determine which inventory items tended to evoke answers that differed from those produced by the standardizing sample.

A system was developed to enable the user of the MMPI to derive several scores from an individual client's test record. Each score represents the degree of similarity between the client's answers and the set of answers that discriminated a particular diagnostic group from the normal sample in the original standardizing studies. For an example of how one of these scales was constructed, see McKinley and Hathaway (1942). For an explanation of the rationale of the MMPI as a measure of personality, see Meehl (1945). Besides the clinical scales, several validity scales (F, K, L, and ?) and a masculinity-femininity scale were included in the inventory.

The procedures by which the MMPI was constructed indicate that the instrument was essentially designed as an actuarial device for predicting psychiatric diagnosis. For this purpose the test proved unsatisfactory (Anastasi, 1954, pp. 553-554). Scores on the separate scales were found not to discriminate among diagnostic groups in subsequent research; and doubt existed as to the value, in any case, of predicting such ambiguous and theoretically vague entities as psychiatric classifications.

Later developments.   Despite its failure to fulfill the promises implicit in its construction, the MMPI has become one of the most popular clinical and research instruments in modern psychology. Efforts to improve and expand it have been virtually continuous since its inception.

The most obvious course of development of an instrument of this type is the devising of new scales that promise greater utilitarian value than those originally proposed. These have appeared in abundance and have claimed to measure everything from the personality concomitants of low-back pain to socioeconomic status and ego strength. Since the pattern of scale construction is much the same in all instances, it is not necessary to examine more than one or two examples to illustrate the method and its rationale.

Wattron (1963) reported a typical study concerned with the construction of an MMPI scale to identify maladjusted prisoners in a correctional setting. Maladjustment was defined as rebellion against prison routine and as recidivism. Three groups were selected. One group was composed of prisoners who had "made good" on parole for five years; the second was composed of inmates confined to prison disciplinary units; the third was composed of recidivists, persons with records of more than one prison sentence. On the basis of MMPI records from one hundred men in each of the first two groups, 72 differentiating items were discovered. A cross-validation study was then conducted by selecting new samples of 150 subjects in the first group, 200 in the second group, and 100 in the third. Total scores on the keyed items were found to discriminate satisfactorily between the parolee and the disciplinary groups but not so well between the parolee and recidivist groups. Item content was not analyzed, and the scale was reported and described in terms of MMPI item numbers only.

In an apparently similar study, Cutter (1964) reported the construction of another MMPI scale. Items were selected by the usual methods, this time to discriminate between the test records of hospitalized sexual psychopaths before and after an 18-month treatment regimen. MMPI responses to individual items were screened twice (cross-sectionally and longitudinally) to produce a final scale of 38 discriminating items. Two validation studies were then conducted to establish the scale's ability to reflect group differences as a function of hospitalization. Content analysis of the items suggested the name applied to the scale by its author—the self-rejection distress scale. It was felt that the scale measured a therapeutically important aspect of the "self-image."

Although this investigation used procedures that are characteristic of actuarial research, it is not purely actuarial in method. It appears, rather, to be an attempt at inductive measurement construction, as described in chapter 3. Cutter's study differs from Wattron's in its emphasis on the nature of the psychological processes underlying observed response differences and in its effort to apply a theoretically meaningful label to the actuarially derived scale. The reader of Cutter's report suspects that this investigator's primary purpose was to discover the kind of personality changes that are brought about by psychiatric treatment of sexual offenders. The name assigned to the scale could scarcely be justified by reference to item numbers alone, and item selection appears to have been used mainly as a guide for the author's inferential processes.

The analysis of Cutter's investigation points up the fact that methods of research are not to be identified solely by procedures employed or by types of measuring instruments used. The intentions of the investigator and the conclusions he feels free to draw are at least as important as the operations he performs. It is perfectly possible to use the MMPI in a theoretical way, as Cutter did; and it will be seen later that it is equally possible to use unstruc-

tured examinations, such as the Rorschach or TAT, in a theoretically uncommitted and thoroughly empirical fashion.

   Profile description.   It has been noted that specific scales of the
MMPI proved to be relatively unsuited to the prediction of psychiatric diagnoses. Because of this failure, it was suggested that
profile information might be more useful than single scores for
general research and clinical purposes. Coding systems were devised
by which an individual subject's overall pattern of separate scale
scores could be expressed in a simple formula and used as an aid to
personality description. An MMPI atlas (Hathaway & Meehl, 1951)
was prepared to present a wide variety of profile types by providing
almost a thousand brief case-study reports describing individuals
who had produced the various scoring patterns. (This atlas might
well have been cited in the preceding chapter as an example of the
use of case studies to demonstrate technique.) Its publication
proved a potent stimulus to the use of the MMPI in clinical examination; for, in actual practice, particular profile shapes were quickly
assigned interpretive significance. MMPI profiles became the basis
for drawing complex inferences about personality dynamics and for
constructing personality descriptions, not unlike descriptions cus-
tomarily derived from projective or interview materials.

   The tendency of clinicians to insist on the inferential use of the
MMPI, despite its actuarial construction, is of only passing concern
to the present discussion. More important is the fact that growing
discontent with this way of using the instrument led to a return to
the actuarial approach in later research. Conditions seemed to demand a reappraisal of psychometric purposes; and the result was
that the predictive goal of the early 1960's became, not to guess at
specific diagnoses, but to replace intuition with data and to compose objective personality descriptions from MMPI profile data.

   To this end, Marks and Seeman (1963) collected masses of
information from more than 1,200 male and female patients
treated for psychiatric disorders at the University of Kansas Medical
Center in Kansas City, Kansas. The MMPI records of these subjects
were classified and ultimately grouped into 16 profile types, or
codes. Additional data on subjects representing each code type were
then summarized and presented in quantified or tabular form,
along with lists of Q-sort items said by psychiatrists and psycholo-

gists, familiar with each case, to be most and least descriptive of patients in each group. Data included such items as age, sex, inpatient and outpatient percentages, psychiatric and other medical diagnoses, personal history (including sibling status, dating habits, criminal records, education, etc.), mental status, symptoms, course in treatment, and a variety of psychometric test scores. Marks and Seeman's study was truly atheoretical, in that no attempt was made to explain its findings. Its intended function was to present material that would be of value, even to readers with different conceptual preferences (1963, p. xvi). More will be said about this investigation when the actuarial method is evaluated in a later section.

Prediction

Marks and Seeman's descriptive purpose contrasts with that of many actuarial studies, which focus more specifically on the use of the actuarial method for making specific predictions of clinically relevant events.

A major characteristic of research that compares clinical with actuarial predictions is its frequent emphasis upon the improvement of practical efficiency and prognostic accuracy. The clinician is sometimes characterized as "a costly middleman who might better be eliminated" (Meehl, 1956, p. 271); the practitioner's obligation to the taxpayer is cited as a compelling reason for him to employ the most efficient (*viz.*, actuarial) methods possible in his work; and cost per unit of service bids fair to become the ultimate measure of value to psychological science (Rimm, 1963).

The question of whether purely statistical predictions are better than clinical judgments first came to the attention of most psychologists in 1954 (Meehl, 1954). The conviction that the clinician is a highly inefficient computer was also expressed by Meehl in his 1955 address to the Midwestern Psychological Association (Meehl, 1956). Since then, the pitting of clinical judgments against wholly empirically derived predictions has provided an absorbing pastime for many research psychologists. One example of a study designed to test the skill of the clinician will suffice to show how the game is played. (The reader should note the actuarial use of a projective examination in this study.)

Grebstein (1963) asked three groups of five judges each to use

Rorschach psychograms to estimate the Wechsler-Bellevue IQ's of thirty VA hospital patients. One group of judges was *naive*; they had taken only an introductory course in the Rorschach. One group was *semisophisticated*; they were graduate students with more course work and clinical experience than the first group. The third group was *sophisticated*; they were professional clinical psychologists with at least five years of experience. The clinicians' competition was provided by a multiple regression equation, constructed by correlating ten Rorschach psychogram scores with Wechsler-Bellevue IQ for one hundred selected cases, other than those rated by the judges. The resultant equation, finally reduced to four factors and a constant, was then applied to predict IQ scores for the thirty original patients. It was found that both the judges and the statistical formula estimated IQ values significantly better than chance, but that degree of sophistication and experience was not a significant factor in determining the judges' accuracy of estimation. (Additional technical discussions of the statistical complexities of this problem may be found in Hammond, Hursch, and Todd [1964] and in Tucker [1964].)

Base rates.   Though not used in Grebstein's investigation, the concept of the *base rate*, a notion borrowed from the principles of Bayesian statistics (Edwards, Lindman & Savage, 1963), is important in establishing a numerical index of the value of a given method of decision making. Briefly, a base rate represents the natural rate of occurrence of a phenomenon in the population being studied. A high base rate is likely to lead the clinician and others to misjudge the value of his services. For example, if 80% of the clients seeking help at a given agency are known to be neurotic, a given diagnostic instrument must demonstrate its ability to improve significantly over the high degree of accuracy that would be achieved by calling all applicants neurotic with no diagnosis at all. The "Barnum effect" is produced by passing off base rate information as if it represented astute and efficient judgment. Thus, a practitioner may state that a given patient is depressed; but this statement is thought to have little diagnostic value if all other patients in the institution are also depressed.

One of the problems with base rate determination in clinical situations arises from the fact that because they involve human judgments rather than concrete objects or things, true base rates are seldom known or easily determined. Neurosis and depression, for example, are not physical existents; they are diagnostic verdicts. An actuarial investigator can count the number of rocks or trees in a field without relying on someone else to point them out; but in a clinical situation he cannot identify neurosis or depression independently of the judgments of the clinicians who assign these terms to particular patients. When he counts diagnostic labels on medical charts, the actuarial investigator does not establish a true rate of occurrence of neurosis or depression; he records only the frequency with which some psychiatrist or psychologist has judged these labels to be appropriate. If he then conducts a research that produces an instrument which identifies depression or neurosis more efficiently than might be accomplished on the basis of simple base rate prediction, he merely puts himself in the position of being able to predict probabilistically judgments that are usually considered valid by definition. Since the judgmental process in diagnosis cannot be avoided, it is hard to see what has been gained by such research. The new instrument may be more accurate than pure guesswork, and it may even predict the behavior of diagnosticians reasonably well; but it scarcely constitutes any improvement in the judgmental process of diagnosis itself.

This is not the place to enter into further discussion of the merits and deficiencies of the case for and against the clinician as a practitioner in applied situations. The argument is not of pressing concern to the science of personality; but it does represent an area of investigation in which the actuarial method has been extensively employed.

A noncompetitive predictive study.   A somewhat different use of actuarial prediction is exemplified by a study by Briggs, Wirt, and Johnson (1961) that attempted to predict juvenile delinquency from MMPI profiles and family history information. These investigators selected a sample of 573 cases from a larger population of 1,958 ninth grade boys, tested by Hathaway and Monachesi (1951) in an earlier research. Their sample was subdivided into two groups: 201 cases that showed delinquency "excitor" signs on MMPI profiles (as established by previous research); and 372 cases that did not evidence such signs.

Social agency files on these cases were then surveyed. Forty-two informational items were identified and grouped into seven categories: family disruption, poverty or need, dissocial behavior, psychiatry for family, marital disruption, inadequate parent-child relationship, and minor psychological problems. The cases were then rated on these categories, according to the number of specific items that applied. For unspecified reasons the investigators elected to deal only with the category (or, better, "subcategory") of family disruption due to disease, a grouping that contained six specific items.

Two levels of delinquency (the criterion) were defined in terms of police contacts after the collection of predictive data. The *less severe* level included all contacts of subjects with the police; the *more severe* level excluded from consideration those contacts involving minor infractions.

Statistical analyses were presented to show the relationship between actual and predicted occurrences of delinquency in the group of boys, who were chosen because of the presence of appropriate signs in their MMPI profiles. Accuracy of prediction was shown to improve as the number of family disruptions due to disease increased and to be higher when the *more severe* criterion of delinquency was employed. It was concluded that the MMPI and case history data satisfactorily identified subsamples that are highly saturated with predelinquent children. The authors characterized their study as "empirical rather than theoretical" but felt that their technique would be useful as a "quasidiagnostic" selection procedure for treatment programs aimed at the potential delinquent.

Several features of this study identify it as actuarial in intent. The definition of delinquency solely in terms of a practical criterion is characteristic of the method, as is the collection of large amounts of miscellaneous, and hopefully predictive, data from test records and social agency files. Also characteristic are the statistical procedures, which were employed not to test hypotheses but to demonstrate that the predictive formula is more accurate, at least in small subsamples, than the base rate.

The study failed to employ all the data available to arrive at the predictive formula. The authors did not explain their reasons for examining only one category of social information instead of all seven. They did suggest, however, that their other case history factors might prove useful in establishing additional predictive formulas. Presumedly, the use of only one of the many possible MMPI profiles that might have been studied was justified by the results of previous actuarial research.

EVALUATION

In its strictest applications, actuarialism is inapplicable to the study of personality as that term is understood here. On logical grounds it is impossible to draw inferences or test propositions about mediating psychological processes through the use of a method that is completely data oriented. Correlation coefficients and predictive formulas are scientifically meaningless in and of themselves. If they do not improve upon or confirm some conceptual understanding of significant processes, they are mere numbers, without theoretical importance.

The evaluation of the actuarial method therefore requires that a careful distinction be made between the needs of personality theory, as a field of psychological science, and the tasks the practitioner is called upon to do by the society that supports him. It is too often argued that the supreme test of a method is its degree of success or efficiency in predicting events in applied situations. It is further argued that by this criterion the actuarial approach has already demonstrated its superiority to personality theory.

The most common reply to this argument is to maintain that the tests by which personality theory and actuarialism are evaluated have been unfairly rigged against the clinician. It is often maintained that the clinician (the presumed representative of personality theory) has been given insufficient information or has been asked to make inappropriate judgments. The counterargument to this reply usually consists of additional research, showing that even when such objections are met, the actuarial approach retains its overall superiority in predicting practical criteria.

Fortunately, more thoughtful restatements of the predictive problem do exist; and some of these are worth considering briefly. Holt (1958) took an integrative position by calling attention to the regrettable fact that the question of predictive validity has become a matter of opposition between clinician and statistical formula, when it does not seem that it was intended to be so in the first place. Holt felt that real needs can best be met by giving up the idea of competition, in favor of a search for the best possible predictive combinations of actuarial and trained clinical judgments.

Taking a different tack, Sines (1964) presented an interesting analysis of the clinical situation, which is based on the argument that the test behavior-life behavior relationship is asymmetrical. He pointed out that most actuarial studies begin with a criterion and search for measurement patterns that correlate with it. By contrast, the clinician begins with measurement patterns and attempts to predict real-life behaviors from these. The actuarial method is thus able to predict successfully only when particular measures are significantly associated with the criterion. The clinician is more likely to recognize that many data configurations may lead to the same predicted behavior. Sines felt that validity studies would be more useful and realistic if they began with measurement patterns instead of the criterion and sought out the practical behavioral concomitants of these patterns. This suggestion seems eminently reasonable, and it deserves close attention in future research.

At this point the clinician qua social servant must be left to resolve his problems of prediction in his own way. The user and developer of personality theory has a different set of issues to face that are more relevant to this discussion. His problem is to recognize that most of the theories he employs were not, in fact, designed to serve the purposes usually imposed upon clinicians by social agencies. They were designed to explain the organized mediating processes of the individual. The measure of their ability to do so is not the degree to which they permit one to make psychiatric diagnoses or to predict success in on-the-job training, as useful as these predictions may be in some situations. The immediate goal of personality research, as such, is no more to predict clinical phenomena than the goal of the learning theorist is to predict the academic success of human children from studies of eyeblink response conditioning.

The scientist has a right to expect, even to demand, that theory be predictive; but what it predicts should be specified by the nature of the theory and by the procedures of the research efforts that operationize it. The prediction from personality theory that a particular client will evidence hostility under a certain set of conditions carries with it the scientific obligation to state how that client's hostility will be manifested and how the specified conditions may be recognized or produced. If the conditions occur and hostility is not evidenced, the theory is disconfirmed. If hostility appears but the conditions are other than those specified, the theory may rightfully be said to be inadequate; but it has not been disconfirmed. If the conditions never exist, the theoretical statements are simply not tested by the case. The proper evidence for hostility may be classes of responses to projective examinations, verbal expressions in an interview situation, overt behaviors on the ward or at home, restlessness and nightmares, or any other manifestation that is consistent with the individual and the circumstances under which he is observed. They must, of course, be made explicit in advance of their appearance; but they need not be universally, socially, or simply defined.

If personality theory has been lax in spelling out the implications and indices of the processes in which it is interested, it is subject to the severest criticism. The actuarial method does a considerable service by pointing out such weaknesses.

Surplus Meanings

It is important to bear in mind that strictly actuarial research does not involve conceptualization; neither predictor nor criterion can be assigned theoretical significance. Within the actuarial framework, therefore, number of arrests is not an index of antisocial hostility; divorce rate is not a measure of marital instability; and hospital discharge is not an index of benefit from therapy. To utilize quantifications as indications of anything other than what they specifically count is to impart to them unwarranted significance and meaning.

Of course, conceptual significance is commonly applied to actuarial measures in actual practice; and it is on the basis of these surplus meanings, expressed or implied, that the usefulness of existing theory or practice is often questioned. It should be evident by now that the mere application of a reliable measuring instrument with a suggestive name does not imply that something relevant to a specific theory of personality is necessarily being measured. Indeed, the actuary should be the first to point out that calling a set of items an anxiety scale in no way establishes that psychology has miraculously developed a test that measures anxiety, as the clinician or personologist understands that term. Still, actuarial investigators are prone to apply conceptual names to their measures; and the frequency with which they do so suggests that actuarial research is rarely as atheoretical as it sets out to be. It is unlikely that any scientific effort is entirely without conceptual underpinnings. Usually the real problem is not whether or not to be theoretical, it is to persuade those who do research to state their implicit theories openly. To be purely empirical in approaching practical problems, there is no special reason why the MMPI, for example, should be so popular as a predictive instrument. The fact that it is frequently used suggests that some idea exists to the effect that it measures something relevant; and it would be helpful to know what that something is. Otherwise, why not expect eye color, basal metabolism, or the page number of the telephone book on which the person's name is listed to work just as well?

These difficulties become most apparent when the phenomena of interest are not the obvious, easily identified type. For example, few knowledgeable psychologists would accept the naive identification of Jung's concept of extraversion with "number of clubs joined" by college sophomores. The distortion of the theoretical notion that is engendered by such an obviously incorrect operationization is so readily apparent that it requires no further discussion. Nevertheless, the relation between theory and measurement is not so clear with respect to all indices. For example, both Meehl (1956) and Marks and Seeman (1963) referred to a study by Halbower (1955) that demonstrated the superior ability of the MMPI profile to predict Q-sort descriptions of personality. It is tempting to conclude from these results that the actuarial method is superior to the clinician in describing personality, since the Q-sort was admittedly designed by Stephenson (1953) to serve exactly that purpose.

The problem is clearly one of surplus meaning. As employed by the actuary, neither the items of the MMPI nor the statements of the Q-sort are inherently capable of describing anything. Since a subject's true or false judgment of the content of specific MMPI items cannot be taken to have any inherent theoretical or descriptive significance, then the placement of various Q-sort contents by clinicians must not be assigned such significance either. To take seriously the item content in a criterion clinician's description of someone else's personality with the Q-sort should make no more sense to the actuarialist than to take seriously the content of a subject's self-description, using MMPI statements.

Marks and Seeman's work (1963) demonstrates this point concretely. The Q-sort employed in this study had been developed on the basis of extensive previous research. It consisted of 108 statements, subdivided unequally into 9 groups of from 3 to 25 statements each. This grouping was based upon what the authors called a "conceptual scheme for personality description"; and the statement classes were labelled in such a way as to suggest that the 9 groups had theoretical significance, for example, motivational needs, areas of conflict, mechanisms of defense, attitudes toward self. Marks and Seeman, however, did not utilize the groupings to arrive at any theoretical characterizations or differentiations among their subject samples. They remained methodologically consistent with their thoroughgoing actuarial approach and simply reported base rates and separate Q-sort statement means for each MMPI type. As indicated by the introduction to their book, however, Marks and Seeman were inclined to feel that the Q-sort arrays they acquired were, in fact, *descriptive* and that the ultimate product of their work constituted something more than a highly elaborate listing of concomitant facts. By giving their findings such significance, they suggest to the reader that their data actually describe personality. This, of course, they do not do. The task of describing personality requires a conceptual integration of data. It implies that statements, items, and numbers are taken to be representations, indicators, or signs of psychological states or processes.

Marks and Seeman's research did not set out to make a contribution to personality theory, and it did not make one. That is unfortunate; for it would be useful to the personality theorist to find out, for example, what types of need structures or defensive postures (as reflected in Q-sort descriptions) tend to be associated with what types of personal data or MMPI responses. To be sure, a well-developed personality theory would even have suggested specific predictions, the confirmation or rejection of which could make a significant contribution to scientific knowledge.

Conservatism

The term *prediction* has been used throughout this presentation without much comment. It is necessary to clarify its usage before proceeding to the discussion of the next method of research. The actuarial method, as such, is not inherently predictive. The results of actuarial investigations are commonly used in predictive ways; but the investigations themselves frequently do not involve any attempt at prognostication. The only predictions of which the actuary may usually be accused are those involved in his initial selection or rejection of predictive measures. If he does not include subjects' house numbers in his data, it is because he believes they will not correlate with his criterion; and that, of course, implies a prediction.

Pure actuarial researches seek out concomitant variations among quantities. They describe concurrences that exist at the time the data were analyzed, and they combine these concurrences in such a way as to make their future use as easy and as efficient as possible. Once these tasks have been accomplished and the resulting formula is applied in a practical situation, the success of the ensuing predictions is entirely a function of the similarity of all relevant conditions to those that existed at the time of the first investigation.

Using the formula in practice, then, tells what probably would have happened if the subject had been a member of the original sample. Even the study by Briggs et al. (1961), cited earlier, was predictive only for the original subjects. Any future use of their formula would necessarily be conservative, since it reflects only relationships between predictors and criteria observed in the past. As long as conditions remain entirely stable, the point is trivial. In certain practical circumstances, however, it may be vitally important to staff and client alike. Suppose, for example, that an actuarial formula is used to predict the diagnoses assigned by an agency's clinical director, who has a marked propensity for calling patients homosexual. If that director should change his diagnostic bias, or if he should be replaced by one who favors compulsivity, rather than homosexuality, as a diagnosis, the formula will fail to adjust. Previously valid diagnoses will then be wrong, and the predictive formula is likely to be discredited before new base rates can be established.

The essential conservatism of the results of actuarial research cannot be denied or ignored. Where the method is applicable, it is critical that the formulas derived from it be as contemporary as possible. Modern computers make it feasible to maintain an almost constant revision and updating of formulas of this type, on the basis of nearly continuous recomputation as new data are supplied. If diagnostic and evaluative procedures do not become static but are constantly being improved, the perpetuation of errors may thus be minimized, though never fully eliminated. If changes in conditions occur, the formula must respond to their effects with minimal delay by suitable adjustments of parameter terms; or it will soon become useless.

References

ANASTASI, ANNE. *Psychological testing.* New York: Macmillan, 1954.

BRIGGS, P. F., WIRT, R. D., & JOHNSON, ROCHELLE. An application of predictive tables to the study of delinquency. *J. consult. Psychol.*, 1961, *25*, 46-50.

CUTTER, F. Self-rejection distress: A new MMPI scale. *J. clin. Psychol.*, 1964, *20*, 150-153.

EDWARDS, W., LINDMAN, H., & SAVAGE, L. J. Bayesian statistical inference for psychological research. *Psychol. Rev.*, 1963, *70*, 193-242.

GREBSTEIN, L. C. Relative accuracy of actuarial prediction, experienced clinicians, and graduate students in a clinical judgment task. *J. consult. Psychol.*, 1963, *27*, 127-132.

HALBOWER, C. C. A comparison of actuarial versus clinical prediction to classes discriminated by MMPI. Unpublished doctoral dissertation, Univer. of Minnesota, 1955.

HAMMOND, K. R., HURSCH, CAROLYN J., & TODD, F. J. Analyzing the components of clinical inference. *Psychol. Rev.*, 1964, *71*, 438-456.

HATHAWAY, S. R., & McKINLEY, J. C. *Manual for the Minnesota multiphasic personality inventory.* Minneapolis: Univer. Minn. Press, 1943. (Revised in 1951, and published by the Psychological Corp., N.Y.)

HATHAWAY, S. R., & MEEHL, P. E. *An atlas for the clinical use of the MMPI.* Minneapolis: Univer. Minn. Press, 1951.

HATHAWAY, S. R., & MONACHESI, E. D. (Eds.) *Analyzing and predicting juvenile delinquency with the MMPI.* Minneapolis: Univer. Minn. Press, 1951.

HOLT, R. R. Clinical *and* statistical prediction: A reformulation and some new data. *J. abnorm. soc. Psychol.*, 1958, *56*, 1-12.

McKINLEY, J. C., & HATHAWAY, S. R. A multiphasic personality schedule

(Minnesota) : IV. Psychasthenia. *J. appl. Psychol.*, 1942, *26*, 614-624. (In Sarason, pp. 2-7 [see References, chapter 1, above].)

MARKS, P. A., & SEEMAN, W. *The actuarial description of abnormal personality.* Baltimore: Williams & Wilkins, 1963.

MEEHL, P. E. The dynamics of "structured" personality tests. *J. clin. Psychol.*, 1945, *1*, 296-303. (In Sarason, pp. 7-13 [see References, chapter 1, above].)

MEEHL, P. E. *Clinical versus statistical prediction.* Minneapolis: Univer. Minn. Press, 1954.

MEEHL, P. E. Wanted—a good cookbook. *Amer. Psychologist*, 1956, *11*, 263-272.

RIMM, D. Cost efficiency and test prediction. *J. consult. Psychol.*, 1963, *27*, 89-91.

SINES, J. O. Actuarial methods as appropriate strategy for the validation of diagnostic tests. *Psychol. Rev.*, 1964, *71*, 517-523.

STEPHENSON, W. *The study of behavior.* Chicago: Univer. Chicago Press, 1953.

STRONG, E. K., JR. *Vocational interests of men and women.* Stanford, Calif.: Stanford Univer. Press, 1943.

TUCKER, L. R. A suggested alternative formulation in the developments by Hursch, Hammond, and Hursch, and by Hammond, Hursch, and Todd. *Psychol. Rev.*, 1964, *71*, 528-530.

TYLER, LEONA E. Toward a workable psychology of individuality. *Amer. Psychologist*, 1959, *14*, 75-81. (In Mednick & Mednick, pp. 22-31 [see References, chapter 1, above].)

WATTRON, J. B. A prison maladjustment scale for the MMPI. *J. clin. Psychol.*, 1963, *19*, 109-110.

6

Factor analysis

Factor analysis has long been used as an aid to the process of induction, and it is the only research method in personality that is identified with particular mathematical procedures. In essence, factor analytic computations reduce large masses of information to manageable proportions by minimizing data redundancies through the systematic analysis of relationships among a variety of measures.

In keeping with present purposes, no attempt is made to describe or explain the mechanics of factor analysis as a set of computational operations. A beginner may appreciate the broad logic of this method with little difficulty; but he is well advised to refrain from undertaking factor analytic research without the benefit of formal instruction in its technical complexities. Without extensive training or at least the aid of a consulting specialist, most psychologists are unable to select appropriately from available mathematical alternatives or to make necessary technical decisions intelligently.

A relatively brief discussion of the rationale of factor analysis and a description of the Thurstone centroid procedure for extracting factors may be found in Guilford's classic book on psychometric methods (1954, pp. 470-538). Various techniques of factor extraction are explained and described in relatively simple terms by Fruchter (1954). A comprehensive, but more difficult, survey is available in Harman (1960). The Fruchter and Harman volumes contain bibliographies for those wishing to pursue the computational aspects of the subject in greater detail. Hall and Lindzey (1957) have presented summarizations of the conceptions of personality built from extensive factor analytic studies by Eysenck and

Cattell and have recommended books by Cattell (1952), Thomson (1951), and Thurstone (1947) as additional sources of technical procedural information.

GENERAL CHARACTERISTICS

Procedures and Decisions

All factor analytic studies begin with the collection of data that are amenable to summarization by means of correlation coefficients. The method is most appropriate for use with a particular correlational index, the Pearson product moment correlation coefficient (r); but estimates of r are often substituted, for computational simplicity or when measurement conditions do not permit the collection of continuous data.

The calculation of a correlation coefficient requires that a number of scores occur in pairs. The numerical index of correlation may be used to specify the degree to which it is possible to guess accurately the scores in one set of data from a knowledge of only the paired scores in the other set. When more than two sets of suitable measures are available, all possible measurement pairs are considered; and a separate correlation value is calculated for each pair (e.g., a with b, a with c, b with c). The results of these calculations are entered into a tabular display, called a *matrix,* which contains the indices of correlation of every measure with every other measure. It also contains indices selected to represent the correlation of each measure with itself (diagonal values). Sometimes, diagonal values of 1.00 are appropriate; sometimes, previously established test-reliabilities are used; as a third possibility, communalities may be estimated and entered into the matrix. Different purposes are served by each alternative, although communality estimates are preferred in most research. The technical reasons for this preference need not be considered, since the important point is that the selection of appropriate diagonal values is only one of many decisions, most of which affect the final results, that the factor analyst has to make in the conduct of an investigation. It is, in fact, characteristic of this method that, despite its complex mathematics, many solutions (indeed, an infinite number) to each specific research problem are possible, depending upon the way certain computational and procedural decisions are made.

Once the correlation matrix has been completed, the process of factor extraction is undertaken. Most of the operations involved in factor extraction are tedious and rather mechanical in nature. They may be performed by hand, although it is far more efficient to have the work done by properly programmed computers. Factor extraction reduces the size of the original matrix by identifying similarities among the various measures, according to the values of their intercorrelations. The result of the process is a second tabular display, smaller than the matrix, called a table of factor loadings. This table shows the number of factors needed to account for the values in the matrix and, when the factors are orthogonal, the intercorrelations of each measure with every resultant factor. The table of factor loadings and the original matrix are redundant; for mathematical manipulation alone permits reconstruction of the latter from the former.

The table of factor loadings that emerges from the extraction procedure is rarely in its most useful or convenient form. Additional transformations of the information it contains (called *rotations*) are required. The logic of rotation may be partially appreciated if one thinks of the factors as axes of a graph and of the loadings of the various measures as points on the graph, showing the spatial relation of each measure to each factor (axis). It will be recalled that, in a geometric representation of this type, axes, or coordinates, may be shifted to any convenient position without destroying the essential relationships the graph displays. For example, in a simple, two-dimensional graph, points that are five units apart on a straight line extending out from the origin might be represented by x, y values of, say 4, 3 and 8, 6 respectively. If the points stand for tests, the axes for factors, and the x and y values of the points for loadings, it is evident that both tests are weighted on both factors. It would now be difficult to interpret the psychological processes represented by the x and y coordinate lines, because the data provide no basis for assigning specific aspects or parts of the two tests to particular factors.

Suppose, however, that both axes were rotated to bring the x coordinate into line with the points. The corresponding x, y values would then be 5, 0 and 10, 0. The straight line distance between the points would remain unchanged, but the relation between them (i.e., their differential loadings on a single factor, x) is now obviously expressed by their new numerical identifications.

Because he always has more measures and factors to deal with than are used in the preceding, oversimplified example and because his measures seldom distribute themselves into convenient clusters, the factor analyst's problem is far more complex than the one just considered. Nevertheless, the goal of rotation is essentially the same as that expressed above. Reference axes are rotated until a useful and clearly communicated organization of the data is developed.

The criteria for most effective rotation are not standard or uniform. Sometimes, insistence on the rigorous application of a test of mathematical simplicity yields loadings that do not satisfy the requirements of maximum psychological meaning. Sometimes, oblique reference axes are more useful than perpendicular (orthogonal) ones. Here again, the investigator must choose among several possibilities available to him.

Mathematics as tools.   Differences among computational procedures and alternatives, especially with regard to rotation, are responsible for possible variation in the outcomes of factor analytic studies; and the student of personality research should be aware of this important characteristic of the method. Present concerns are with broader issues however; and other aspects of the factor analytic approach are more pertinent to this discussion, which is concerned primarily with overall research strategy.

Mathematical operations, no matter how complex, are tools to be used to serve research purposes. How well and how appropriately they are applied depends, to a large extent, upon how well an investigator understands their technical details; but it also depends upon knowing when to apply them. Saws, for example, are handy instruments; and there are many types and designs available. Knowing the difference between a crosscut and a ripsaw is useful only if the job to be done calls for the use of saws rather than pliers in the first place. The following discussion concentrates on the features and uses of factor analysis as a type of research tool, rather than on differences among the various specific computational procedures that may be applied once the method itself has been selected.

TYPES OF DATA

Factor Analytic Research Designs

Six basic factor analytic research designs were originally suggested by Cattell (1946). These designs are commonly referred to by the letters *O*, *P*, *Q*, *R*, *S*, and *T*; and they differ in the kinds of data they employ and in the nature of the factors they yield. In the following sections, *R* and *Q* are considered together because they are *single occasion* designs; both utilize large numbers of scores and relatively large numbers of subjects, although all measures are taken on all persons only once. *P* and *O* are treated together because they are *single subject* designs, in which large numbers of scores are obtained from one person on many occasions. *S* and *T* are treated together because both are *single score* designs, in which large numbers of subjects are measured on a single function on several occasions. The differences between design pairs, in terms of factor yields, will become apparent in succeeding sections. (A helpful, nontechnical summary of the various designs is also available in Fruchter [1954, pp. 202-204].)

R and Q. The research design most commonly associated with the factor analytic method is the type designated *R* by Cattell. In this design, subjects, preferably a large number, are administered a battery of tests or quantifiable examinations at one time. The resulting measures are intercorrelated to determine which tests or numerical indices belong together as factors. For example, twenty attitude scales of twenty items each might be administered to a large sample of subjects. Suppose that a factor analysis of the resulting data indicated that most of the differences among subjects on these scales could be accounted for by four independent factors. The investigator is then in a position to construct four new or revised instruments of perhaps twenty items each (a total of eighty items) that will distinguish among individuals as efficiently as the original instruments, which involved a total of four hundred items. Furthermore, if he interprets his results in a theoretically meaningful way, he stands to gain important insights into the structure of attitudes, as measured by the types of scales he used.

Q-design also involves obtaining many scores (usually from about 30 to about 150) from a number of subjects. Instead of factor analyzing tests, however, the subjects themselves are intercorrelated with each other. For technical reasons, *Q* studies do not usually use standard psychometric instruments but sets of statements, called *Q* sorts, that are arranged by a subject to describe the events or psychological entities of interest to the investigator (Stephenson, 1953, pp. 47-61). The form of the arrangement is specified in advance, and the investigator is interested in how statements are organized into the final description. He is concerned with the patterning of statements, much as a clinician might be interested in the *shape* of a profile of test scores, quite independently of the absolute values of the scores themselves.

In *Q*-designs, if two persons organize the descriptive statements in very similar ways, the resultant *r* between them will be high and positive. If their patterns of response are unrelated, the *r* between them will approach a chance value of zero. If the patterns are systematically dissimilar, the *r* will be high and negative. Factor analysis of these data then tells the investigator which sets of response patterns, provided by his subjects, belong together. By inference, he therefore knows which *persons* tend to be similar. The result is a typology, a classification of people, rather than of measures as in *R* design.

In a *structured* *Q* sort the descriptive statements that the subjects use are purposefully selected to represent particular theoretical variables. Usually, equal numbers of statements are identified with each theoretical category or each end of a postulated personality dimension. When a structured *Q* sort is employed, the investigator may examine the distributions of items with particular theoretical meanings, in the average or composite response pattern of each person-type. He may thereby arrive at theoretical characterizations of the groups of persons that comprise each factor in his results.

No generally accepted *Q* sorts exist as standard devices for the assessment of personality organizations, but a variety of specific *Q*-sort instruments has been originated for particular research projects. A list of 1,197 "phenotypic personality traits," many of which are suitable for use in *Q* sorts, has been prepared by Meehl, Schofield, Glueck, Studdiford, Hastings, and Hathaway (1959).

P and O.   Less common than R or Q in the familiar literature on personality is *P-design*. In this design a number of normative measures are obtained several times from a single subject. Intercorrelations are determined among measures, and the final factors reflect the stability of relations between tests or indices over time. In *P*-designs, two measures correlate at a high level only if the relation between them remains stable during all testings. Suppose, for example, that on the first administration of the battery, a subject obtains high scores (compared to standardizing groups) on two tests, both of which demand maximum speed of response. If, on later administrations of the battery, his performances on these two tests tend to decrease and increase together, perhaps as a function of fatigue and rest, the intercorrelation between the tests will be high. The resultant factors therefore reveal the similarities among measures that tend to vary together consistently on the various testing occasions.

O-design is rare in psychological research. It is similar to Q-technique in its focus on *patterns* of relations among measures. In this case, however, occasions instead of people are intercorrelated; for the investigation has only one subject. Factor analysis of *O*-data leads to statements about similarities and differences among testing situations. An example of a study using *O*-design is presented later.

S and T.   *S-design* involves the intercorrelation of persons, on whom a single measure has been taken on a number of occasions or under a variety of conditions. The result of a factor analysis is a typology, as in Q-design; but here the subjects are grouped according to the similarity of their patterns of responses on repeated measurements with a single test. *S*-design might be used in personality research to classify persons according to mood patterns over time, as measured by a single euphoria-disphoria index for example. It could also serve to classify persons according to their differential susceptibility to states of anxiety or stress, as measured in a number of environmental situations designed to arouse such conditions.

T-design also involves obtaining a single score from each of many persons on many occasions or under many conditions. Here, however, the occasions or conditions, rather than the persons, are intercorrelated. When only two administrations are used and when conditions are as similar as possible on the two occasions, the design merely constitutes an assessment of the test-retest reliability of the measuring instrument. If the number of administrations is increased and the conditions are varied, T-design becomes a device for examining similarities among situations with respect to a single variable. If differences among individuals do not change under altered measurement conditions (if the correlation between situations is high), the investigator infers that the conditions themselves are functionally similar. T-design could be extremely useful for factor analyzing a variety of experimental conditions that are designed to produce the same central states, for example, gratification, frustration, anxiety, stress.

EXAMPLES

Relevant examples of certain varieties of factor analytic research are difficult to find. R and Q are best represented in the existing literature. P- and O-designs are rare, but not entirely unheard of. S- and T-designs are practically nonexistent, and no examples of these are presented.

R-design

The bulk of factor analytic research uses R-designs. By no means is all of this research relevant to the interests of the personality theorist, but several concrete examples will serve to suggest its possibilities.

A common use of factor analysis is to simplify measurement techniques. To this end, Kassebaum, Couch, and Slater (1959) administered the MMPI to 160 college freshmen and factor analyzed the scores of these subjects on 32 scales designed for this instrument. Three factors were extracted, and these were identified by the properties of the various scales that were highly saturated in each. The first factor was named ego weakness versus ego strength. The second factor was named introversion-extraversion. The third was tentatively named tender-minded sensitivity; but it was found to account for so little variance that it was not considered further. The investigators also calculated what they called "fusion factors" (i.e., factors lying midway between the reference axes of the original factors).

The most significant aspect of this study is its suggestion that complex personality measures may be essentially classifiable into two groups: those that measure ego strength and those that measure introversion-extraversion. The investigation suggests the radical simplification of measurements and concepts that may be possible through the use of R-designs with standard psychometric instruments.

Rorschach responses were similarly factor analyzed by Geertsma (1962). Using data from 157 normal subjects, collected by a previous investigator, 20 coded responses and psychogram ratios were factor analyzed to simple structure. Since the seven factors obtained were intercorrelated, a second-order factor analysis was performed. That is, the factors themselves were combined into two, more inclusive factors. It is not necessary to consider Geertsma's results in detail. Suffice it to say that his primary factors were similar to the customary scoring categories for this examination and seemed to justify the scoring procedures commonly used in coding Rorschach responses. The second-order factors appeared to distinguish between cognitive activities and affective processes, a distinction that is already familiar to Rorschach workers.

Nichols and Strümpfer (1962) performed an interesting R-design study on the well-known draw-a-person test, which is often proposed as a measure of personality variables. Drawings of human figures were obtained from 107 male college students and from 90 male VA patients. Of the VA patients, 30 were psychiatrically normal, 30 were diagnosed as neurotic, and 30 were diagnosed as schizophrenic. These drawings were evaluated by a wide variety of methods suggested in the literature. In all, 32 scores were included (one of which simply identified the sample to which the subjects belonged) in an overall factor analysis. A second factor analysis, using somewhat fewer scores but including a score for adjustment, was performed on data from the VA patients alone.

The first factor analysis produced four apparently meaningful factors. Factor I appeared to relate primarily to the overall quality of the drawing. Factor II was a group membership factor, separating VA from college subjects. Only the sample identification score and the highly correlated age score were heavily loaded in this factor.

Factor III was loaded only on measures of the size of the drawings. Factor IV was defined by the scores identified with the variable, "aggression." The analysis of data from the VA sample alone also yielded four factors, a quality factor, a size factor, a defensiveness or constrictiveness factor, and an adjustment factor. No drawing variable had its major loading on the adjustment factor.

The authors felt that most of their data could be accounted for by differences in sheer overall quality of the drawings. Despite the pervasiveness of this factor, however, neither it nor any specific score correlated to any marked degree with gross adjustment. It was concluded that specific aspects of figure drawings that might be indicative of the personality of the individual producing those drawings are not likely to be evident in group research because of large individual differences in overall quality of the drawings themselves.

An important feature of this study was its use of a factor analysis of data from the VA sample to test the proposition that varying levels or types of adjustment (normal, neurotic, schizophrenic) are systematically reflected in features of the human figure drawings which can be scored. Failure to find a factor which was heavily loaded in both adjustment scores and indices of drawing characteristics was used as evidence to disconfirm this proposition and, by implication, to cast doubt on the more general notion that personality characteristics are reflected in human figure drawings in uniform fashion by all persons. It is not essential to consider the adequacy of the study as hypothesis-testing research; but the reader should find it worthwhile to perform his own evaluation, as an exercise in methodological criticism.

Q-design

Studies using Q-designs are comparatively infrequent, but they do appear occasionally. Q-designs require factor analytic procedures and the use of Q-sort instruments. It is important to remember, however, that only a small percentage of studies that use Q-sort instruments employ them in factor analytic fashion. As previously mentioned, Q sorts are measuring devices constructed according to Stephenson's original suggestions. They are often called "ipsative" because they measure variations of a number of scores obtained from a single individual around his own mean. By contrast, standard psychometric tests are "normative" because they measure variations of single scores obtained from many individuals around a norm, or group average (Broverman, 1962). Q sorts need not be subjected to factor analyses, and frequently they are not. A survey of researches that use Q-sort instruments in a variety of ways, not all of which are factor analytic, has been provided by Wittenborn (1961).

One of the best known factor analytic studies using Q-design was reported by the originator of the technique (Stephenson, 1953, pp. 167-172). From an examination of Jung's writings, Stephenson collected about two thousand statements describing introverted and extraverted personality types. From this pool of items, 121 were selected to form a sample of Q-sort statements for research purposes. Fifty subjects used these statements to describe "an ideal extravert," "an ideal introvert," and their "usual self." Three descriptions were obtained from each subject. As is usual in Q-sort research, each description was obtained by having subjects categorize the items according to how much each statement was "like" or "unlike" the psychological entity identified by the instructions. The frequency of items in the various categories was such that the overall distribution approximated the well-known normal curve. According to the degree of similarity between an individual's descriptions of the two "ideals" and his "self," 15 subjects were selected who described themselves as being much like their own conception of either the extravert or introvert. (These subjects were 8 women who described themselves as introverts and 7 men who described themselves as extraverts.) Self-descriptions of the selected subjects were then intercorrelated, and a factor analysis was performed on the resulting matrix. Two main factors were identified and found to meet the criterion of simple structure after rotation of the axes. That is, persons who were high on one factor were low (or unsaturated) on the other. The two factors corresponded very closely to the subdivision of subjects according to the self-ideal correlations described above. The men, who identified themselves as extraverted, comprised one factor; the women, who identified themselves as introverted, comprised the other. The factor loadings of the self-descriptions of the remaining subjects were then determined; and the identity of each, as extravert or introvert, was assessed and tabulated. It was concluded that the two-factor structure provided an adequate descriptive frame of reference for data from all subjects, and it was inferred that evidence in support of Jung's typology had been obtained.

It is interesting to note that, on an individual basis, introversion and extraversion tended to be negatively correlated. That is, if a particular person described himself as being like the introvert, he described himself with the same Q-sort items as being the opposite of the extravert (high negative correlation). The factor structure, however, described independent factors, rather than the two ends of a single dimension. This means that if one knew a single subject to be strongly and positively saturated on the introversion factor, one could not predict that the same individual would be strongly and negatively loaded on the extraversion factor. The types, then, are not opposites, as would be suggested by data from individuals; they are simply different.

Another Q-sort study employing factor analytic methods was conducted by Nadler and Shontz (1959). In this research, the Q-sort instrument was composed of 63 items designed to describe workers in the sheltered shop of a rehabilitation agency. Descriptions of 28 workers were obtained, not from the workers themselves but from their supervisors. Since two supervisors described each worker, it was possible to ascertain the degree of agreement between supervisors and to construct composite descriptions of each worker. Interjudge reliability was considered satisfactory, and a factor analysis of the composite descriptions was executed. Six factors, or personality types, were thus identified.

Besides the Q-sort items themselves, two sources of information were available for discovering the nature of these factors. The first consisted of agency records on each subject, containing such data as age, sex, performance IQ, and work ratings in the shop. These were correlated with subjects' loadings on the various factors. By this means, the first factor was identified as a work-orientation factor, because subjects with high loadings on it strongly tended to be rated as being good workers. The second factor was identified as "intellectual deficit," since subjects with high loadings on this factor had very low performance IQ's.

The second source of additional data was descriptive case history information available on all subjects. Interpreted qualitatively, these materials, combined with an analysis of the content of Q-sort items descriptive of subjects of various types, then led to the naming of the rest of the factors. The nature of these factors is not especially important, because the purpose of Nadler and Shontz's study was not to identify types that could be generalized to all sheltered-shop situations. It was intended only to establish that personality patterns or types provide meaningful descriptions of clients in such settings. In this, the authors felt that they were successful.

P-design

P-designs have not yet become popular in personality research, and a pointedly relevant example is not available to the author. Fruchter (1954, pp. 186-191), however, summarized a P-design study by Cattell, Cattell, and Rhymer (1947), which involved the successive readministration of a battery of tests, yielding 14 separate measures, to a single subject on 55 days. Four resultant bipolar factors were found to account for much of the variance in the data. Considering the large amount of information drawn from this subject, it is evident that factor analysis is a most useful device for condensing and summarizing complex relationships of this sort.

P-design may be used to confirm, in individuals, factors discovered by conventional R-technique studies. Unique P-factors may also serve a useful purpose in describing the organization of traits or abilities in particular individuals. Holtzman (1962) has called attention to the special statistical dangers inherent in P-design research, because it involves repeated measures on the same subject. His criticisms apply to designs other than P as well; but they are highly technical and need not be considered in detail here.

O-design

An interesting, though not readily available, example of the use of O-design is Bowdlear's study of a single person with idiopathic epilepsy (1955). Using a theoretically structured group of descriptive Q-sort statements, Bowdlear asked this subject to describe himself under a variety of specified conditions. For instance, he described himself as he is when he is angry, when he is having a seizure, when he is with his girl friend, and so forth. A total of twenty-five psychologically important occasions or conditions were thus described and factor analyzed to determine which produced similar psychological states (i.e., self-descriptions) in the subject. Analysis of item contents then served to characterize the occasion-factors in theoretical terms.

O-design offers as yet untapped possibilities for the study of organizational changes over time or in a variety of situations with known psychological properties. Combined with the strategy of the representative case, described in a later chapter (chapter 11) it is perhaps one of the most promising and least appreciated research designs available to the personologist.

S- and T-designs

As indicated above, no examples of the use of S- and T-designs are available to the author. These designs appear to hold great promise for the study of personality, but their real potential cannot be evaluated until they are more commonly used in research.

EVALUATION

Criticisms and Problems

Most legitimate criticisms of factor analytic research arise from concern over the lack of uniqueness in factor solutions to correlation matrices and from doubts about the value of inferences drawn from these solutions, once they are obtained.

Lack of uniqueness. Indeterminateness of outcome is an advantage for purely descriptive or inductive research, since it provides a flexibility that permits the investigator to derive maximum meaning from his data. But it can be troublesome when a study is designed to answer fairly specific research questions. Indeed, the more pointed the purpose of an investigation, the more bothersome this feature of the method tends to be. The lack of uniqueness in factor analytic results can easily leave one in doubt as to whether a specifically presented solution is necessarily the best the data have to offer. The previously cited study by Geertsma (1962), for example, constituted a reanalysis of data originally obtained for a factor analytic study by Wishner (1959). Wishner tested three major hypotheses (and a fourth that did not concern Geertsma) and reported confirmation of the first, no confirmation of the second, and some support for the third. By contrast, Geertsma's reanalysis produced only partial support for the first two of Wishner's hypotheses. The only differences between the two studies were computational; they concerned the number of factors extracted and the technique of rotation.

When specific hypotheses are at stake, it does not seem desirable for the outcome of an investigation to be so subject to after-the-fact influence that radically different conclusions may be drawn, as a function of who performs the statistical operations; and this certainly seems to be a weakness in the factor analytic approach to some kinds of research questions. It is possible that the development of more satisfactory and universally acceptable criteria for factor extraction and rotation will reduce the importance of this objection to the method as a hypothesis-testing device. In the meantime, however, the relevance of the criticism must be recognized and admitted in any attempt to evaluate factor analysis as a research strategy.

Problems of interpretation. Even if factor analysts came to agree completely about when to stop extracting factors and how to rotate axes, the general problem of interpretation would remain unsolved; for the factor analytic method exerts little control over the inferential processes of the investigator. The theoretical significances of all the measures used in a factor analytic study are rarely specified in advance; and if they could be, it would often be unnecessary to do the factor analysis. Thus, the investigator is rarely constrained by rigorous a priori rules of correspondence to interpret his factors in any particular way. Indeed, it is often said of factor analysis that "you get out of it only what you put into it." If what is put into the matrix is sufficiently vague, the researcher may get out of his results almost anything that pleases him. It is often noted that interpretations of factors are not, in reality, names of things; they are tentative labels assigned to data congruencies. It is possible to attach any of a number of labels to a given factor structure, even to one that has been confirmed by successive investigations. Which of these labels may be correct can sometimes not be decided until more controlled research has been used to verify propositions derived from theories in which the various labels play correspondingly different conceptual roles.

For the interested reader, a comprehensive and not-too-technical discussion of some of the problems of inference faced by factor analysts is available in Coan (1964). This article deals with the various possible levels of correspondence between statistical results and inferred conceptual factors. Although it has particular relevance for factor analysis, the article also deals with matters that are of concern to the psychologist interested in more general methodological problems in personality research. (See also Royce [1963].)

Strengths and Potentialities

On the basis of criticisms such as those presented above, it is sometimes argued that factor analytic research, like case studies, can only suggest hypotheses, and that its usefulness is confined to the preliminary, exploratory stages of scientific investigation. Like most generalities of its type, this statement sounds reasonable; but it greatly oversimplifies important issues.

Some hints of the real possibilities of the factor analytic method for research in general psychology have been provided by Guilford (1961), and his statement provides a good starting point for the balance of this evaluative discussion. Guilford felt that the results of properly executed factor analytic research are capable of providing the basis for constructing comprehensive theories of behavior. He criticized current users of this method for their focus on the relatively restricted problem of merely reducing data to simple and convenient form. That type of research, he felt, is unlikely to produce information of basic theoretical interest.

In contrast to the view that is most often expressed (that factor analysis is not useful for testing hypotheses), Guilford complained that many factor analytic studies are unproductive primarily because they do not state or test hypotheses. It is necessary, he felt, to ask questions before collecting data. For example, a particular factor structure may be predicted from theory, and tests may be selected or specifically constructed for a research battery, to reflect the traits or abilities with which that theory is concerned. Variables may be manipulated by systematically altering test contents, instructions, or response requirements (note the introduction of an experimental attitude). From such variations, changes in factor structure, as suggested by theory, may be anticipated; and the success of these anticipations will indicate the usefulness of the theory from which they were derived.

Guilford stressed the identification of factor analytic method with theoretical approaches that are concerned with what goes on inside the organism, rather than only with what is directly observable about the organism's behavior. Although factor analysis is objective in the sense that it employs measures of overt responses (e.g., test scores), its ultimate concern is with "psychological properties of a central nature." The theories it produces are likely to emphasize functional totalities and organizations. Unlike the behaviorist, the factor theorist does not back off from a concern for central variables or from an interest in the whole functioning individual.

Guilford's remarks were concerned primarily with the use of R-designs in factor research, since his own extensive work with the method employed these designs almost exclusively. His comments apply to all the factor analytic designs, however; and many of them have meaning for all forms of research in personality.

Hypothesis testing.   When factor structures that may be similarly interpreted appear repeatedly in a series of independent investigations using a variety of different measuring instruments, increased confidence may be placed in the generality of inferences drawn from the data. Even greater weight is put on investigations in which emergent factor structures are successfully predicted on the basis of existing concepts.

If predictions of factor structures are considered *hypotheses*, it follows that this method can be used for hypothesis testing. It is often argued, however, that hypothesis testing requires the use of experimentation; and factor analysis is a descriptive, rather than an experimental, research strategy. This argument carries little weight, since it has already been noted that there is no inherent incompatibility between the experimental approach and the use of factor analytic research designs. It is regrettable that the experimental attitude is not more common in research that uses factor analytic designs; but failure to use a method well scarcely proves that proper use of it is impossible.

Even when deliberate experimentation is not employed, there

are some kinds of theoretical propositions that may be satisfactorily investigated by factor analytic means. There is, after all, something to be said for a theory that predicts relations among a group of persons, measures, or situations with a high level of consistency. A theory of motivation, for example, that is repeatedly confirmed by factor analyses of different sets and types of motivational measures, administered to samples of a wide variety of subject populations, would not be far amiss in claiming for itself a high degree of generality. Neither would a typology that repeatedly appears in Q-design analyses, when measurement contents and subject groups are purposively varied to provide a wide sampling of both. By the same reasoning, a theory that specifies genotypic similarities and differences among phenotypically different experimental situations (occasions) could gain strong support from the results of a properly executed study using T-design and factor analytic mathematical procedures.

The major advantage of this method is that it deals directly and explicitly with complexly patterned information; and the personality theorist has a right to feel that the study of his subject requires research that does not sacrifice the integrity of persons or situations by compelling a piecemeal examination of isolated part processes. Indeed, many of the strengths and weaknesses of the factor analytic method parallel those of personality research in general. The personologist has to recognize that his research results may not often be definitive or unequivocal, and that many of the phenomena he studies can be satisfactorily explained in more than one way. If this recognition makes him uncomfortable, he can find solace in the fact that his approach, like the factor analytic method, has the compensatory merit of dealing with human behavior and experience in a way which recognizes the integrity of the person and which preserves the necessary properties of the events it proposes to investigate.

The Unfamiliar Methods

Since few examples of some factor analytic designs are available in the literature, it is worthwhile to consider for a moment a hypothetical example of how these might be used productively. A relatively simple investigation, that might interest a student of personality, would involve examining a number of subjects several times with the same instrument. The instrument should measure a function which is likely to change in response to situational variations; thus the function should not be something like intelligence, life style, or ego strength. It might, however, be something like tension or mood. If crude estimates were considered satisfactory, subjects might be asked merely to rate their general subjective states on several scales, for example, tense—calm; sad—happy; weak—strong; fearful—confident. An enterprising teacher might decide that the members of his class could perform this task each day after class sessions are over. (At least that would assure a common time of day and known, if not entirely stable, environmental conditions. The instructor would know, for example, which data were collected on days when examinations are given.)

The result would be a volume of data that could be treated in several ways by factorial techniques. A single composite index of euphoria-disphoria might be constructed, and S-design might be employed to group subjects according to the similarity of their mood patterns over the course of the semester. It will probably appear from this analysis that some persons are "in phase" with each other (that is, they constitute a type), while others are "out of phase." If the class is a relatively informal one, in which students get to know each other well, sociogram information obtained at the end of the semester might permit the testing of hypotheses about the influence of mood correspondence (sympathy or antipathy, in the true senses of the words) on social choice. The proposition that choices within types will be more frequent than choices across types could then be evaluated statistically. In addition, much would be learned about the characteristics of mood fluctuation, from an examination of the differences between types on actual self-ratings.

The same data might also be handled in other ways. Self-ratings on specific items from, say, the most popular or most academically successful student might be selected for analysis in a P-design. A factor analysis would then reveal the structure of the various self-ratings that this person made over the course of the semester. A similar factor analysis of data from the least popular or least successful student would provide a suggestive contrast to the first procedure. Depending on the nature of the course, predictions might be made about the resulting differences.

Using the composite index, T-design might be applied to an analysis of the class situation itself. Selected periods that ought to influence overall mood might be specially chosen for inclusion in the matrix. For example, the investigator might include several examination days, several days between examinations, several days on which possibly disturbing material was discussed, and so forth. Factor analysis of these data would reveal the relation between situational characteristics and mood ratings, by grouping the occasions according to the similarities and differences among the responses they produce.

The possibilities inherent in even such an apparently simple study as this have by no means been exhausted by these alternatives. The suggested study may nonetheless be sufficient to convince the reader that the factor analytic method has potential that has largely gone unrecognized. More important, it should convey the impression that a well-defined subject of inquiry and a few hypotheses, no matter how tentative, are vital to the conduct of this type of research.

Measurement

When all is said that is to be said about the factor analytic method, per se, one difficulty still remains to be resolved. It is the difficulty of measurement. Factor analytic research, like most research, can be no better than the measurements it employs. The example above was qualified by the phrase "if crude estimates are considered satisfactory." It is unfortunate but true that crude estimates are often considered satisfactory too early in the research process. Guilford advised that systematic variations in measuring instruments provide a useful means for evaluating hypotheses in factor analytic research. He is undoubtedly correct. It is very rare, however, to find an investigator who follows Guilford's advice. It is just as rare to find that instruments included in factor analytic studies have undergone adequate pretesting and validation to justify their inclusion as indices of anything at all. Indeed, some measurement problems of particular importance to factor analytic research, which have, as yet, no satisfactory solutions, can be identified (Holtzman, 1962; Sundland, 1962).

The possibilities of factor analysis as a method of test development have probably been insufficiently appreciated by personality theorists. Cattell (1963, pp. 430-431) noted the resistance among many psychologists to the idea that "factor analysts are in a sense instrument makers and others are instrument users." Yet, it seems reasonable to suppose that careful investigations based on factor analysis, by "mental measurement specialists," have the potential to provide devices for assessing meaningful personality processes in theoretically acceptable ways. Personality research is in dire need of such measurements, and personologists would be ill-advised to ignore suggestions that might improve the situation.

The weaknesses of measuring instruments, of course, cannot be held responsible for the weaknesses of the methods that employ them. Still, it does seem that factor analytic research is particularly prone to include poorly developed instruments. Perhaps it is necessary to view this method, not merely as a way to simplify and classify heterogeneous data, but as a way of obtaining systematic, meaningful, and carefully derived information that bears directly upon issues of theoretical importance, before this problem will be resolved.

References

BOWDLEAR, C. M. Dynamics of idiopathic epilepsy as studied in one case. Unpublished doctoral dissertation, Western Reserve Univer., 1955.

BROVERMAN, D. M. Normative and ipsative measurement in psychology. *Psychol. Rev.*, 1962, *69*, 295-305.

CATTELL, R. B. Personality structure and measurement. I. The operational determination of trait unities. *Brit. J. Psychol.*, 1946, *36*, 88-103.

CATTELL, R. B. *Factor analysis: An introduction and manual for psychologist and social scientist.* New York: Harper & Row, 1952.

CATTELL, R. B. Concepts of personality growing from multivariate experiment. In J. M. Wepman & R. W. Heine (Eds.), *Concepts of personality.* Chicago: Aldine, 1963. Pp. 413-448.

CATTELL, R. B., CATTELL, A. K. S., & RHYMER, R. M. P-technique demonstrated in determining psycho-physical source traits in a normal individual. *Psychometrika*, 1947, *12*, 267-288.

COAN, R. W. Facts, factors, and artifacts: The quest for psychological meaning. *Psychol. Rev.*, 1964, *71*, 123-140.

FRUCHTER, B. *Introduction to factor analysis.* Princeton, N.J.: Van Nostrand, 1954.

GEERTSMA, R. H. Factor analysis of Rorschach scoring categories for a population of normal subjects. *J. consult. Psychol.*, 1962, *26*, 20-25.

GUILFORD, J. P. *Psychometric methods.* (2nd ed.) New York: McGraw-Hill, 1954.

GUILFORD, J. P. Factorial angles to psychology. *Psychol. Rev.,* 1961, *68,* 1-20.

HALL, C. S., & LINDZEY, G. *Theories of personality.* New York: Wiley, 1957.

HARMAN, H. H. *Modern factor analysis.* Chicago: Univer. Chicago Press, 1960.

HOLTZMAN, W. H. Methodological issues in P-technique. *Psychol. Bull.,* 1962, *59,* 248-256.

KASSEBAUM, G. G., COUCH, A. S., & SLATER, P. E. The factorial dimensions of the MMPI. *J. consult. Psychol.,* 1959, *23,* 226-236.

MEEHL, P. E., Schofield, W., Glueck, B. C., Jr., Studdiford, W. B., Hastings, D. W., & Hathaway, S. R. *Minnesota-Ford pool (reduced) of phenotypic personality items.* Minneapolis: Univer. Minn., 1959.

NADLER, E. B., & SHONTZ, F. C. A factor analytic study of motivational patterns in a sheltered shop. *Pers. Guid. J.,* 1959, *37,* 444-450.

NICHOLS, R. C., & STRÜMPFER, D. J. W. A factor analysis of draw-a-person test scores. *J. consult. Psychol.,* 1962, *26,* 156-161.

ROYCE, J. R. Factors as theoretical constructs. *Amer. Psychologist,* 1963, *18,* 522-528.

STEPHENSON, W. *The study of behavior: Q-technique and its methodology.* Chicago: Univer. Chicago Press, 1953.

SUNDLAND, D. M. The construction of Q-sorts: A criticism. *Psychol. Rev.,* 1962, *69,* 62-64.

THOMSON, G. H. *The factorial analysis of human ability.* (5th ed.) Boston: Houghton Mifflin, 1951.

THURSTONE, L. L. *Multiple factor analysis.* Chicago: Univer. Chicago Press, 1947.

WISHNER, J. Factor analyses of Rorschach scoring categories and first response times in normals. *J. consult. Psychol.,* 1959, *23,* 406-413.

WITTENBORN, J. R. Contributions and current status of Q methodology. *Psychol. Bull.,* 1961, *58,* 132-142.

7

Correlational method

The correlational method is one of the most popular of the various approaches to the empirical study of personality. Perhaps that is because it superficially appears to be the simplest research strategy available and because the data it employs usually have an aura of natural authenticity that appeals to the personologist's interests.

Technically, correlational research is distinguished by its identification of relevant theoretical variables with measured, rather than with systematically produced, differences among subjects. It is sometimes described by saying that it compares one set of responses with another, drawn from the same group of subjects. This statement is inaccurate, however, since it does not identify the most important feature of the method. Correlational research does use response relations as basic data, but it is always primarily concerned with the theoretical inferences that may be drawn from the demonstration of these relations. It never treats responses as conceptually barren observations of simple empirical facts. The importance of this feature of the method will become clearer as the discussion proceeds.

NATURE OF CORRELATION

Before considering in detail the various uses of correlational research, it is necessary to discuss the broad concept of correlation itself. In the preceding chapter, the correlation coefficient was said to provide an index of the degree to which one set of scores could be accurately estimated from the knowledge of another set of scores obtained by the same subjects. Historically, use of the correlation coefficient has been associated with research on individual differences. There still exist groups of psychologists who are very much concerned with knowing the degree to which it is generally possible to predict behavior in one situation from a knowledge of behavior in another. The personnel psychologist, for example, wishes to know how well responses to an employee selection test correlate with actual performance on various jobs. The clinical psychologist wishes to know which responses to examinations like the Rorschach or the MMPI correlate with the presence or absence of psychopathological conditions. It has already been suggested that actuarial research is always correlational in character, since its concern is primarily for "what goes along with what" in the applied situation.

The usual correlational index (the Pearson product moment r) is derived from the mathematical manipulation of scores obtained from individuals, considered in relation to the total sample. But a more inclusive, abstract concept of correlation as a means for dealing with research data does not preclude the possibility of comparing groups as wholes with each other.

Consider the possible use of the correlational method to investigate the relationship between ego strength and adaptation to stress. If a suitable measure of ego strength were available and if a suitable test situation could be constructed so that adaptation to a standard stress condition could be sensitively assessed, there is no reason why an investigator could not simply calculate a correlation coefficient of the usual kind between subjects' scores on the two measures and draw his conclusion from the size and significance of that figure. The raw data might look something like those in Table 1.

Suppose, however, that measures permitting accurate discriminations among individual subjects were not available. The investigator might be able to classify his subjects satisfactorily into, say, only five groups on ego strength because he does not feel confident of discriminations among subjects within groups. His data would then look more like those in Table 2. Instead of calculating a correlation coefficient, the investigator would probably now employ analysis of variance, a statistical technique by which the differences among the means of the various ego strength groups on the stress-response measurement may be tested for significance. Observe that the research problem is still essentially correlational. Previously measured subject differences on the independent variable are systematically compared with obtained subject differences on the dependent variable. All subjects are exposed to the same stress situation (i.e., there is no differential manipulation of conditions as a function of the groups to which subjects are assigned). The only difference between this study and the one suggested above is that, here, the concern is with group rather than with individual differences.

Table 1——Fictitious data for calculating a product moment correlation between ego strength and adaptation to stress

SUBJECT	EGO-STRENGTH SCORE	ADAPTATION SCORE
A	16	8
B	17	12
C	19	14
D	23	6
E	25	5
F	26	11
G	27	7
H	29	13
I	30	5
J	31	4
K	32	12
L	33	10
M	35	15
N	36	11
O	38	9

Table 2——One possible grouping of data from Table 1

GROUPS	EGO-STRENGTH LEVELS*	MEAN ADAPTATION SCORES
ABC	very low (17.3)	11.3
DEF	low (24.7)	7.3
GHI	intermediate (28.7)	8.3
JKL	high (32.0)	8.7
MNO	very high (36.3)	11.7

* In order of increasing ego strength scores (independent variable); group means in parentheses.

Suppose, further, that the investigator were to classify his subjects into only two meaningful groups on both variables. The analysis of his results then constitutes no more than a comparison of the absolute number of subjects in *high* and *low* ego-strength groups who respond more or less "adaptively" to stress (see Table 3). Although he is now using frequency counts and a 2 × 2 contingency table instead of individual scores and a product moment coefficient, his study remains correlational in character. Indeed, it is often the case that in this type of research the same data may be analyzed in a variety of ways, some of which, at first sight, may not appear to involve correlation at all.

Table 3——Second condensation of data from Table 1

EGO-STRENGTH LEVEL	ADAPTATION LEVEL	
	BELOW MEDIAN	ABOVE MEDIAN
low*	4	3
high	3	4

* Low and high groups include subjects below and above the median subject. (H, with a score of 29, has been dropped.)

The point of all this is that correlational research is not exclusively identified by the use of obviously correlational statistics. Its essential features are its identification of variables in terms of measurements of already existing subject characteristics, rather than in terms of manipulative operations performed by the investigator, and its use of a single, standard test situation for all subjects, rather than a different set of treatments for each research group.

The correlational method is obviously not characterized by a high degree of control over relevant variables. Indeed, Cronbach (1957) said of the correlational discipline that it is used to study "what man has not learned to control or never can hope to control." In this sense, correlational research lies in a border region between methods that are entirely descriptive (case studies, actuarial investigation) and methods that are experimental in character. Correlational research is commonly used to verify hypotheses; but no controls are exerted on the research situation other than those implicit in the measures that are taken on all subjects.

Another important lesson in our hypothetical example is that the classification of subjects into groups, according to pretest values obtained on a measure representing the independent variable, is, in actuality, an admission of lack of faith in the measurement of that variable. A reconsideration of the data will help to clarify this statement. In Table 1, it is assumed that every score on both measures is subject to a certain amount of error; but if the instruments are sufficiently sensitive, the amount of error in particular scores may not be sufficient to raise doubts about the placement of individuals in the overall sample. If the limits of uncertainty for any ego strength value were, for instance, plus or minus .25 points, then every subject is quite accurately represented by the score assigned him. These limits would suggest, for example, that subject F's true score probably lies between 25.75 and 26.25, while subject G's true score lies somewhere between 26.75 and 27.25 (F and G obtained raw scores of 26 and 27, respectively). The investigator does not know the exact score difference between these two subjects, but he may feel reasonably certain that G has a higher score than F. There is, therefore, no a priori necessity for him to lump these two subjects together in one group and treat them as if their combined performances were best represented by a single mean value of 26.5.

If, however, the error of measurement were sufficiently large to prohibit making distinctions among individual subjects, the investigator might feel more certain of himself if he combined groups of similar scores and represented the whole group by a single average value. Thus, if the error of measurement in the two cases cited above were 1, 2, or 5 points, it might be best for research purposes to combine subjects into groups. The combining might take place in many ways, depending upon the magnitude of the error of estimate. The most gross method would be to combine the seven highest-scoring subjects into one group and the seven lowest-scoring subjects into another (the *median split*, as in Table 3). Another possibility would be to attempt to assure group differences by taking only the five highest and the five lowest subjects and eliminating the five middle-scoring subjects altogether (*extreme groups* design). With smaller errors of measurement, other possibilities would be to divide the sample into high, middle, and low thirds, or into fifths (as in Table 2). The end of the process of subdivision is, obviously, to divide this sample into fifteen subgroups of one subject each. In this case, discrimination is again considered sufficiently fine to distinguish among individual subjects; and the investigator is back to running a straightforward study of correlated individual differences, just as if he had not subdivided his sample at all.

There are some technical differences between the group comparison situation and the straightforward correlational situation. When there is more than one subject in each comparison group, the deviation of each subject from the mean of his own group is considered to constitute "error." This contrasts with the straightforward correlational situation, in which the source of error is considered to reside in the measuring instrument. A second difference is that multiple group comparisons may be statistically significant when a nonlinear relationship exists between the measured variables, since the statistical devices that are usually employed are sensitive to all variations among means, not just to those that change uniformly with increases or decreases in the variable according to which subjects have been grouped. These differences are important in some research situations; but they are not matters of immediate concern, since they are more statistical than methodological in nature.

This discussion has become rather more technical and statistically complex than might be wished. It is important, however, to establish the identity of the correlational method and to clarify the fact that it is, indeed, a research strategy and not just a statistical technique or a specific type of procedure. Research strategies do not exist in statistics, per se; they are reflected by the selection of designs and statistics for particular purposes. It is now appropriate to examine more carefully the purposes of correlational research.

HYPOTHESIS TESTING

Although it has been mentioned before, it is worth reviewing the notion that in most psychological research designed to verify theory by predicting specific behaviors in standard measuring situations, at least two classes of variables may be distinguished. The first comprises the *independent* variables: those that are presumed, on theoretical grounds, to determine the outcome of the investigation. The ideal of pure experimentation is to alter independent variables systematically so that they operate at various levels of known intensity. The second class comprises *dependent* variables, the values of which are presumed to be determined by the values of the independent variables, as long as other relevant research conditions are randomized or held constant.

The basic logic of deductive hypothesis testing is that theory must dictate some relationship between a set of independent variables and a particular dependent variable. Research then constitutes the transformation of this relation from abstract, theoretical terms into measurements of responses (representing the dependent variable) that occur when determining conditions (representing independent variables) are either purposely set at selected values or are measured, so that their values are known before the dependent variable is assessed.

If a psychological investigator cannot actually manipulate the levels at which an independent variable operates, he may employ other strategies to accomplish a comparable purpose. As suggested above, one possibility is to select subjects who themselves represent different levels of the variable. For example, if an investigator cannot make people bright or dull, he can, at least, measure intelligence and separate his subjects into bright and dull groups. If he cannot manipulate anxiety levels successfully, he can select anxious and nonanxious subjects, as defined by scores on a suitable measuring instrument, for comparison on some behavior that he thinks will be affected by anxiety level. When he uses this approach, he is employing what is here called the *correlational method*.

The investigator must assume that the only systematic differences among his subjects are reflected in their pretest scores and that, in all other respects, they are equivalent. Otherwise, he cannot be sure that the relationship he evaluates is precisely the one he intended. The establishment of a lack of systematic differences, other than those accounted for by the independent variable, is commonly accomplished by taking additional measures of the subject samples and by establishing that no variations that are significantly correlated with the independent variable exist among subjects or between subject groups on these indices.

If significant covariance is found, it may sometimes be handled by arguing on theoretical grounds that these particular relationships are not actually relevant or important. A second alternative is to employ statistical adjustments, which remove from the data the effects of unwanted correlations between the independent variable and other irrelevant conditions. Partial correlation or analysis of covariance is usually used to serve this purpose. An even more suitable, though less common, possibility is to remove these correlations in advance by dropping or adding selected subjects in the research sample, on the basis of available information about their individual characteristics.

In personality research, samples are often equated (i.e., correlations with the independent variable are eliminated) with respect to such variables as age, sex, and intelligence; sometimes educational status and socioeconomic status are also considered. It is not uncommon for these "matching" variables to be chosen because convenient measures of them are available, rather than because theory or previously obtained knowledge dictates the necessity for their inclusion. Needless to say, this practice leaves something to be desired as far as scientific method is concerned.

Once having obtained subjects that are not systematically different, or groups that are reasonably well matched, except for known differences on the independent variable, the investigator places his subjects in a standard test situation. The test situation is selected to provide an operational definition of the dependent variable. Its conditions are held constant, but subjects' responses are expected to vary in accordance with their standing on the independent variable. For example, if the study were concerned with the relationship between anxiety and learning, high and low anxiety groups (as identified by pretesting) could be exposed to identical learning situations; and appropriate acquisition or extinction scores from the two groups could then be compared as a test of the hypothesis that anxiety influences learning rate. Under ideal conditions, a correlational research fully identifies the independent variable with the pretest measure, according to which groups are selected; and it fully identifies the dependent variable with the responses to the final testing situation. It follows, then, that valid measurement, per se, is critical to the success of this type of research.

Inference

If an investigator collects two sets of data on a single sample of subjects and compares these sets of data statistically, there is nothing inherent in his procedure that requires identifying his study as correlational research as that expression is used here. He may simply be seeking an empirical relationship, as the actuarial investigator does, with no concern whatsoever for the meaning of the relationship, once it has been described. In actuarial research a measure is simply a measure; in the extreme, it is assigned no meaning whatsoever. In correlational research, however, a measure stands for, represents, or defines a variable or an aspect of a variable. Research results are related back by inference to theoretical statements, which are then judged to be confirmed or unconfirmed on this basis.

The strength of the correlational approach is obvious. If the right kind of theoretical question is asked and if it is answered by appropriate research designs and procedures, the investigator has achieved far more than is accomplished by reporting simply the presence or absence of a relationship between two sets of otherwise meaningless numbers.

The weaknesses of the method are of two general types. First, there are the weaknesses of the measurements that are frequently used in correlational research; but these weaknesses plague all research in personality, and no further discussion of them is required at this point. Second, there are important problems of inference and these need to be considered in some detail.

The beginning scientist is often warned that correlation is not cause. That is, the fact that two observations tend to occur together consistently does not mean that one of the observed events causes the other. We are especially prone to make causal interpretations when the temporal relations between observed events are consistent. When A always occurs before B and B never occurs except after A, it is difficult to avoid drawing causal inferences. Indeed, for some, these conditions may be exactly what is meant when it is said that A causes B. A problem may arise, however, when it is noted that even causal relations depend in some ways upon the observation of correlations. Thus, the student finds himself having to learn that correlation is not cause but also having to learn that cause cannot be inferred without proving the existence of meaningful correlations.

It is not necessary to go further into the philosophical aspects of causality to uncover the problem with correlational research. It is plain that if A is not merely correlated with B, but actually *causes*

B in the historical sense described above, then B does not simultaneously cause A. For example, if a research is designed to show that hormonal disturbance of some specific type causes anxiety, the same research cannot, at the same time, show that anxiety causes hormonal disturbances. Both propositions may be meaningful and testable, particularly to a holistic theorist; but each demands a different kind of investigation.

To confirm the first proposition would require, at the very least, that two groups, equated for initial anxiety levels, be used. One group would then be subjected to appropriate hormonal disturbance, perhaps by way of the injection of a drug; the other group would probably also receive an injection, but the substance injected would be inert. Measures of aroused anxiety would assess the dependent variable, and it would be expected that anxiety scores for the hormonally disturbed group would be higher than for the group receiving the inert injection. It would also be desirable to show that after the effects of the drug wore off, both groups were again equivalent on the anxiety measure.

To confirm the second proposition would require groups of subjects that are hormonally equivalent, according to some standard physiological test. One of these groups would be exposed to a situation designed to arouse anxiety. The other might be exposed to a similar situation that lacked only the anxiety-producing elements. If the proposition were true, the anxious subjects would evidence subsequent hormonal disturbance, while the nonanxious would not. Once again, it would be desirable to retest for hormonal condition after the anxiety of the treated group has been removed or alleviated.

Neither of the suggested studies is correlational in character, for both define the independent variable in terms of experimental manipulations. A typically correlational study might test the first proposition by selecting subjects who naturally displayed appropriately different hormonal balances and by measuring their anxiety in another test situation that is the same for all subjects. The test of the second proposition would not be essentially different. Subjects, selected because pretest scores indicated different levels of anxiety, would also be tested for hormonal imbalances. The only differences in procedure might be the order in which the two test scores were obtained and the variable according to which the sample was split, if classifications of subjects or extreme groups designs were used.

Implied in this characterization of correlational research is the idea that the approach often constitutes a substitute for experimentation. A helpful way of conceptualizing the use of correlational research to test hypotheses is to consider that *with respect to independent variables, measurement substitutes for manipulation.* Often the substitution takes place because direct control is out of the question. In testing a developmental hypothesis about the psychological conditions that predispose people to neurosis, it is patently impossible to control such conditions over a sufficient period of time to make experimentation feasible. Sometimes also, the substitution takes place because direct manipulation would be unethical. Few investigators would wish to induce, for example, academic failure in a subject, merely to study its effects on his personality. There are a variety of reasons, including simple convenience, for substituting measurement for manipulation. Whatever they may be, however, their effect is always to produce a correlational investigation instead of an experiment.

If these descriptions of the experimental and correlational approach have been clear, it should be obvious that, in many studies that employ the correlational method, dependent and independent variables are fully interchangeable. Suppose, for example, that the previously cited study (chapter 3) by Greenfield and Fellner (1963) had, in fact, demonstrated a reliable correlation between ego strength and the presence or absence of certain psychic experiences (castration fear and rejection) in college subjects. Disregarding the inadequacies of the measures in this study, it would still not be possible, on the basis of this research alone, to say whether different psychic experiences are responsible for the levels of ego strength displayed by the various groups or whether differential levels of ego strength made these groups correspondingly more or less susceptible to the psychic experiences ascribed to them. Causal relations are difficult to pin down, at best. In correlational research they can be nearly impossible to determine.

In examining correlational investigations, it is an interesting exercise to consider how each study might be rationalized if dependent and independent variables were reversed. In a few cases it will be seen that the reversal is sufficiently absurd to justify the study on the grounds that only the proposed variable identifications make sense. In many cases, explanations of results are just as feasible in one direction as the other: these studies, are, of course, ambiguous. Finally it often happens that intriguing new theoretical ideas are suggested by reversed interpretations. It might be well for investigators to take some such ideas seriously in deriving suggestions for future research.

Correlational Hypotheses

It is not unusual to find correlational researches that do not clearly distinguish independent and dependent variables and that do not mention causal relations. Frequently the investigator seems to be saying that his theory only predicts relationships among variables and that his study is designed merely to examine for the presence or absence of those relationships. Hypotheses are stated directly in correlational terms.

The statement of hypotheses in limited correlational form may or may not indicate that the investigator is concerned with historical cause-effect relations. In some research reports, the use of such hypotheses seems merely to signify the author's awareness of an inherent weakness in his research strategy. Predicting only the existence of a correlation, then, may be just a cautious way of stating a proposition that actually has cause-effect implications. In other investigations, however, correlational hypotheses do not seem to imply any concern with the determining conditions of observed behavior; relations between independent and dependent variables seem not to be at issue in the first place. Studies of this sort are usually designed to establish relationships among various measures of a single, broad theoretical construct. Basically they are predictive only in the sense that particular significant relationships are specifically anticipated before data are collected. Such studies serve much the same purpose as certain forms of factor analytic research, but they focus on a limited number of correlation values rather than on extensive matrix arrays.

The use of correlational hypotheses as substitutes for direct cause-effect propositions is implied in a research by Morrow and Berger (1964), which examined the relationship between prejudice, as measured by a Likert-type rating scale, and the reasons for committing criminal acts, given by penal-psychiatric patients in response to an interview situation. One stated hypothesis was that the explanations given by highly prejudiced men would stress external causes of the crime, while those given by men with little prejudice would be more introspective in form, stressing emotional struggles and strivings. The second hypothesis was that the former group would display more concern for status and the need to prove manliness, while the latter would display more concern for self-expression, achievement, and so forth.

Detailed research procedures are not of immediate concern, although it is worth noting that Morrow and Berger felt that their hypotheses were confirmed by the data. The real problem with this study is the use of the word "hypothesis" in the context of its clearly correlational methodology. At no point did these authors discuss the causal relations implicit in their study. Of course, they recognized that the retrospective nature of the interview situation was inconclusive as to the actual factors operating at the time of the criminal offense; but that is a separate question that is not relevant to the point of the research.

There are at least two reasons for supposing that these investigators did have in mind a distinction between independent and dependent variables. First, it would not make obvious theoretical sense to suppose that perceiving external causes for one's own antisocial behavior causes a criminal to become prejudiced or unprejudiced; the reverse formulation is a more acceptable alternative. Second, the authors referred to earlier work on the authoritarian personality to provide theoretical support for their investigation. Familiarity with this work indicates that the reasons stated by the interviewees are to be viewed as a specific product of their previously established personality organization (authoritarian or nonauthoritarian, as indirectly measured by a scale of prejudice), rather than the opposite. In that sense it may be said that their personalities caused them to perceive their own actions in particular ways.

Many correlational studies appear to involve at least an implicit set of cause-effect statements. Framing hypotheses only in terms of specifically predicted relationships, however, is a way of avoiding firm commitment, when the method does not permit the confirmation of causal propositions. When the situation is such that only one interpretation of the data makes sense, no particular harm is done; but when ambiguity is possible, it would certainly be helpful to make alternative interpretations explicit and to consider their relative feasibility as explanations of obtained results.

An illustration of correlational research that does not involve causal relations is afforded by Fisher and Fisher's study of the correlations among responses to four indices of body sensation and experience (1964). The purpose of this investigation was to validate Fisher and Cleveland's scheme for rating body boundary definiteness from responses to projective inkblot tests—the so-called barrier score (1958). In one study, these barrier scores were correlated with subjects' reports of the origins of bodily sensations while in a relatively relaxed state. A second study correlated barrier scores with retrospective reports of body experiences. A third study correlated these scores with reported bodily sensations when subjects thought they had been administered an active drug (actually an inert substance). Finally, in a fourth study, barrier scores were correlated with subjects' selective recall of learned verbal material, referring to internal and external body sensations. Each study was presented as the test of a hypothesis, and confirmation in all studies required statistically significant values of rank order correlation coefficients between projective test scores and specifically obtained indices. (In general, these were found.)

Again the pertinent question is the meaning of the term *hypothesis*, as used in this research situation. The barrier scores that were derived from responses to projective examinations can hardly be construed to measure a variable that is in any essential way different from those variables assessed by the other instruments. Indeed, the main purpose of these studies was to establish that, despite their procedural dissimilarities, all the tests employed measure the same psychological characteristic. It is almost impossible to identify dependent and independent variables, because the four studies seem to be based on the unifying proposition that the properties of an underlying organizational structure (the body image) determine subjects' responses to all the instruments. Confirmation of the investigators' hypotheses does not establish that variations in one variable (the dependent) are systematically caused by variations in another (the independent). It establishes that a number of assessments of the same complex central process correlate significantly in predictable fashion.

These investigations might just as well have been conducted as a part of a more inclusive factor analytic research. A wide variety of measures of body-related psychological part-processes might then have been included in the test battery, along with measures of other processes that are psychologically important, but that are not expected to reflect specifically body-related experiences. The projective index could have been included as a "marker" or "criterion" variable, to aid in making decisions about the rotation of reference axes and in the interpretation of obtained factors. Although the factor analytic approach would make greater demands on particular subjects, it seems likely that this method would have provided more information about the theoretical structure of the body-image concept and that, in the long run, it would have done so more efficiently than the method actually selected.

ADDITIONAL EXAMPLES

Personality and Conditioning

Spence and Spence (1964) have reported a straightforward example of the correlational method. These investigators used instruments purporting to evaluate personality characteristics, as measures of the independent variables: anxiety, neuroticism, extraversion, and rigidity. The dependent variable constituted performance on an eyelid conditioning task, in which the same subjects who responded to the personality tests were conditioned to respond with an eyeblink to a 500-cycle tone. The unconditioned stimulus was a puff of air administered after the sound of the tone. The actual measure of the dependent variable was the number of conditioned responses (eyeblinks following tone) emitted on thirty trials, following thirty initial "training trials." One hundred sixty college students served as subjects.

The results of this study were reported in the form of a matrix, in which the intercorrelations among all measures were presented. It was found that the measure of conditioning correlated significantly (though at rather low levels, r = approximately .20) with the measures of anxiety and neuroticism but not with the measures of extraversion or rigidity. In actuality, the highest correlations that were found existed among the measures of the independent variables. Anxiety, as measured by the Manifest Anxiety Scale, and neuroticism, as measured by the Maudsley Personality Inventory, were closely related ($r = .798$). The two measures of rigidity were also related, though not so strikingly ($r = .391$). Other correlations among independent variable measures suggested a possible relationship between anxiety and neuroticism, on the one hand, and rigidity, on the other. *Hy* (hysteria) scale scores from the MMPI were also examined as a possible measure of extraversion but were found to be significantly correlated with scores on the Maudsley Extraversion Scale only for female subjects.

Since a true conditioned response is involuntary, an additional analysis was conducted of data from 17 subjects who had given more than 50% *voluntary* eyeblink responses in the conditioning situation. (Voluntary responses can be distinguished from involuntary responses if careful observations are made. See Spence and Ross [1959].) The results of this analysis were not different from the general findings and need not be considered further here.

As might be expected, this study somewhat confuses its implications for learning theory with its focus on personality characteristics as independent variables. The anxiety scale, though classified as a personality measure, was also used as an index of drive. Similarly, the measure of extraversion was used as an index of subjects' tendencies to build up *reactive inhibition* at differing rates. The main purpose of this study seemed to be to show that drive, rather than rate of accumulation of reactive inhibition, is the critical determinant of conditioned responsivity. Other personality measures were not given precise learning theory counterparts, but they were included apparently because previous work and other considerations suggested their possible usefulness.

There is no point in pursuing the questions of measurement that are raised by this investigation. These have already been discussed in chapter 3; and the concern of this summary is only for the structure of the study. This research is plainly correlational in character. It is apparent that drive level and rate of accumulation of reactive inhibition were intended to be independent variables. Rate of emission of conditioned eyeblinks was clearly the dependent variable. It makes no sense to suppose that the emission of conditioned eyeblinks determines subjects' scores on the various pretests; but it does make sense to propose that pretest scores, in some sense, cause or determine eyeblink emission.

The study is therefore a substitute for experimentation, since no attempt was made to make subjects neurotic or anxious (to manipulate what the authors call drive level) or to make them differentially extraverted (to manipulate their supposed rates of accumulation of reactive inhibition). Instead, pretest measures were used to identify the natural operating levels of these variables, and straightforward correlations were calculated between these natural operating levels and the measure of the dependent variable. Experimentation, as that term is used here, would require an entirely different set of rules of correspondence between theory and investigative procedure than are employed in this research.

Other investigators might have handled the data from this study differently. One alternative would have been to divide subjects into groups, according to scores on the most relevant pretest indices. Four such groups might be formed: high anxiety, high extraversion (HH); high anxiety, low extraversion (HL); low anxiety, high extraversion (LH); and low anxiety, low extraversion (LL). Means of these groups on the conditioning measure could then have been compared by appropriate techniques (specifically, analysis of variance). If drive were more related to conditioned response performance than is reactive inhibition, it would be expected that the HH and HL groups would show more eyeblink reponses than the LH and LL groups. No significant difference would be expected between the HH and LH combination, on the one hand, and the HL and LL combination, on the other. Indeed, some such analysis of grouped data might have been more appropriate to the problem than the one employed, because the use of straightforward product moment correlation coefficients suggests a concern for individual differences that does not exist in this investigation.

An additional indication that the study is a substitute for experimentation derives from the observation that the purposes of these investigators could not have been served by an inductive approach to their data. Since a complete matrix of intercorrelations is provided, it might be supposed that factor analysis would be appropriate. Such is not the case, however; for this study clearly identifies the particular correlations that are of major concern to the evaluation of the hypotheses. All other correlational indices in the matrix are incidental to the primary purposes of the research. It is true that another investigator with other interests might utilize these same data to advantage in a factor analytic study. But the truth of that assertion only serves to reinforce the basic principle that research methodology resides at least as much in the intentions of the research worker as in the procedures he employs.

Aggression and Dependency

A profitable illustration of the correlational approach in personality research is afforded by Kagan's study of the relationship between aggression in preadolescent boys and the appearance of dependency themes in fantasy stories (1958). The report of this investigation is particularly well-organized; it is a good example of expository clarity in scientific writing. The study proposed to test the hypothesis that the combination of dependency upon parents and parental nurturance would lead to an inhibition of aggression in a child, out of fear of loss of love. By the same token, minimal dependence in combination with parental rejection would be expected to lead to more ready expression of overt aggression, since the loss of love is less dangerous to the child under these conditions.

These hypotheses lead directly to the identification, in theoretical terms, of an independent variable (level of dependency plus parental nurturance) and a dependent variable (overt aggression) in this investigation. The "rules of correspondence" provided by the author were relatively uncomplicated. Aggression was measured by teachers' ratings of 118 boys in a public school. (Since each child was rated by only one teacher, inter-rater reliability could not be determined.) Twenty-one extremely aggressive and twenty-one extremely nonaggressive boys were selected to provide contrasting groups for study. The independent variable was assessed by having all selected subjects tell stories to pictures depicting situations that would presumedly arouse fantasies (and, hence, stories) reflecting themes of dependency, nurturance, anger toward parent, parental anger toward child, and punishment of child by the parent. The stories were later scored by two judges, who performed their task without knowledge of the aggressivity ratings of the subjects. The subjects were also asked questions, designed to determine who is the "boss" of the house, which parent is most likely to be obeyed, and which parent is the primary agent of punishment.

Results in predicted directions were obtained on most fantasy themes. In general the mother appeared to dominate the homes of the nonaggressive children more than of the aggressive children. The findings were seen as confirming the hypothesis.

This study illustrates an interesting feature of the correlational method. Although it is common to identify levels of the independent variable by splitting subjects into groups on a pretest of that variable, in Kagan's investigation it was the dependent variable that was so identified. Actually it makes little practical difference which variable is treated in this manner; the correlational character of the study is unaffected in either case. Basically, this investigation compares the responses of subjects in one situation, namely, the classroom, with their responses in another, the story-telling session. Except for the fact that the measure of aggression (at least) is probably too crude to justify the procedure, there is no reason why extreme groups had to be selected or why straightforward product moment correlations could not have been computed between two appropriate sets of measures from all 118 boys. By the same token, there is no methodological reason why the fantasy measures could not have been used as a sample-splitting device, so that ratings of aggression could have been compared for the dependent-nurturant group and the nondependent rejected group. This design might follow the theoretical model slightly better than the one that was actually used; for the theory says, in effect, that if one knows a child's family situation, one can predict the amount of aggressive behavior that will be displayed, because the former causes the latter.

The study also makes apparent an essential weakness of the correlational approach. Cause-effect relationships are actually made no clearer by the outcome of this research. The data may be taken to support the stated hypotheses, but they also provide equal support for entirely different propositions. Given these findings, it is easy to say that aggressive children tend to provoke (cause) rejection and enforced independence from their parents. Similarly, nonaggressive children may tend to become dependent because they lack the constitutional vigor to take care of themselves in normal everyday situations; they may therefore tend to evoke nurturant behavior from their parents in order not to jeopardize their own security. Although these statements reverse the cause-effect sequence proposed by Kagan, they are as much supported by his findings as their opposites; and they might make a good deal of sense to harassed parents of aggressive or dependent children.

To argue that *both* sets of cause-effect relations are true may also make good theoretical sense. Indeed, it seems reasonable to suppose that rejection provokes aggression and that aggression, in turn, provokes further rejection. But the important point is that the data from this study do not establish the validity of this type of "vicious circle" causal explanation with any greater certainty than it establishes the validity of its components. If the study does not prove that either relation is valid individually, it cannot prove that both are valid simultaneously.

Direct experimentation might be used to bring greater control into research on the problem. For example, a group of children could be made aggressive; and changes in fantasy production could then be examined for increased evidence of rejection and independence. Or, children could be encouraged to become dependent; and behavioral observations could then be made to examine for changes in aggressive activity. If suitable comparison groups were included, such studies might be useful. Of course, they would not reveal much about the sorts of developmental sequences Kagan had in mind in his hypotheses, since they would not reflect the long-term and often subtle influences that occur in the natural home situation. At the very least, the correlational method has the merit of interfering minimally with processes of that type.

Affective Responsivity

An example of a research in which the correlational approach may not have been as useful as some other method is afforded by Block's study of affective responsivity (1957). From a sample of seventy medical school applicants, all male, two groups of twenty subjects each were selected for comparison on a variety of personality-test measures. Selection of extreme groups was made on the basis of subjects' galvanic skin response to a standard test situation, in which each subject was asked to lie about his choice of a number from 1 to 5, or about his choice of one of six months or six colors. Two raters examined the resulting GSR records and selected the extreme *reactors* and *nonreactors* for further study.

No significant differences were found between these groups on a medical college admissions test, on grade point average, on a college level vocabulary test, on the Gottschaldt test (hidden figures), or on three indices of originality. (These results were taken to mean that the difference between groups could not be ascribed to intelligence. The interpretation is curious, since some of these instruments measure functions that are not ordinarily expected to correlate with intelligence.)

Each subject had also been assessed by five psychologists, using a 115-item, descriptive Q sort (reliabilities of agreement not reported). Composite descriptions of subjects in the two groups were compared by unspecified statistical tests, and some Q-sort statements were found to discriminate between groups. Similarly, an adjective check list was employed by seven other psychologists to describe each subject. (All subjects had been observed for an 18-hour period in a variety of situations.) Again, although levels of interjudge agreement and type of statistical test employed were not specified, some differentiating adjectives were discovered. Certain statements from the MMPI and from the California Psychological Inventory were also found to discriminate between reactors and nonreactors. The specific items were not identified by the authors, but a summary of a content analysis was presented.

On the well-known rod-and-frame test, reactors were found to be more influenced than nonreactors by the position of the misleading frame in their perceptual judgments of verticality. On a test of resistance to group consensus regarding the solution to a problem, reactors were found to express less confidence about their judgments, but to be no more conforming, than the nonreactors. Finally, it was reported that systolic blood pressure of the reactors was raised significantly more than the blood pressure of nonreactors following exposure to a "stressful psychodramatic situation."

On the basis of these findings the reactors were characterized as "dependent, dreamy, idealistic, and suggestible." Nonreactors were characterized as "relatively cool, evasive, opportunistic, and independent." It was suggested that affective responsiveness is a general dimension of personality that is manifested in a variety of cognitive, visceral, and motoric ways.

In this study it is not easy to identify independent and dependent variables, nor is it obvious why the same results could or should not have been analyzed by selecting extreme groups on any measure other than GSR responsiveness. Clearly the author did not intend to prove that GSR reactivity caused the other obtained differences; but this simply implies that there can be no reason other than convenience for using the particular analytic procedure employed. The data describe a series of relationships among a variety of measures, and not all possible relationships among them at that. Neither they nor the apparent purposes of the study demand a particular statistical treatment. It should be remembered that this researcher was repeating earlier work by another investigator and saw some merit in following similar procedures. Nevertheless, it should also be noted that, by separating subjects according to their performances on, for instance, the rod-and-frame test, these results could just as easily have been used to examine another concept, namely, field dependence versus field independence, a dimension of personality proposed in Witkin, Lewis, Hertzman, Machover, Meissner, and Wapner (1954). Similar splits on other variables could probably have been used to examine a variety of other possible concepts.

It is not easy to see why this investigation utilized an extreme groups design. A more generally useful approach might have been to apply a straightforward factor analysis to much of the data. The curious reader is left wondering whether the hypothesized outcome, a dimension of affectivity, would have been confirmed by this more obvious and appropriate treatment of the available empirical information.

Diagnostic Studies

One of the most popular uses of the correlational method is in the comparison of groups of subjects with differing psychiatric diagnoses. No essential difference, except in specificity of measurement, exists between the research that employs a standard test instrument for the selection of subjects and the one that uses instruments, even poor ones, applied by others in previous situations. There is nothing to prevent the investigator from equating antisocial behavior with the number of times a judge has pronounced sentence on a person. Neither is there anything to prevent him from assigning theoretical significance (if he can find any) to grades in college, number of jobs held, eye color, or chronological age. Any index that differentiates subjects and makes conceptual sense may serve the purpose, at least as far as the properties of the method are concerned.

Since psychiatric diagnoses are readily available to many psychologists, these are often used as indices of independent variables in correlational investigations. Naturally, the impossibility of equating any psychiatric diagnosis with a particular theoretical variable makes this practice questionable at best; but the questionability of a practice has little bearing on the frequency of its actual use.

A diagnostic study of some interest for this discussion was reported by Daston (1964), who intended to test the hypothesis that chronic schizophrenia is, in reality, a form of brain damage. The research samples consisted of 21 brain-damaged, 21 chronic schizophrenic, and 13 acute schizophrenic subjects. Diagnosis, then, identified the levels, or conditions, of the independent variable. It was reported that educational level was approximately equivalent for the three groups but that the brain-damaged subjects were slightly older than the others (on the average), and that verbal IQ differences existed among the three samples (acute schizophrenics were highest, chronics were lowest).

All subjects were administered a perceptual incongruity test, which consisted of a single photograph of a series of buildings, one of which, because of peculiarities of its construction, appeared to be two-dimensional. The subjects were expected to detect an incongruity in this picture, and ratings were assigned according to the readiness with which they did so. Previous research had established that brain-damaged persons, as a group, have difficulty identifying the incongruity the picture poses.

The hypothesis of this study was expressed in empirical terms by the statement that "there should be no differences between groups with organic brain syndromes and groups of chronic schizophrenics in verbal identification of a three-dimensional spatial incongruity." Implied, but not expressed, was the prediction that differences between these two groups and the group of acute schizophrenics would be evident, with the acute schizophrenics expected to do better on the test.

Analysis of the results revealed that the acute schizophrenics recognized the incongruity most readily, the brain-damaged subjects were next, and the chronic schizophrenics did most poorly of all. A significant difference between the scores of the acute and the chronic schizophrenics was reported and was interpreted to mean that the "schizophrenic process itself" probably could not account for the results. Whether the difference between the acute schizophrenics and the brain-damaged subjects was significant was not stated in the report.

It was concluded that the hypothesis was not supported; however, the proposition that chronic schizophrenia is associated with brain damage was not rejected. The suggested reason for the obtained results was that the group of chronic schizophrenics had spent a long period of time as residents of medical settings, while the group of brain-damaged subjects entered the institution directly from the community. It was proposed that this experiential difference accounted for the significance of the performance difference between groups.

There are several interesting aspects to this investigation. First, there is the questionable, some would say controversial, matter of attempting to prove a hypothesis by predicting the existence of no significant difference between the critical groups. Second, there is the question of whether performance on the particular task that identified the dependent variable actually measures brain damage, or whether it is more likely to reflect something broader, perhaps a more general state of cognitive disturbance, such as might arise from many sources, including, for example, acute anxiety, intense emotion, or (as suggested by the author) prolonged isolation from the normal stimulus environment. Third, and most important from the point of view of the correlational method, there is the effort to explain a predictive failure by finding variables other than the independent variable on which the critical groups differ.

The first question will not be dealt with at length, since it involves a problem in scientific method that would take the present discussion too far from its intended course. (The interested reader may pursue the matter further by examining the articles by Grant [1962] and Binder [1963].)

The second feature of the investigation is worth considering in somewhat greater detail. The proposed correspondence between central nervous system condition and perceptual test performance is highly questionable at best. The equation of brain damage, as a physiological condition, with performance on a perceptual task implies a simple correspondence between bodily and behavioral events that simply does not exist. If it did, the accurate diagnosis of brain damage would be far easier than it actually is. Furthermore, the study implies that this perceptual test is also capable of measuring degrees of brain damage. The results would then suggest, paradoxically, that chronic schizophrenics are more brain-damaged than brain-damaged persons. This paradox explains why the results had to be accounted for in other terms—it is the only way to explain the findings without either abandoning the hypothesis or rejecting the perceptual instrument as a valid index of brain damage. It therefore became necessary to find some characteristic other than brain damage on which the groups differed. The alert reader might observe that levels of intelligence could have served this explanatory purpose nicely, since the groups arranged themselves in the same order on measures of IQ as on the perceptual incongruity task.

This brings the discussion to the third feature of the study, the attempt to explain unsatisfactory empirical results by turning to criticisms of sample constitution. Correlational method is based on the premise that the groups to be tested are equivalent, *except* for their differences on the independent variable. If this premise is not reasonably well satisfied before the study is begun, it is, perhaps, best not to conduct the research. There is often something to be learned from the failure to achieve predicted results in a well-conducted research; but that something should comprise more than simply the recognition of an avoidable methodological error (such as the failure to equate groups for intelligence).

A final important note on this investigation must be made. Since differences were found on the perceptual task between acute and chronic schizophrenic groups, it was stated that the results could probably not be explained in terms of the schizophrenic process alone. This interpretation is acceptable only if one presumes that a theoretically meaningful entity, called the schizophrenic process, exists and if one presumes that the nature of this process is the same for persons diagnosed as acute schizophrenics and persons diagnosed as chronic schizophrenics. Since there is a variety of schizophrenias, since a wide range of individual differences exists even within diagnostic categories, and since the criteria by which these diagnoses are made are by no means uniform, it is doubtful that many theorists would accept such a conclusion. Diagnostic studies are probably best conducted as actuarial researches, at least when standard psychiatric nomenclature, with its conceptual obscurities, provides the criteria against which measures are evaluated. Diagnostic research is a hazardous business.

Mixed Designs

Correlational and experimental methods are often combined in personality research. Investigators are frequently interested in the differential effects of a manipulated variable on the behavior of groups that are known by pretest to differ on an important, related personality characteristic.

To take a relatively simple example, consider the popular studies on the relation between anxiety and learning. Hypotheses might be formulated regarding the relative ease with which anxious and nonanxious subjects learn different kinds of material. A correlational approach might be used to select groups of anxious and nonanxious subjects. Experimental manipulation could then be used to expose half of each group (randomly selected) to one type of material to be learned, while the other half of each group is exposed to a contrasting type of stimulus. (See also Mednick's previously cited validation study of the remote association test (1962), in which creative and noncreative subjects were exposed to differential reinforcement on a paired associates selection task.)

In statistical terms, it is often said that this type of investigation is concerned with the *interaction* of two variables. It is generally argued that the use of such cross-classification designs is more efficient than the conduct of a number of separate correlational or experimental studies would be. Interactive designs of this type are becoming increasingly popular in personality research; but they are often highly complex and difficult to analyze. We have already seen how difficult it can be to conduct well-planned researches of the simplest varieties. Mixed methodologies are even harder to handle properly. Some less complicated examples of mixed methodologies are presented in later chapters. For the present, however, they have been avoided; and only relatively pure representations of the correlational approach have been illustrated in the preceding sections.

EVALUATION

No scientific method is without its pitfalls; and it is always easier to find fault with someone else's work after it is completed than to execute the perfect investigation oneself. A large number of correlational studies are subject to severe criticism; but the excoriation of particular investigations does not necessarily imply that the method itself has nothing to offer the study of personality.

Perhaps the most difficult problem with the method is recognizing when and how it is being used. For the investigator who is planning an empirical study, it is imperative that a method be *selected*, and not just fallen into without a thought. An ideal correlational research that is intended to test a predictive hypothesis involves a clear identification of independent and dependent variables and clear rules of correspondence that relate these variables to the indices that represent them. It requires that the demand for samples which are equivalent, except for their differences on the independent variable, be met as nearly as possible. It is also necessary that statements about cause-effect relationships be carefully considered and properly qualified in the final report of the investigation.

Natural Processes

The major advantage of correlational research to the study of personality is its relative lack of interference with natural processes, particularly as they influence the level or condition of independent variables. The personologist recognizes that it is not possible to produce such important global characteristics as extraversion or introversion, dependency or independence, prejudice or tolerance, feelings of inferiority or of self-confidence, meaningfully and at will in a psychological laboratory. He would much prefer to permit natural processes to manipulate his variables for him, especially when it is possible to measure their level later with a fair degree of accuracy. He can then test hypotheses about the influence of this manipulation with a minimum of concern about the artificiality of his procedures. Kagan's study (1958), cited above, on the relation between aggression and dependency in children, provided a good illustration of this point. It was noted that certain kinds of experiments could have been run to test Kagan's hypotheses, but it was also observed that the manipulation of these variables in a laboratory would by no means be equivalent to their manipulation by parents in a home situation. The difference between the experimental and correlational approach in this case might even be so great as to raise doubt about the equivalence of the hypotheses under the two sets of investigative conditions.

Looked at in this way, the often expressed notion that correlational research is only to be used when experimentation is impossible cannot quite be taken at face value. It is true that experimenters cannot manipulate long-range, complex situations, such as home environments. It is also true that there are a great many variables psychologists would probably not manipulate even if it were in their power to do so. We would not wish to talk a subject into hanging himself, even if we were sure it could be done and even if we knew that someone would be around to cut the subject down before he really hurt himself. Nevertheless, psychologists are interested in the effects of home environments and in the characteristics of persons who attempt suicide, even if they do not perform experiments on these subjects. It is in such instances that correlational research is used to good advantage.

The fact that experimentation is sometimes not possible is only part of the reason for choosing a correlational approach. More important is the consideration that experimental manipulation is often a very poor substitute for the real thing. The loss of precise control over all aspects of the situation that produces differences in the level of the independent variable may be more than compensated for by the greater relevance of the real situation, with all its complexities, to the personality theorist. When the investigator is interested in the study of whole people, as they exist in their everyday lives, and when he meets the requirements of the method, he need not apologize for his use of correlational approach.

The Individual in Correlational Research

It has already been shown that the study of group trends in predictive correlational research is a consequence and admission of our inability to describe the individual accurately. It follows, then, that when the structure and measurement of a concept is well understood, large sample research should become unnecessary.

As an extreme example, suppose that it were possible to identify, by specific measurement, a single person who is, in almost all respects, a pure extravert and another who is an equally pure introvert. Suppose, also, that it could be established that these two persons are otherwise equivalent, for all practical and theoretical purposes. Predictions from theory could be made about differences in the responses of these two subjects to a variety of test situations that identify important dependent variables. The test of the theory would then depend upon its ability to explain and predict individual behavior. Although it uses only two subjects, the research would still be correlational, and it would be well suited to its purpose. The personality theory that could not predict individual differences under these ideal conditions could certainly not be considered adequate as a general explanation of behavior. Correlational research that utilizes only massed data runs the risk of absorbing the very phenomenon in which the personologist is most interested, the individual person. Loss of the individual perspective is not demanded by correlational research strategy, but it is often an unfortunate consequence of an investigator's overconcern for the conduct of large sample investigations.

Conclusion

The correlational method has a deceptive appearance of simplicity. From a mechanical standpoint, it is usually an easy matter to obtain several measures from a group of subjects and to examine the relationships among them; and from a theoretical standpoint, it is rarely difficult to find some reason for doing so. The major strategic appeal of the method is its apparently happy marriage of descriptive research design and the hypothetico-deductive approach to scientific investigation. It thus appears to offer the possibility of verifying theoretically derived propositions without the bother of conducting actual experiments and without the artificiality that experimentation often introduces through its almost necessary interference with the natural processes of behavior.

A closer examination of the method shows that it is by no means the final solution to the problem of research in personality. When carefully developed and properly qualified, a correlational investigation can provide confirming evidence for propositions that cannot be fairly evaluated in any other way. It is also useful in studies that examine the expression of global personality characteristics in specifically predicted behaviors, as in the study by Morrow and Berger (1964). Finally, it is often helpful when employed as a kind of "miniature factor analysis" in concurrent validation research, where significance and direction of correlations of selected measures with a criterion instrument are predicted. But the method is certainly inappropriate for examining cause-effect relations, as these are usually understood by the experimentalist; and it is a serious (though frequent) mistake for any investigator to conclude that his correlational findings are sufficient, in and of themselves, to establish the validity of causal propositions of the traditional, historical type. It is probably fair to say, therefore, that the most serious error in using the correlational method arises from investigators' tendencies to assign it powers of proof that it does not possess, and thus to draw unwarranted conclusions or inferences from the data it provides. Personality theories will probably always have to be justified empirically by a variety of research methods, no one of which is fully adequate to the task of verification, but all of which contribute in some way to the overall purpose of understanding and explaining the organization of individual behavior. Among these methods, the correlational strategy is certain to occupy an important position. It is a dangerous method, because it tempts the unwary to conduct hasty research and to draw unwarranted conclusions; but if it is viewed in proper perspective and employed with appropriate caution, it can make a not inconsiderable contribution to the growth of psychological science, as the personologist sees it.

References

BINDER, A. Further considerations on testing the null hypothesis and the strategy and tactics of investigating theoretical models. *Psychol. Rev.*, 1963, *70*, 107-115.

BLOCK, J. A study of affective responsiveness in a lie-detection situation. *J. abnorm. soc. Psychol.*, 1957, *55*, 11-15. (In Mednick & Mednick, pp. 307-313 [see References, chapter 1, above].)

CRONBACH, L. J. The two disciplines of scientific psychology. *Amer. Psychologist*, 1957, *12*, 671-684. (In Mednick & Mednick, pp. 3-22 [see References, chapter 1, above].)

DASTON, P. G. Space perception in chronic schizophrenia and brain damage. *Percept. mot. Skills*, 1964, *18*, 183-190.

FISHER, S., & CLEVELAND, S. E. *Body image and personality*. Princeton, N.J.: Van Nostrand, 1958.

FISHER, S., & FISHER, RHODA L. Body image boundaries and patterns of body perception. *J. abnorm. soc. Psychol.*, 1964, *68*, 255-262.

GRANT, D. A. Testing the null hypothesis and the strategy and tactics of investigating theoretical models. *Psychol. Rev.*, 1962, *69*, 54-61.

GREENFIELD, N. S., & FELLNER, C. H. Differential correlates of physical handicap and obesity with grade point averages in college males and females. *J. clin. Psychol.*, 1963, *19*, 263.

KAGAN, J. Socialization of aggression and the perception of parents in fantasy. *Child Develpm.*, 1958, *29*, 311-320. (In Mednick & Mednick, pp. 328-335 [see References, chapter 1, above].)

MEDNICK, S. A. The associative basis of the creative process. *Psychol. Rev.*, 1962, *69*, 220-232. (In Mednick & Mednick, pp. 583-596 [see References, chapter 1, above].)

MORROW, W. R., & BERGER, A. Prejudice and the offenses of penal-psychiatric patients. *J. clin. Psychol.*, 1964, *20*, 218-225.

SPENCE, K. W., & ROSS, L. E. A methodological study of the form and latency of eyelid responses in conditioning. *J. exp. Psychol.*, 1959, *58*, 376-381.

SPENCE, K. W., & SPENCE, JANET T. Relation of eyelid conditioning to manifest anxiety, extraversion, and rigidity. *J. abnorm soc. Psychol.*, 1964, *68*, 144-149.

WITKIN, H. A., LEWIS, HELEN B., HERTZMAN, M., MACHOVER, KAREN, MEISSNER, PEARL B., & WAPNER, S. *Personality through perception*. New York: Harper & Row, 1954.

8

Natural process research

In the preceding chapter it was noted that the correlational method is often used as a hypothesis-testing strategy, in which measurement substitutes for controlled manipulation of independent variables. In such cases, it is generally presumed that nature has administered the necessary experimental treatments before research is actually undertaken. The major advantage of this approach was said to be its minimal interference with natural processes. Its implicit disadvantage arises from the fact that the investigator frequently has little information about the status of his subjects before the natural events of interest occur, and he usually has little control or knowledge of the actual circumstances under which experimentally relevant changes take place.

It often happens that an investigator has an opportunity to observe subjects before and after, and sometimes during, the occurrence of an important event in their lives. In the clinic, for example, patients, who are about to undergo any of a number of kinds of therapeutic interventions, may be available as subjects before therapy, while treatment is underway, and after it has been completed. In industry, administrative actions that effect personally important changes in wage or working conditions or that involve the assignment of promotions or transfers may stimulate the study of employee response. The military service, educational institutions, indeed almost all settings in which psychologists work, afford opportunities for the study of naturally occurring events.

Characteristics

The general model for what is here termed *natural process* research is the model for all experimentation. An independent variable (or, generally, in this method, a complex set of independent variables) is set at different levels (conditions being otherwise as similar as possible) so that its influence upon a dependent variable may be determined. In natural process research, changes in independent variables are of a type that normally occur without the experimenter's intervention. Dependent measures are selected because it is anticipated that changes in independent conditions will influence particular kinds of behavior significantly.

Naturalness. As used here, the word *natural* should not be taken too literally. It certainly should not be interpreted to mean "without artificial intervention," for most therapeutic efforts and administrative decisions are highly artificial in one sense of the word. What is natural about this type of research is that the investigator does not actually perform an experimental manipulation. The changes he studies result from events over which he exerts a minimum of systematic control; they would occur whether they were the subject of experimental investigation or not.

The research by Riklan, Zahn, and Diller (1962), in which before-and-after human figure drawings were used to examine the effects of chemosurgery of the basal ganglia on patients with Parkinson's disease, qualifies as one that employs natural change. Although chemosurgery could hardly be called a spontaneous occurrence, this study is natural because the investigators evaluated the effects of events that would probably have taken place even if their research had not been conducted. Specific experimental purposes did not generate systematic efforts to control the investigative situation. Patients were not purposefully selected and administered their disease; the course and extent of surgery were not dictated by a prescribed research objective; even the decision to perform surgery was undoubtedly independent of the investigators' interest in studying its effects on figure drawings.

A still more obvious use of natural changes in independent variables is represented in the study by Gottschalk, Kaplan, Sleser, and Winget (1962), in which five female subjects recorded the onset and duration of their menstrual cycles and signs of ovulation, to provide indices of the level of a naturally changing somatic condition. Each subject also free associated into a tape recorder every day, to provide verbal data that could be examined for evidence of anxiety and hostility, the dependent variables.

Two hypothetical examples. The characteristics of this method and the intended meaning of the term *natural* may be further elaborated in two rather extreme, hypothetical research projects. Consider the not unusual problem of evaluating the effects of a therapeutic drug on the behavior of psychologically disturbed patients. One way to accomplish the evaluation would be to select a homogeneous group of disturbed subjects and to divide them randomly into two or more experimental subgroups. One group (the null standard) would be designated to receive a placebo, that is, a prescription that is in every way like the drug, but that lacks the active, presumedly therapeutic, substance; each of the other groups would be assigned a particular dosage of the drug. Measures of behavior would be taken before and after treatment and compared among groups, to determine the effects of the various dosages. To make certain that observed differences between groups are due solely to the operation of the drug, care would be taken in advance to insure that all subjects are otherwise treated in exactly the same way between drug administration and final evaluation of its effects. To guarantee this, the whole experiment might well be conducted within the confines of the laboratory or experimental ward. All subjects might be scheduled to enter the experimental situation together. They could then be brought closer to the desired pretest equivalence by subjecting them to a supervised common regimen of activity and diet for several days. Predrug tests would be administered, after which drugs and placebos would be supplied in dosages of predetermined size. Care would be taken to be absolutely certain that no subject takes either more or less of the prescribed substance than he is allowed by the research plan; and, ideally, no patient would be permitted to take any medicine other than the one under investigation. Double-blind or multiple-blind procedures would be instituted, to make sure that neither the subjects nor the personnel administering the drugs know the dosage levels given to each patient. If behavior ratings were employed as measures, the judges who provide these ratings would also be kept in ignorance of subjects' group identities. Even the person who performs the final statistical analysis might remain uninformed of many research details until his work is complete. Throughout the experiment, no subject would be permitted to deviate from the activity or living schedule of the entire group. All patients would remain under strictest observation and control until the research was complete.

The obvious purpose of an experiment like this is to determine the effect of the drug in isolation. It is good research, but it clearly does not qualify as one that studies natural changes in an independent variable.

Another way to perform the evaluation of this drug would be to permit patients to enter the clinical situation in their usual fashion and to undergo the routine diagnostic work-up, so that treatment recommendations might be made in the customary way. All patients, for whom the drug is recommended, would receive it. Dosages would be determined by the practicing physician who is responsible for the patient, by his customary methods (usually cut-and-try); and no effort would be made to interfere with or control the physician's judgment regarding the best dosage level for any particular patient. The effectiveness of the drug would be judged in terms of a comparison between patients' pre- and post-treatment status, as determined by measures of appropriate dependent variables. Between the beginning and the end of the study, little or no effort would be made to assure equivalence of other research conditions within the treatment group; these would probably be assumed to influence all subjects in approximately the same ways.

A study like this would represent the simplest form of research that employs natural changes in the independent variable. Its purpose may appear to be the same as that of the first study, but its method differs in one critical respect—it conscientiously avoids all but the most necessary interference with normal institutional routine. It is actually designed to examine the effects, or effectiveness, of the drug under conditions that represent, as nearly as possible, the ordinary situation of the patient.

To some investigators there can be no argument strong enough to justify research of this second type, when controlled experimentation is possible. The first study, described above, would be granted

the scientific approval of authorities who feel that the only worthwhile test of a drug is an examination of its effects in isolation, that
is, with no other contaminating variables operating. However, the
argument for the second, more naturalistic study also has merit. It
is, simply, that, if you want to know the real effects of a drug when
it is an integral part of a regular treatment regimen, it is absolutely
essential to permit that regimen to function with a minimum of
outside interference. Some further implications of this argument
will be considered in a later section; at present, it is necessary to
examine in greater detail the features of natural process research
itself.

CONTROLS

The purposely simplified hypothetical example presented
above was not intended to convey the impression that every research
which takes advantage of natural changes in independent variables
avoids all possible control over the investigative process. Indeed,
many such studies introduce a variety of direct and indirect controls
that complicate their design and make identification and clear-cut
classification difficult. There are several ways to achieve the objective of control without destroying a study's identity as natural process research. One is to conduct the study in a laboratory setting, so
that research conditions may be held relatively constant. Another is
to use data from comparison groups that undergo no change or that
experience different kinds of changes in the independent variable.
These devices by no means exhaust the available alternatives; but
they are rather commonly employed, and they are sufficient to illustrate the point.

Use of Laboratory Settings

Provided that it is possible or feasible for the natural change of
interest to occur in a laboratory environment, this type of research
may be conducted under highly controlled research conditions. An
example of such a study is the investigation by Goodenough, Shapiro, Holden, and Steinschriber (1959) of the relationship between

eye movements and electroencephalograms, on the one hand, and dream recall, on the other. One major hypothesis of this research was that when subjects are asleep, dreams occur during periods when eye movements are taking place. The study may be viewed, in part, as an attempt to validate an index of dreaming against a criterion of dream recall. An additional purpose of the study was to examine differences between subjects who described themselves as frequent dreamers and subjects who described themselves as infrequent dreamers. This latter purpose was served by the correlational method; hence the investigation involved a mixed design. Its correlational aspects need cause no further concern here, for only the first problem is relevant to the present discussion.

Following procedures similar to those developed by Dement and Kleitman (1957), the experimenters brought subjects into a laboratory, where each slept for three, not necessarily consecutive, nights. Electrodes were attached to the subject's head to provide measures of eye movements and frontal, parietal, and occipital electroencephalograms. Electroencephalographic records were used primarily to provide indices of depth of sleep. When a period of eye movements was detected by the experimenter (who was in another room, watching the recording apparatus), a bell was rung in the subject's room as an awakening stimulus. The subject had previously been instructed and trained to respond by answering a bedside phone (which would turn off the bell) and by reporting immediately whether he was dreaming and the content of any dream recalled. To provide comparison data, the subject was also awakened during periods of ocular quiescence and asked to give a similar report. As expected, dream recall occurred more frequently when subjects were awakened during periods of ocular movement, and it was concluded that the combination of EEG and eye movement measures seems to provide an objective criterion for determining when dreams occur.

Although conducted in a laboratory, this study qualifies as one that examines natural processes, because the levels of the independent variable (presence or absence of eye movements) were observed, rather than intentionally induced, by the investigator. The study might be subject to criticism on the grounds that sufficient artificiality was introduced into the observational situation to raise doubt about the meaningfulness of the changes that occurred. A most important problem arises from the fact that it was necessary to disrupt the natural independent variable cycle (by waking the subject) in order to assess the status of the dependent variable (to acquire the report of the presence or absence of a dream). Other criticisms might be developed from the facts that subjects were not tested in their own beds or in familiar environments, that they had electrodes attached to their heads, and that they were asked to do something they do not normally do: to remember the contents of all their dreams. Under these conditions, there may be good reason to doubt the possibility of bringing about either a state that can be legitimately called natural sleep or sets of cognitive conditions that can be validly identified as dreams. Even the use of electroencephalographic indicators to confirm that subjects were, in fact, asleep does not lay these doubts to rest; for such measures are far from being universally accepted as valid. The authors themselves noted the concern that exists in some circles over the evidence that EEG "sleep" may appear even when a subject is behaviorally awake (see Kleitman, 1957).

Despite the fact that it is not difficult for an advocate of naturalism in the research setting to find fault with this study, it is hard to imagine how it could have been conducted very differently. Eye movements and electrical activities of the brain cortex can only be assessed in an artificial situation; and in the final analysis, there is presently no way to know whether a person is dreaming except to wake him up and ask him. Furthermore, it would hardly be feasible to set up the elaborate instrumentation involved in this research in every subject's bedroom in his own home. Under such circumstances, it is certainly more desirable to use the laboratory than to abandon entirely the prospect of conducting a useful investigation.

At this point it is perhaps appropriate to describe briefly another study of the relation between eye movements and internal cognitive states (Antrobus, Antrobus, & Singer, 1964). In this research subjects were told to manipulate their own thoughts in particular ways (e.g., to indulge in a secret wish, to make thoughts race as fast as possible). Electro-ocular activity was the dependent variable; and values on this index were predicted to vary systematically, as a function of the type of cognitive activity induced by the instructions. The principles that are discussed in the next chapter will make it clear that, despite its superficial similarity to the investigation described above, this study does not employ natural changes in the independent variable. It is, rather, an attempt to manipulate remotely a psychological state which normally does not occur in the laboratory situation. The study is mentioned at this point merely to make more clear the difference between laboratory experimentation of the natural type (as represented by the work of Goodenough et al.) and experimentation in which the independent variable is systematically set at prescribed levels by actions of the investigator.

Comparison Groups

Prechange measures as comparison data. As in all research in which the effects of changes in variable levels are of interest, natural process research requires the use of some standard to which the influence of the altered variable may be compared, so that a judgment of the significance of this alteration may be made. In the structurally simplest forms of natural-change research, the standard is the behavior of the subjects before the experimental change takes place. Some obvious examples of such studies are the previously cited research by Gottschalk et al., on the influence of menstrual changes on anxiety and hostility, the second hypothetical study of drug effects, and the study by Goodenough et al., on the relation between eye movements and dream recall.

The use of subjects as their own comparison standard is usually possible in most natural process research, since it is common for the investigator to have information about his subjects before the event in which he is interested takes place. When several serial events are involved, and if subjects are tested frequently over relatively long periods of time, the research product is a *longitudinal* investigation, of the type already familiar to students of developmental psychology. (Hopefully it is obvious by now that the classical *cross-sectional* design is correlational in character.)

As employed in studies of development or of other sequential changes, such as might occur in prolonged psychotherapy, for instance, longitudinal research is often considered to be descriptive rather than experimental. But many such investigations fit the logic of natural process research quite nicely. The complex alterations that are characteristic of somatic growth or decline constitute read-

ily identifiable changes in independent conditions. Data from repeated tests of important responses constitute measures of dependent variables.

It is always important to consider the intentions of the investigator when evaluating or classifying a longitudinal study. A research on bone development in a group of children may be no more
than a descriptive survey of change that happens to be correlated
with time (chronological age); the investigator may not be concerned with the underlying processes that cause the observed alterations. Similarly, a study of emotional development may constitute,
in the investigator's mind, merely a cataloguing of emotional responses, arranged according to the ages at which they appear.

If measures of bone development were undertaken on a special
group of children (for example, before and after exposure to radia-
tion in the explosion of an atomic bomb), or if the cataloguing of
emotional responses were undertaken on a group of children exposed to a particular socioeconomic environment, the identification
of the studies as natural process research would be clear. Similarly,
if an investigation concerned the development of, say, children's
fears, as they reach and pass the age of puberty, it would be at least
implied that the investigator considered puberty (a somatic condition) to determine or to have effects upon the content of the fears in
which he is interested.

Since before-and-after data are usually available in natural
process research, it should go without saying that subjects should be
used as their own comparison standard whenever possible. As desirable as self-comparison may be, however, it may leave certain questions unanswered. In particular, it fails to account for the possibility that observed changes in dependent variable values might have
occurred solely as a function of the passage of time between test and
retest. For this reason, it is often necessary to include additional
comparison groups in the research design. As indicated earlier, the
inclusion of such groups is one way to bring greater control into the
overall experimental situation.

There are at least three types of comparison groups that are
commonly employed. One type is implicit in character; the second
consists of subjects who are specifically selected for research purposes; the third contains subjects for whom the occurrence of a
normally expected change has been artificially curtailed.

Implicit comparison groups. When appropriate comparison subjects are not available, an investigator may use existing knowledge of psychological processes to substantiate his claim that without the occurrence of the natural change in the independent variable the observed change in the dependent variable would not have taken place. When describing the emotional development of children in slums, for instance, the results might be contrasted with existing, accepted information concerning emotional development under more normal conditions.

Sometimes an implicit comparison group consists of subjects examined in other investigations. For example, evidence from previous research may be cited to show that scores on the measure selected for assessing the dependent variable do not change over a given period of time under ordinary test-retest conditions. When such evidence is available, it is generally better to use it than simply to assume temporal stability of responses. A study such as the one by Cutter (1964) cited in chapter 5, which examines changes due to hospital treatment, but which does not provide at least implicit support for the presumption that observed changes in the research group cannot be accounted for by the passage of time alone, leaves itself open to possible criticism for its omission.

Selected comparison groups. In some investigations it is possible to find subjects who are, in most important respects, similar to the experimental subjects, but who either undergo no change in the independent variable or experience a different kind of change from that which characterizes other research groups. When such comparison subjects are available, it is desirable to obtain dependent variable measures from them at the same times at which the other research groups are examined. In this way maximum control is exerted over possibly influential environmental conditions If the naturalness of the research method is to be preserved, it is important that these groups not be established by any investigator-initiated manipulations; otherwise, a mixture of methods results. Mixed-method studies of this type are discussed in the next section.

Good examples of the various sorts of comparison groups that may be used in a methodologically consistent natural process research are to be found in the previously cited research by Riklan et al. (1962), on the effects of chemosurgery on drawings of the human figure by patients with Parkinson's disease. The primary research group in this study consisted of 47 Parkinsonians, all of whom underwent chemosurgery. The subjects constituted a "consecutive series," although those who were mentally defective, who had histories of mental illness, or who were preoperatively judged to be pyschotic had been eliminated, and only patients who underwent unilateral surgery were represented in the sample. This primary research group was subdivided into two comparison groups, according to the side of the brain on which the operation was performed. In addition, two more groups of subjects with Parkinsonism, who did not undergo surgery, were selected to provide further comparison data. Both groups were equated with the primary research sample for age, sex, length of illness, and neurological condition. The first of these groups was tested twice in three weeks; the second was tested twice, with an average time interval of nine months between testings. Finally, an implicit comparison group was invoked by calling attention to previous research findings, indicating that figure drawings by non-Parkinsonian adults do not change markedly over a period of months.

The design of this study not only illustrates how selected and implicit comparison groups may be used in research that employs natural changes of independent variables, it also demonstrates the use of *preselection* of subjects as a way of establishing favorable research conditions. The purpose of preselecting subjects is to insure that those in the final sample will be normally sensitive to the natural change and will be likely to respond in typical, rather than idiosyncratic, fashion. In this type of research, preselection is always a process of exclusion; it involves eliminating subjects who actually undergo, or who would otherwise be eligible for, the experimental change, but who are inappropriate to the investigation, for reasons that can be clearly specified in advance. Preselection is common in many methods of psychological research. It tends to produce uniform samples of subjects and, thus, to reduce "within-groups variability." Overenthusiastic preselection obviously reduces sample size, especially if matched comparison groups are also employed. It may decrease the generality of findings, if it eliminates representatives of important subject groups. If preselection is carried to the extreme, the result is a research on one subject, about whom a great deal is known before the investigation takes place. This approach to research is considered in the chapter that describes the method of the *representative case.*

Directly controlled comparison groups.   Because naturally available comparison groups are sometimes very hard to find, investigators frequently supplement the method of natural changes by exerting direct controls over certain groups of subjects, who then serve as a null standard for the evaluation of the research outcome.

This mixture of methods is well represented in a research by Kalin (1964), which studied the effects of alcohol, drunk at fraternity parties, on memory for TAT stories. Natural change in the independent variable was permitted at one party: subjects drank as much as they wished, but records were kept of the amount consumed. No consumption of alcohol was permitted at the other party, where only soft drinks were served. Interestingly, subjects in the directly controlled group responded negatively to the lack of naturalness of the direct controls imposed; they became angry at the prospect of a "dry" party and had to be promised a keg of beer to induce cooperation.

Another form of mixed design is represented in some forms of treatment research. Sometimes subjects are randomly assigned to drug and placebo groups. Both groups are then treated naturally, that is, no further attempt is made to regulate or manipulate dosage levels or research conditions. Direct control is introduced in such studies by the fact that the active substance is deliberately withheld from the placebo group, by actions of the investigator. A study by Helper, Wilcott, and Garfield (1963), that is cited later in this chapter, serves as an example of this type of research.

MORE EXAMPLES

A Study of Psychotherapy

A most informative illustration of natural process research is afforded by Murray's study of some aspects of the process of psychotherapy with a single client (1954). Murray reported his investigation as a case study, perhaps because he felt, as many do, that it is not possible to conduct an experiment on only one subject. In actuality, his work constituted an investigation of the effects of psychotherapy (a complex independent variable) on certain aspects of personality functioning and behavior, as suggested by theory.

Using verbal statements produced by a single client in therapy as data, Murray had independent judges draw inferences about the degree to which the subject's verbalizations reflected *hostility* or *defense*. These personality variables were selected, in part, because a theory of conflict suggested the prediction of a reciprocal relationship between them: when one is high, the other should be low. It was also anticipated that the process of therapy itself would be such as to produce an overall increase in hostility and a correlated decrease in defense.

Hostility statements were further classified according to whether hostility was directed toward the client's mother, his aunt, other people, general situations and groups, the therapist, or a vague "home" situation. *Defense* statements were classified into those representing intellectual defenses and those representing physical symptoms and discomforts. Apparently, specific predictions were not made about all subcategories; but it is unlikely that advance hypotheses were entirely lacking. The subcategories of hostility were later used to demonstrate that, as therapy progressed, hostility was displaced from its presumedly true object, the mother; and the nature of the categories was taken to reflect a gradient of displacement away from this true object to psychologically more distant persons and things.

The single subject of the study was seen for 17 hours of psychotherapy. The initial interview was not used, nor was the thirteenth interview, which, for some reason, was not phonographically recorded. The remaining 15 hours of therapy were replayed to three judges, who classified every meaningful statement according to the scheme described above. Interjudge reliabilities were found to be satisfactory (r's from .86 to .98).

The number and percentage of hostility and defense statements (all subcategories combined) were plotted graphically against the progression of therapeutic hours. Hostility statements were shown to increase gradually, while defense statements were shown to decrease gradually. Furthermore, as predicted by the theory of conflict, a high rate of production of one kind of statement in any given hour was regularly associated with a relatively low rate of production of the other.

Similar graphic displays showed a gradual increase in hostility toward the mother for about six consecutive hours. There followed several hours of hostility toward the aunt and a subsequent series of hours of hostility toward others. Hostility for any particular person was shown to decrease as new, more distant objects for anger became the targets. The gradient of displacement, associated with the general increase in hostility level over all the therapeutic hours, was invoked to explain this succession of events.

Finally, it was graphically demonstrated that the *intellectual* and *physical complaint* defenses were inversely related for several hours. Following a therapeutic interpretation of the latter, intellectual defenses rose briefly; but the two were eventually brought into a balance that was then retained throughout therapy. After this, both forms of defense tended to decrease.

Data were presented on a second case (referred to, interestingly enough, as "a natural experimental control for the first") to support the proposition that punitively interpreted defenses tend to decrease following the administration of the interpretation.

It is important to bear in mind that this study did not involve any direct experimental manipulations. The therapist was permitted to function entirely naturally. There is no suggestion that he was ever asked to provide interpretations of any special kind at any special times or that his actions with his client were in any systematic way influenced by the conduct of this investigation. Yet it remained possible to study the processes involved and to relate findings to a meaningful conception of therapeutic change.

Murray's study is particularly interesting because its findings served as a source for hypotheses that were later tested in a directly controlled research on rats. That study will be analyzed in chapter 10.

Hunger and Learning

Personality theory is heavily loaded with concern for motivation, and there is some reason to doubt that drives aroused in a laboratory setting accurately reflect the properties of motivational states as they occur in everyday life. Consequently, an examination of the effects of naturally operative motives is of considerable interest. An example of such a study, on the influence of hunger on paired-associate learning and recall, is provided in a research report by Epstein and Levitt (1962).

Using members of college fraternities, these investigators obtained hungry subjects by testing men at 5:00 p.m. and at 6:30 p.m., before and after the regular evening meal. There were two testing sessions: one involving the learning of the paired associates list; the other involving recall, recognition, and relearning of the original list. One fourth of the subjects (15) were hungry at the first, but not at the second session. One fourth were hungry at both sessions. One fourth were not hungry at the first session, but were at the second. One fourth were not hungry at either session.

The learning task consisted of food-related and non-food-related words, paired in such a way as to produce six sets of two paired words each. One set consisted of two pairs of food-related words with high association value (e.g., cheese, cracker). Another set consisted of two pairs of food-related words with low associative value (e.g., cake, ham). Two similar sets of non-food-related pairs and two sets of mixed pairs (one food-related and one non-food-related word) of high and low associative value were also constructed. The non-food-related words were all names of household objects (e.g., stair, ceiling, carpet).

Despite the rather low level of drive arousal involved in this research, hunger was found to favor more rapid learning. Selective recall of food words in hungry subjects was also found to be facilitated, but only when hunger was not present at the time of learning. Further, it was found that relative facilitation of learning or of selective recall of food-related words occurred at the expense of a retardation in the learning or recall of non-food-related words.

In discussing their results, the authors described this study as empirical, which presumably means that they felt uncommitted in advance to specific predictions of outcome. Actually, of course, an investigator implies the existence of hypotheses whenever he identifies an independent variable and takes the trouble to examine as carefully as was done here the relationship between its various levels and responses to carefully constructed measures of dependent behavioral phenomena. Whether formally expressed or not, specific hypotheses are always automatically manifested in the statistical comparisons that are made and in the conclusions that are drawn from any research.

Some comment must be made about the properties of the learning and memory tasks, in contrast to the naturalness of the independent variable in this research. It might be argued that paired associates constitute a nonrealistic set of stimuli, or even that variables other than learning and memory might have been more appropriately employed in a study that was intended to be as naturalistic as possible in all respects. Perhaps so, but the intention of these investigators was to employ a natural situation only in identifying the conditions of the independent variable. The research can be characterized as a study of whole-part relations, that is, of the influence of a globally organizing mediating state (an aroused motive) on certain behavioral part processes. As such, it serves a useful purpose; and it stands as an example of an effective experiment on natural processes.

Two Studies of Treatment

As suggested by the Epstein and Levitt study of the effects of hunger on learning and retention, natural process research may be highly focused in intent. A comparable level of intentional specificity is sometimes reflected in natural process investigations that evaluate the effects of treatment regimens. .

One such study, on the effects of chlorpromazine on learning, retention, and motor performance in emotionally disturbed children, was reported by Helper et al. (1963). Their study constitutes a mixture of natural process and direct control methods, and was cited as such in a previous section of this chapter.

Thirty-nine children, admitted to an inpatient service of a psychiatric institute, served as subjects. Nineteen were assigned (randomly) to a drug group; twenty were assigned to a placebo group. Various types of psychiatric disorders were represented in the subject samples, although no subjects displayed initial symptoms that contraindicated the use of chlorpromazine. (Certain other preselection criteria were also employed, but these need not be detailed.) The procedure for drug administration was the same as was normally used in clinical practice. Dosage levels were adjusted by the physician, according to apparent individual need and response. The study was of the classical *double-blind* type. Neither the persons administering the drug and testing its effects nor the subjects themselves knew who was receiving the active substance. An additional precaution was to have the drug administered by a psychiatrist who was in no other way connected with the study.

The measures of dependent effects were straightforward. A paired associates task, involving associations between pictures of children and assigned names, and a serial learning task, in which pictures of familiar items served as stimuli, were the basic materials for studying learning and retention. Three forms of each task were prepared. The subjects learned the first forms during the predrug assessment period. The second and third assessment periods (on-drug and post-drug) involved relearning one previously experienced list and learning one new form of the tests. A standard digit-span test was also employed. In addition, the following performance measures were obtained at each assessment period: stylus tapping rate, number of O's dotted on a mimeographed page in one minute, and Porteus Mazes.

The effects of chlorpromazine were found to be specific to the paired associates learning and to the Porteus Mazes. Performance on both tasks showed a decrement in the drug group between pre-drug and on-drug evaluations. The decrement was reversed when administration of the drug was stopped. The authors speculated that the drug might affect the ability to sustain "active attention to novel and significant details." It neither improves nor affects adversely performance on other learning or motor tasks. The high degree of focus of this research is indicated, in part, by the fact that, despite the extensiveness of the data and the care with which they were analyzed, no general statements were (or could be) made about the overall effectiveness of the drug as a therapeutic agent. As in Epstein and Levitt's study, the purpose was to examine the effects of a global state (induced by chlorpromazine) on particular, dependent reponses.

An interesting contrast is the follow-up study of psychiatric patients, reported by Lewinsohn and Nichols (1964). This investigation is too complex to be presented in detail, but a general outline of its design will convey its relevant characteristics.

The subjects were 45 patients from a psychiatric hospital who had received various forms of treatment and who had been discharged for six months without rehospitalization and were willing to return for reassessment. Three interview ratings were available on all subjects. The first interview was taken at admission, the second at discharge, the third at the time of the follow-up investigation. Staff psychologists performed the interviewing and rating tasks, and a standard scale was used for quantifying the ratings. A follow-up psychiatric rating was also obtained. A psychiatrist familiar with the case examined each patient at follow-up time and retrospectively rated his status as it had been at admission and at discharge; he also rated the patient's present status, on the basis of his interview with him. Data from a battery of psychological tests and examinations, administered at admission, at discharge, and at follow-up, were also available. The tests were the MMPI, the IPAT Anxiety Questionnaire, the Rotter Incomplete Sentence Blank, the Gorham Proverbs Test, the Shipley-Hartford Retreat Scale, and the draw-a-person examination. A staff social worker also interviewed a responsible relative of the patient and made a rating of preillness, and follow-up social adjustment.

Since most of the instruments yielded multiple indices, it is obvious that the amount of data makes it impossible to summarize the findings succinctly here. Many of the measures were found to be sensitive to change, and most such changes seemed to occur between admission and discharge. The results were seen as offering "little support for the hypothesis that treatment begins a process of change which continues after the termination of treatment." As compared to the investigation of the effects of chlorpromazine, this research is not sharply focused on specific dependent variables. A large battery of measures of a large variety of functions provided data for answering very general questions.

An investigation such as this could be conducted to serve either of two possible purposes. It could be a study of measurement validity, or it could be a research on treatment effectiveness (as it was for these investigators). The question of purpose is critical; for two entirely different investigations may be supposed to have taken place, depending upon how the research is defined. If it was designed to test the validity of a number of measures of therapeutic change, then the existence of such change would have to be assumed, so that inferences could be legitimately drawn about the sensitivity of various instruments to it. If, however, the research was intended to be an investigation of the effectiveness of therapy, then precisely the opposite set of assumptions would have to be made. In this situation, the validity of the instruments would have to be assumed; and the problem would be to determine whether any changes actually took place as a result of treatment. Either of these purposes could be served by this type of research; but it would be awkward and usually unsatisfactory to attempt to do both at the same time. More will be said of the multiple index problem in the section on *evaluation*.

A Study of Stress

One of the objections to much of the laboratory research on a topic such as stress is that it often fails to produce personally meaningful psychological effects on subjects because of the artificiality of the laboratory setting. One way to solve this problem is to try to deceive the subject, so that he will believe he is involved in a personally meaningful task. This approach will be considered in the next chapter. A better way is to employ subjects who are, by the very nature of their life circumstances, having experiences that possess a high probability of being stressful.

Janis (1958) attempted this by intensively studying patients before and after undergoing surgery. He justified the use of these subjects by presenting a detailed analysis and description of the typical experiences of surgical patients.

Janis reported the results of three studies in his book, but the second (actually, the first, in terms of the order in which they were conducted) is of most immediate concern. This study reports the impact of surgical experiences on twenty-two patients in a general medical hospital. Structured preoperative and postoperative interviews were supplemented by behavioral observations on the wards to provide the data for the investigation. An important correlational element was introduced into the design by dividing the subjects into three groups (high, moderate, low) according to the level of preoperative fear displayed by each.

Detailed summaries of individual cases were presented to support the investigator's conclusions. Briefly, these were that postoperative behavioral and emotional disturbances are most likely to occur in patients with extremely high or extremely low preoperative fear; they are least likely to occur in patients with moderate anticipatory fear. Postoperative reactions were not found to be related to the type or severity of the surgery performed.

Janis criticized his own study, because the single investigator who collected the data in both the preoperative and postoperative situations also performed the analysis of the results. He cautioned that these procedural defects could easily have introduced bias into the findings. It would certainly have been desirable to use multiple data collectors, who were uninformed of each patient's preoperative status; and the analysis of data would have been improved if independent judges had rated the interview and ward behavior records. These are fundamental problems of research design that have important implications for the conduct of this type of investigation. They do not, however, reduce the value of Janis' study as an illustration of the use of naturally occurring situations in personality research.

A less telling criticism of this study, also put forth by the author himself, is that the "case study method" it employs can justify only "suggestive," but not "definitive," conclusions. The easiest answer to this objection is that the research does not, in fact, employ the case study method; it is a natural process experiment. What make it appear to be something else are its intensive study of individual subjects and its reliance on qualitative data. The intensive study of individuals is possible, even desirable, in many types of personality research; it is therefore not a reliable identifying feature of the case study or of any particular method. By the same token, the mere fact that results are essentially qualitative does not identify an investigation as a case study. Although Janis' data could have been quantified in any of a number of ways, the fact that they were not does not alter the basic strategy according to which they were collected.

For those who prefer large samples and more quantitative data, it should be noted that one of the other two studies reported in Janis' book is a survey research (N=149), in which college students retrospectively reported personal surgical experiences. As an interesting contrast, the third research is an intensive natural process study of a single subject in psychotherapy, who underwent minor surgery during the course of her psychoanalysis. The reader should find it worthwhile to analyze and compare all three of Janis' investigations, as contributions to the advancement of our understanding of individuals' reactions to stressful life situations.

EVALUATION

The evaluation of a particular study that uses natural changes depends, of course, upon the relationship between its purposes and its procedures. No special merit attaches to any research except in terms of the degree to which its purposes are adequately served. For instance, the use of elaborately defined comparison groups may not always have an advantage over the use of subjects as their own comparison standards. Nevertheless, certain consequences tend to follow from the selection of particular research designs within the general natural process method. It is therefore worthwhile to consider the possibilities and limitations of some of the available alternatives.

Sharpness of Focus

All natural process studies employ complex independent variables; that is a property of the method that is inherent in its definition. But not all of them are concerned with complex dependent variables. In the examples, the study of psychotherapy, the study of the effects of hunger, and the study of the effects of chlorpromazine were all rather sharply focused on specific dependent measures. By contrast, in the follow-up study of psychiatric treatment, the dependent effects that were of interest were at least as complicated as the treatment variables themselves.

It is evident, therefore, that the investigator has a decision to make with respect to the complexity of the dependent effects he wishes to examine and with regard to the level of specificity with which they are to be measured. Highly focused studies that use single indices of specific dependent variables pose few problems of interpretation. When multiple indices of complex dependent variables are employed, however, the measurement situation may easily become ambiguous.

A research that is intended to evaluate the effectiveness of a clinical treatment regimen could employ a variety of standard psychological tests and examinations in the traditional before-during-after fashion. Such a study would almost certainly show that some measures reveal change while others do not. These results are easy to predict, for they are almost universal in this kind of research. The investigator is then left to decide, first, whether those measures that show change did so merely by chance (as is always a possibility when shotgun testing is employed) and, second, what any actually significant changes mean. It is tempting at that point for him to conclude, all too hastily, that the treatment was effective and that the tests on which change was demonstrated are valid, while the rest are not and should not have been included in the first place.

Also, there is the problem of interpreting the overall meaning of the changes that are found. If only 25% of the measures show improvement, albeit statistically significant improvement, is that sufficient to judge that the treatment is effective? Unless one is certain of what is being measured and of the investigator's degree of advance commitment to each instrument, that question and similar questions can be very difficult to answer. In many such studies it would be better to employ global indices of improvement, if these can be reliably obtained, than to rely on vast batteries of tests and examinations that produce highly specific data of doubtful significance. When the question to be answered is global to begin with, it makes more sense to approach the problem meaningfully than to sacrifice the value of an investigation merely to gain an appearance of elaborate quantification.

Comparison Data

We have noted that many studies that investigate natural changes use subjects as their own comparison groups and that self-comparison data should be used in virtually every study of this type. Mention has also been made (in an introductory chapter) of the problems associated with the selection of comparison groups, composed of subjects other than those who undergo changes in the independent variable. Many such problems can be reduced to the usual question of the equivalence of research conditions among groups. Unfortunately, there is no simple answer to the comparison group problem. Psychological investigators who wish to work with human beings have virtually no opportunity, and often very little desire, to raise them like laboratory rats in cages under fully controlled conditions of heredity and environment; and the personologist ought to be more interested in people as they are than in isolated variables anyway. It therefore seems reasonable to require that the difficulties of the method of natural changes be faced directly. Comparison subjects should always be as closely matched on relevant variables as the situation permits. Still, it is as important to admit errors that cannot be avoided as to eliminate those that can; and the research worker may as well realize at the outset that it is almost impossible ever to establish exact equivalence among groups in natural situational research. This is a weakness of the method that limits the precision of most studies that employ it. It constitutes the price that must be paid for the obvious benefits the method makes available to the study of personality by empirical means.

Effects of Settings

The examples used throughout this chapter have shown that natural process research is not necessarily *naturalistic*. The essential properties of the method do not exclude the possibility of conducting a natural process study within the confines of the laboratory. In the final analysis, it is the lack of investigator influence on independent variable levels that identifies this approach. Research conditions may be rigidly regulated, and the dependent variable response situation may be closely confined, without necessarily destroying the methodological identity of a natural change study.

In the study of personality, specifically, there are definite advantages to the conduct of natural process research in settings that are as close to real life as possible; and it is obvious that the more controls an investigator imposes upon his research, the less naturalistic his study can be. Whether he likes it or not, the psychologist finds himself repeatedly faced with a kind of "uncertainty principle." If he wishes to be completely confident of the nature of the specific conditions and variables in which he is interested, his control over the situation must usually be so complete as to raise doubt about its validity as a natural event. Personality processes are notoriously susceptible to change, as the artificiality of the situations in which they are aroused increases. Indeed, it follows from the general definition of personality that it is logically impossible to isolate and manipulate part processes as independent variables and still have a research on personality. The very process of isolation too often destroys the entity that is being investigated.

Naturalistic research has a strong appeal for the personologist; but it is not hard to see how he might find himself having to defend his most naturalistically useful investigations against the charge that he does not know for certain what it is that has been manipulated. If he seeks to acquire greater certainty of definition, he almost invariably winds up controlling so many variables that he is uncertain that it is, indeed, an aspect of personality that is being studied anymore. Consider the study in which hunger was manipulated by testing subjects before and after their regular dinner hour. There are, of course, no guarantees that the supposedly hungry subjects had not actually eaten something, perhaps a candy bar, just before appearing for testing; neither can one be certain that the subjects who were exposed to their dinners actually ate them. It is always possible that the food on a particular night was so terrible that most subjects refused to eat it, decided to go to their experiment and to pick up a hamburger later. Even if subjects verbally claimed that they had or had not eaten, or that they were or were not hungry, conservative methodologists would take very seriously the possibility that they might only be trying to please the investigator by telling him what they think he wants to hear. In fact, one could insist that the only way to be sure subjects are hungry is to keep them under surveillance in the laboratory for the required period of time. That, of course, is exactly what the personologist wants to avoid.

Studies of clinical treatment effects can be placed in the same sort of dilemma. If there is minimal interference with the daily routine of the patients during the conduct of such a study, the findings will be highly meaningful in terms of the effectiveness of the treatment in a complex but real-life therapeutic program. At the same time, the researcher may be hard put to prove that the treatment under investigation was the *only* variable that operated differentially in the two groups. Even when subjects are randomly assigned to two experimental groups, there are so many possibilities for difference in the usual institutional setting that it is nearly impossible to evaluate them all. It may be that, quite by chance, one group of subjects has more members in occupational therapy than the other, that one group has closer contacts with home and family, is exposed to better therapists, is more intelligent, contains more males, is slightly older or younger, and so on ad infinitum. If the investigator attempts to overcome such objections by selecting only matched pairs of subjects for study, he obviously improves his control over the sampling process; but at the same time he interferes with the natural procedures by which patients are ordinarily assigned to treatment regimens.

There are other problems too. Even when a mixed method is used to produce a carefully regulated double-blind study of drug effects, it is difficult to prevent staff members who work with subjects from guessing which subjects are on which preparation. Should the drug have side effects, even subtle ones, that tip off its presence, these guesses might well assume a value that exceeds chance expectations; and differential staff treatment of the two groups might follow. The subjects are also capable of comparing their reactions among themselves and are likely to be able to detect which of them are on which compound.

The critical question the investigator must answer is, "How natural must the situation be to answer the kind of question the research intends to ask?" If, as a non-personologist, he is interested in the relationship between food deprivation (as opposed to hunger) and some presumedly related response process, a laboratory study will suit the purpose best. If he wishes to know how damage to a particular portion of the brain, as a result of cranial surgery, affects specific responses, and if he is not concerned with evaluating the therapeutic success of such surgery as part of an overall institutional program, then a maximum of direct control over all aspects of the research is clearly called for.

If, however, the purpose of a study were to examine the influence of hunger, as it is likely to be experienced in real life, on behavioral functions, then the investigator would do well to accept some uncertainty of control and to utilize natural alterations in the independent variable if he can. Similarly, if a study proposes to investigate the effectiveness of an overall treatment program with and without the addition of a new therapeutic agent, the investigator is best off in the long run if he manipulates that program as little as possible.

Beecher's work on the experience and alleviation of pain is precisely relevant to this point (1956; 1959a; 1959b; 1960). His observations have revealed that many laboratory investigations of pain and analgesia make little positive contribution to solving the problems of human suffering as it occurs in real life. Preparations that seem to relieve pain adequately under the controlled conditions of the laboratory often fail to do so on the surgical wards of hospitals, while substances that would seem, by laboratory experiment, to have no value for reducing pain frequently are highly effective in the clinical situation. There is, therefore, a need for more research that deals directly with the problem of alleviating suffering as it occurs in real life, and for less concentration upon learning how to reduce pain in laboratory situations that are so artificial that the effects they produce have little or no generalizability to the clinical situation. Beecher's work makes very clear the importance of naturalistic research when the investigator's concern is with real life phenomena rather than with events that take place only in the laboratory setting.

The Individual

Natural process research sometimes involves only one subject, as in the cited study of psychotherapy (Murray, 1954). Suppose, then, that a personologist is in a position to study a single person intensively while that person undergoes a natural situational change of some importance to his behavior. This investigator could utilize the event for formulating and testing hypotheses about his subject. His theoretical formulation could reasonably be expected to specify which personal conditions of his subject are relevant and which are irrelevant to the predicted effects of the natural situation. It should specify with equal clarity the nature of the changes or consistencies that would be evident following the occurrence of the event. He would then be in a position to conduct a research that would permit him to make preliminary judgments about the validity of his theoretical conceptions.

His work with this subject has all the earmarks of a scientific investigation. And, if another subject is available who is very much

like the first on other important variables but who does not undergo the same natural situation—*voilà*, he has comparison data. If
yet a third subject can be found who is very different from the first
on most relevant variables and who undergoes a similar natural
situational change, he has even more comparison data. Finally, if a
substantial number of adequately understood and properly selected
cases can be studied, a series of experiments may be composed; and
these may be reported in summary form as a single investigation.

Under favorable conditions of measurement and theoretical
sophistication, there is no need for large experimental or comparison samples. Single subjects, well understood, may prove to be more
useful to a science of personality than large groups, about whom
almost nothing is known. This argument is more fully developed in
chapter 11.

Conclusions

Well-chosen natural changes provide the experimental variations par excellence for the student of personality. The reality and
psychological significance of the effects of many life events can
scarcely be denied; and there is little doubt that natural processes
are of more interest to the personologist than artificially produced
ones. Think of some familiar variable, such as frustration, and contrast the usual laboratory effort to produce it with its manner of
occurrence and its effects when it occurs, as it so often does, in
everyday life. One wonders why psychologists insist on attempting
to produce such states artifically, when it is evident that the best
way to study them is to observe people in the conduct of their
ordinary affairs.

There are also circumstances under which natural process research is the only possible or feasible means by which complex
variables may be studied. It is the only method that permits the
study of the effects of such events as tornadoes, earthquakes, floods,
bombings, disease. Laboratory psychologists are likely to turn away
from these research interests, with the comment that the variables
are too complex and the conditions and controls too uncertain to
make experimentation worthwhile. The personologist is likely to
hear this as "I don't like those grapes, they're sour anyway," for
these are the kinds of problems that interest him. He finds them

challenging and exciting, and he is unwilling to concede that they should be avoided because they cannot be artificially reproduced.

The method of natural processes can easily be misapplied. Indeed, it is often carelessly employed. Measurements are poorly selected and interpreted; situations are sometimes overcontrolled; valuable data are sometimes ignored or never collected; purposes are often poorly matched to procedures. The most obviously useful researches that study the effects of natural changes seem to be those which investigate whole-part relationships and those which are designed to validate measuring instruments. The study of personality is intimately identified with a concern for the effects of total organizational states on specific behaviors or processes, and it is quite likely that this method is the best for demonstrating and evaluating such effects. The measurement problem in personality research is also so dependent upon establishing the true-life significance of personality measurements that it is almost inevitable that research which takes advantage of natural changes will be found to serve the purposes of validation better than any other so far considered. It seems to follow, then, that if we wish to study personality in a meaningful way, that is, as a naturally occurring event, we must accept the consequences of that wish and study its natural manifestations.

References

ANTROBUS, J. S., ANTROBUS, JUDITH S., & SINGER, J. L. Eye movements accompanying daydreaming, visual imagery, and thought suppression. *J. abnorm. soc. Psychol.*, 1964, *69*, 244-252.

BEECHER, H. K. Relationship of significance of wound to pain experienced. *J. Amer. Med. Ass.*, 1956, *161*, 1609-1613.

BEECHER, H. K. Generalization from pain of various types and origins. *Science*, 1959, *130*, 267-268. (a)

BEECHER, H. K. *Measurement of subjective responses.* New York: Oxford, 1959. (b)

BEECHER, H. K. Increased stress and effectiveness of placebos and "active" drugs. *Science*, 1960, *132*, 91-92.

CUTTER, F. Self-rejection distress: A new MMPI scale. *J. clin. Psychol.*, 1964, *20*, 150-153.

DEMENT, W., & KLEITMAN, N. The relation of eye movements during sleep to dream activity: An objective method for the study of dreaming. *J. exp. Psychol.*, 1957, *53*, 339-346.

EPSTEIN, S., & LEVITT, H. The influence of hunger on the learning and recall of food related words. *J. abnorm. soc. Psychol.*, 1962, *64*, 130-135.

GOODENOUGH, D. R., SHAPIRO, A., HOLDEN, M., & STEINSCHRIBER, L. A comparison of "dreamers" and "nondreamers": Eye movements, electroencephalograms, and the recall of dreams. *J. abnorm. soc. Psychol.*, 1959, *59*, 295-302. (In Mednick & Mednick, pp. 402-413 [see References, chapter 1, above].)

GOTTSCHALK, L. A., KAPLAN, S. M., SLESER, G. C., & WINGET, C. M. Variations in magnitude of emotion: A method applied to anxiety and hostility during phases of the menstrual cycle. *Psychosom. Med.*, 1962, *24*, 300-311.

HELPER, M. M., WILCOTT, R. C., & GARFIELD, S. L. Effects of chlorpromazine on learning and related processes in emotionally disturbed children. *J. consult. Psychol.*, 1963, *27*, 1-9.

JANIS, I. L. *Psychological stress.* New York: Wiley, 1958.

KALIN, R. Effects of alcohol on memory. *J. abnorm. soc. Psychol.*, 1964, *69*, 635-641.

KLEITMAN, N. Sleep, wakefulness, and consciousness. *Psychol. Bull.*, 1957, *54*, 354-359.

LEWINSOHN, P. M., & NICHOLS, R. C. The evaluation of changes in psychiatric patients during and after hospitalization. *J. clin. Psychol.*, 1964, *20*, 272-279.

MURRAY, E. J. A case study in a behavioral analysis of psychotherapy. *J. abnorm. soc. Psychol.*, 1954, *49*, 305-310. (In Mednick & Mednick, pp. 414-422 [see References, chapter 1, above].)

RIKLAN, M., ZAHN, T. P., & DILLER, L. Human figure drawings before and after chemosurgery of the basal ganglia in Parkinsonism. *J. nerv. ment. Dis.*, 1962, *135*, 500-506.

9

Remote control of independent variables

Natural process research often seeks to employ alterations in independent variables that are of unquestionable validity because of their personal significance or their imbeddedness in the context of the ongoing lives of subjects. In many such investigations, mediating processes, such as those that are of interest to the personologist, may readily be presumed to be involved in determining research outcomes. In some instances the success of the natural event in accomplishing its research objective is readily inferred from the properties of the event itself. For example, it is more reasonable to suppose that highly potent occurrences, such as surgery, flood, tornadoes, and bombings, generally arouse stress than to argue that they do not. Sometimes, however, the success of natural events in altering mediating psychological processes is not so readily apparent. For instance, an investigator interested in the effects of natural fatigue and rest might elect to test his subjects just before bedtime and just after breakfast. This plan might be questioned on the grounds that the investigator cannot know for certain that his subjects are actually fatigued or rested when they are supposed to be. Furthermore, the study might be criticized because the definition of fatigue is too nonspecific: fatigue and rest may not be equivalent conditions for all subjects; the common laborer may not become tired in the same way as the businessman; the nurse's fatigue may be quite different from that of the housewife or bookkeeper.

One answer to this type of criticism is to conduct a more rigidly controlled, laboratory research, so that the relevant variable, fatigue, may be effectively simplified and isolated for study, that is, to adopt the method of direct controls. Although that method is not discussed in detail in this chapter, its features must be described briefly here, so that the more immediate relevant method of remote controls can be viewed in a proper perspective.

It may be recalled from an earlier discussion (chapter 2) that direct control exists when a variable is fully identified with the operations by which it is observed or manipulated. In the *method of direct controls* all research variables are exhaustively defined by the rules that specify how they are measured, altered, or held constant. It follows, then, that descriptions of a completely directly controlled research in terms of concepts and variables, on the one hand, or in terms of procedures and observations, on the other, are redundant. Figure 1 shows the interchangeability of variables and operations that characterizes this approach to psychological investigation.

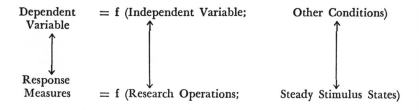

Figure 1——Model for direct control experimentation.

Figure 2 shows the organization of a *remotely controlled* investigation, in which all variables and conditions are indirectly or partially identified and controlled. In this research, stimulus states and changes represent externally imposed efforts to influence variables that are conceptual in nature, that is, they are defined by a theory or model. The downward direction of the two arrows on the right in this figure suggests the deductive process that is involved in designing such a study: abstract theoretical constructs are narrowed down to concrete and specific research operations that are expected to control the independent variables and research conditions of interest.

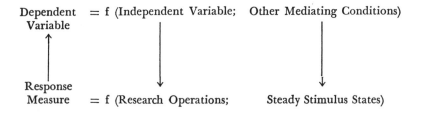

Figure 2——Model for remote control experimentation.

In research that is also remotely controlled with respect to the dependent variable, responses are viewed as partial products of processes that are incompletely manifested in any specific aspect of observable behavior. Here, the upward direction of the arrow on the left in Figure 2 suggests the process of inference that is involved in interpreting the outcome of such a study: concrete responses provide evidence for drawing conclusions about the condition of a more abstract theoretical construct.

It is not necessary for a single investigation to be completely identified with one or the other model; in fact, combinations of direct and indirect identifications in the same experiment are frequent. It is possible for independent variables to be controlled remotely, while research conditions and dependent variables are equated with stimulus states and responses, respectively. This might be the case in a research designed to study, say, the effect of experimentally induced anxiety on conditioned response production. It is also possible, in principle, for independent variables or conditions to be directly equated with stimulus manipulations, but for the response measure to be considered to be only an indirect index of dependent processes. An example of such a study might be one in which conditioning procedures are used to define a variable, such as frustration, and in which the dependent effects (e.g., aggression) are viewed as central in nature, that is, remotely represented by the observed response.

This chapter is concerned essentially with problems of control of the independent variable. All the examples have in common their efforts to produce known states of these variables by remote means.

Characteristics

The requirements for a well-executed remote control research can be stated with some clarity. First, the investigator must have a definite hypothesis to be tested. The hypothesis must state, in conceptual terms, the nature of the independent and dependent processes or variables that are of major concern. Second, the method by which the manipulation of the independent variable is to be accomplished must be specified. This specification requires also that other conditions which might influence results, but which are not relevant to the hypothesis, be taken into account. Third, the measures of the dependent variable must be selected.

So far, the design problem is no different from that involved in any experimental investigation. The next step, however, is critical. Fourth, the relations between the physical-social-environmental features of the study and the concepts it is intended to examine must be clearly understood. These relations must be explicated for independent variables, research conditions, and dependent variables, separately considered.

Hypothetical example. For the sake of exposition, let it be assumed that an investigator decides that both the independent variable and the research conditions which interest him are partially or indirectly reflected in the rules of correspondence that represent them (i.e., are remotely controlled). For the sake of concreteness, let it also be assumed that he is interested in studying the influence of pain on learning.

When this investigator decides upon a method for inducing pain, one major problem is to assure himself and his eventual readership that his method works. An obvious way to deal with this problem would be to use a measure of pain that does not depend on learning, as learning is assessed in the experiment. Carefully recorded and evaluated behavior ratings (e.g., grimacing, signs of muscular tension, verbal comments such as "ouch") would be a possibility. Measures of physiological events known to be specifically correlated with pain would also serve the purpose, if such could be found. A post-experimental interview, in which subjects are asked directly whether they experienced pain, could also be employed.

An additional precaution would have to be observed; for it must be remembered that it is just as necessary to establish convincingly that a process is not operating when it is supposed to be absent as it is to establish that it operates when its presence is expected. A group that is supposed to be pain-free is unacceptable if a measurement of the effectiveness of stimulation shows that the members of the group actually (even if for unknown reasons) experience pain. Assessments of subjects' reactions to presumedly null conditions are just as important as assessments of their reponses to manipulations designed to intensify the independent variable.

The effectiveness of remote controls is sometimes established, at least in part, by the selection and testing of comparison groups. In our hypothetical research on pain, such groups might be needed to establish that it is indeed pain, and not some other research condition, that causes the results to come out as they do. If, as in the study by Barber and Hahn (1962), the pain stimulus were "immersion of the hand in icewater for three minutes," it might be considered desirable to utilize another group that immersed their hands in lukewarm water for three minutes, to provide assurance that the effects on learning were not attributable to some unknown reaction to simply sitting with the hand in water for three minutes. If, for some strange reason, it were thought important to determine whether having the hand wet for three minutes made a difference, another group would have to be added that sat with their hands in an empty bucket.

As mentioned in previous chapters, there is no simple solution to the problem of selecting comparison groups; groups must be selected to answer as many meaningful questions about possibly influential conditions as can be handled. These groups must be composed of subjects that are as nearly as possible equivalent to those actually included in the experimental sample. In practice, equivalence is generally assumed if subjects are randomly assigned to the various conditions in the order of their appearance for participation in the experiment.

A word must be said at this point about the practice of attempting to make stimulus manipulations so potent and powerful that no subject could fail to respond to them in some way. In our hypothetical example, pain could almost certainly be produced by inducing third degree burns over a large percentage of every subject's body; and few would doubt the effectiveness of the procedure. Quite aside from the fact that one can go to jail for doing such things, there are important ethical considerations involved in such practices. Attention is called to section 4.3 of the *Ethical Standards of Psychologists* (1953), which covers the problem.

Suppose, then, that the investigator has arrived at a satisfactory solution to the problems posed by the independent variable and by other research conditions. There remains the issue of the measurement of the dependent variable. Since this has been discussed in previous chapters, suffice it to say that lack of commitment to measures of dependent variables is invariably a sign of inadequate advance preparation for a research effort. The least valuable studies in the literature are those which explain away negative findings solely in terms of inadequacies in measurement. No presumably controlled research should be published which offers this type of excuse to explain failure to confirm an hypothesis.

Incidentally, a satisfactory relation between a concept and a measure is not necessarily simple or direct in nature. It need not be argued that dependent variables should be exhaustively defined only by overt responses that are taken at face value. In personality research the most important measures are often those which are derived from observable behavior by way of the judgments of trained and reliable experts. These may be quite complex and extremely indirect; for it is possible that, in some investigations, highly divergent responses (e.g., attack and flight) might both be judged to be manifestations of the same state (e.g., anxiety) by sophisticated judges. Certain kinds of phenomena, such as dream contents, can be studied only in this way if one is interested in their psychodynamic significance rather than in the simply counted properties of their manifest report (see, for example, Hall, 1964). Indirect measures are perfectly acceptable, provided that their reliability is firm and that the investigator is willing to make the necessary degree of commitment to their representation of the processes he is studying.

In the present example concerning the influence of pain on

learning, it might be that classical laboratory techniques for measuring learning would provide adequate indices of the dependent variable. In this case, there would be little problem of assessment; for the procedures are well known and most psychologists are already familiar with the limits of their generalizability. So long as the investigator's interest is primarily in establishing the reality of the influence of a global organizing state upon a specific response process, this technique would be quite acceptable. Naturally, if the term *learning* were to have broader significance than that (e.g., the achievement of mastery), measurement problems similar to those already considered would have to be faced and resolved.

Problems and Principles

The key question in all remote control research is whether or not imposed controls have produced desired effects. This issue cannot be ignored, and it will be met with in every research example that follows.

In practice, the effectiveness of a manipulation of an independent variable is often simply assumed. The mode of manipulation is described in detail, and the reader is expected to be convinced by this description that it must be effective. In direct control research, in which a manipulation is actually equated with, and may be considered a definition of, the independent variable, this assumption is clearly warranted—in fact, it is necessary. But an investigator cannot have his cake and eat it too. If he chooses to use direct controls, he cannot argue later that his research was ineffective because his manipulations failed to produce the desired mediating effects. Neither can he legitimately exclude subjects because of their failure to respond. By the same token, if he chooses to employ remote controls, he is obliged to establish the effectiveness and specificity of his manipulations. In the ideal case, of course, these would be so certain that no subjects are eliminated for failure to respond appropriately. Failing that, it is essential to know which subjects respond in which ways, so that proper and objective assignments can be made, without reference to outcomes on measures of the dependent variable.

It is often necessary to conduct separate researches, prior to the experiment proper, to discover the most appropriate manipulations and the best measures of their adequacy. Sometimes, previous results obtained by other investigators are sufficient to establish the effectiveness of a specific manipulation. For example, a whole series of measures of the success of a particular film in producing stress were studied in research reported by Speisman, Lazarus, Davison, and Mordkoff (1964). This report provides evidence of the effectiveness of the film in serving its purpose. It also reveals the complex nature of the stress response and demonstrates that the pattern of reaction is a function of both the content of the film (subincision among Australian aborigines) and the personality of the viewer.

The problem of assessing the effectiveness of remote controls is compounded by the fact that one is not always able to determine when they are being used. Unfortunately for the reader of research reports, investigators' attitudes toward the relation between controls and concepts are too seldom explicitly stated. Explication is essential in almost all studies of complex psychological processes. The need for it is certainly obvious in research on sensory deprivation, for instance, where it is important to know whether deprivation, per se, is defined solely by the operations of eliminating and depatterning the stimulus field, or whether it is more accurately described as a probable effect on the subject's central organization, as it is influenced by these operations. No specific examples of sensory deprivation research are presented in this chapter, but the reader will find it worthwhile to examine the subject for himself. Two good places to begin are the collection of papers edited by Solomon, Kubzansky, Leiderman, Mendelson, Trumbull, and Wexler (1961) and the symposium by Freedman, Reisen, Held, and Teuber (1961). The former describes several research procedures in detail and attempts theoretical integrations of findings. The latter deals with research procedures and data in more summary fashion and focuses primarily on conceptual organizations of results. These works provide a background for the examination of later investigations in the area as well as some specific illustrations of problems in research planning and design.

Cognitive dissonance. One of the best specifications of criticisms to be leveled at remotely controlled researches is contained in Chapanis and Chapanis' critique of the studies on "cognitive dissonance" (1964). It is worth the space it takes to summarize this paper briefly. First, it is necessary to sketch the theory of cognitive dissonance and to present an example of a typical research on the subject.

The theory of cognitive dissonance proposes, roughly, that people prefer consistency to inconsistency in their actions, knowledge, opinions, and beliefs. It states that, when inconsistency exists, change will take place in such a way as to restore consistency to the total system (Festinger, 1957). In general, research which purports to confirm this theory attempts to demonstrate that an induced increase in dissonance (independent variable) produces changes in expressed knowledge, opinions, or beliefs (dependent variable) which restore consistency to the cognitive system. A typical research on cognitive dissonance involves bringing the subject into a situation in which his beliefs are contradicted by his experiences. Tests of his beliefs then indicate their degree of change to restore balance to the cognitive system.

A representative study of this general type was reported by Festinger and Carlsmith (1959). Subjects were brought into a room and administered a series of presumedly boring motor performance tasks. The experimenter behaved in such a way as to "make it convincing" that this constituted the complete experiment. (First deception.) Later the subjects were told that they were really part of another experiment, in which one group is given no introduction to the motor performance tasks, while a second group is told beforehand by a hired "stooge" how much fun the tasks will be. (Second deception.) The group of thus prepared subjects was then divided into three subgroups. The first group (null standard) merely waited in another room for four minutes. The second and third groups were persuaded to play the part of stooges. It was explained to them that the regular stooge was not there and that the experimenter was desperate to obtain a temporary replacement for him. Subjects in the two groups were told that they would be paid one dollar and twenty dollars, respectively, to do the job. (Third deception.)

The experimental subjects were then led back to the waiting room, where they were introduced to a genuine stooge, posing as a real subject, who responded to their comments, first by saying that she had heard the experiment was boring and then by listening quietly and acceptingly. (Fourth deception.) The conversation between the subject, who thought he was a stooge, and the real stooge, who knew she was a stooge, was surreptitiously tape recorded. (Fifth deception.)

The experimenter then entered, removed the real stooge, took the subject's phone number, ostensibly because he might be needed again in the future, and led him to another interviewer. The interviewer asked questions about how interesting the tasks were, how important they were, and so forth. The real purposes of the study were finally explained, and the subject was asked to return the money he had been paid. Surprisingly, although some subjects had refused to act as stooges, all who had agreed to do so returned the money willingly.

Dissonance was supposed to have been aroused in this experiment by the pressure on the subject to describe as enjoyable a task that was, in reality, boring. Greater dissonance was expected in the one dollar group, because the magnitude of the reward was presumed to be just barely sufficient to induce the "forced" activity as stooge. The results were judged to confirm the hypotheses.

Chapanis and Chapanis (1964) attacked experiments of this type on several grounds. They doubted the investigator's certainty that the manipulations successfully produced only the desired effect, that is, dissonance. They also suggested that manipulations of the type usually employed in these studies probably arouse other central states and processes "which could contaminate or even account for the findings." For several such researches they suggested some apparently reasonable alternatives. In the study summarized above, they indicated dissatisfaction with the basic conception of the research. It had been called a study of "forced compliance," yet no evidence was provided to show that the subjects felt forced or that they necessarily complied, in the sense of doing something they really would rather avoid. In addition, there was the question of believability; for it seemed to Chapanis and Chapanis that the offer of a twenty-dollar reward for a few minutes work is sufficiently implausible to raise doubt, even in the mind of a college student.

Chapanis and Chapanis also pointed out that, in several studies of cognitive dissonance, subjects seem to have been discarded after the data had been analyzed. This is a tricky business, for if carried out carelessly, it can nullify the whole scientific process. Suppose that an investigator decides to validate a measure of anxiety by attempting to induce such a state in a group of subjects and testing the prediction that their before and after scores on his test should differ significantly. If he then evaluates the success of his induction by whether or not subjects' scores actually change in the expected direction, and if he discards subjects who do not show such changes, he is obviously assuring himself that the validity of his measure will be confirmed. This is a clear-cut example of what can happen when the effects of a remote manipulation are not assessed with another instrument, that is uncontaminated by the measure of the dependent variable. Fortunately, few researchers commit such blatant methodological errors as this. Unfortunately, however, minor errors of this type do tend to creep in if the possibility of their occurrence is not obviated by the research design; and these can be difficult to detect.

Certainly there are conditions in remote control research under which the elimination of subjects from a group is quite acceptable. These conditions exist when a satisfactory, independent assessment of the effectiveness of the remote manipulation is available. In a study of cognitive dissonance, for instance, subjects who did not demonstrate evidence of having actually experienced dissonance (e.g., those who expressed in an interview no feeling of discomfort over the allegedly dissonant situation into which they had been put) could be discarded before the data are analyzed. In fact, there is no reason why subjects who did not react appropriately to the manipulations could not be used as a comparison group of nonresponders.

A rejoinder. So that both sides of the argument over cognitive dissonance may be fairly considered, it should be noted that, shortly after the appearance of the Chapanis and Chapanis critique, Silverman (1964) undertook a defense of work already done on the subject. In essence, Silverman argued that the alternatives to cognitive dissonance theory, suggested by Chapanis and Chapanis as explanations for specific research outcomes, are either unsatisfactory or insufficient to the purpose. Furthermore, he defended the general methodological point that subjects may be dropped from a study, even after the results have been examined, so long as it is not the dependent variable itself that serves as the criterion for their exclusion.

The present discussion suggests that Silverman's latter conclusion may be technically correct, but that other procedures are much to be preferred. It is clearly best to identify the criterion for possible subject exclusion *before* any experimental data are collected and to drop subjects, if one must, *before* the results are analyzed. It may not always be possible to meet this standard of caution; but it is certainly well to approximate it as nearly as one can in all studies that remotely manipulate independent variables and experimental conditions.

The Compromise

It should be apparent from what has already been said that, as far as personality research is concerned, many studies that employ remote controls may be characterized as attempts to produce in the laboratory changes in independent variables that normally do not take place there in any meaningful way. The method may therefore be viewed as a compromise: an attempt to reconcile naturalism with the method of direct control. The purpose of this compromise is twofold. First, it reduces the inconvenience of natural process research, which requires that the investigator seek out his variables in the complex and often scientifically inconsiderate realm of daily existence. Second, it gives the research product an appearance of respectability in the eyes of those who admire direct controls and laboratory manipulations for their own sake.

The effectiveness of this compromise is to be evaluated more fully later. For the present, it is enough to say that it is doubtful that any single method can successfully bridge the gap between the natural complexities of life and the oversimplifications and artificialities of the laboratory. Nevertheless, the method of remote controls has useful contributions to make to the study of personality, when it is properly exploited.

EXAMPLES

Specific research has already been cited, but a few more examples of the method may be helpful. It is especially important for the personologist to understand the method of remote control, for it is one of the most popular and commonly employed experimental approaches; it is also one of the easiest methods to employ poorly.

Emotion

Fear and anger. A research by Ax (1953) on the physiological differentiation between fear and anger provides an instructive illustration of the method of remote controls. In Ax's study, subjects were brought into the laboratory and were tied into the complex electronic apparatus involved in recording such physiological responses as pulse, heart stroke volume, respiration, skin temperature, galvanic skin response, and blood pressure. Despite its actual purpose, the research was described to these subjects as an investigation of differences between hypertensive and nonhypertensive persons. (As we have seen, the presentation of misleading information is common in remote control studies. In this case, the deception constitutes an attempt to control "other mediating conditions" by inducing a common expectancy state in all subjects.) Fear and anger stimuli were then introduced into the experimental situation, and subjects' physiological reactions to these stimuli were measured.

The fear stimulation consisted, first, of a gradually increasing electric shock to one finger. When the presence of the shock was spontaneously reported by the subject, the experimenter first expressed surprise and then alarm. He became excited and confused and told the subject that a dangerous short circuit had just occurred in a high voltage circuit. Sparks were made to fly around the apparatus to enhance the effect. After five minutes, the experimenter assured the subject that the short circuit had been repaired and that all was now safe.

The anger stimulation was produced by a polygraph operator, described to the subject by the experimenter as a substitute who had previously been fired for incompetence and arrogance, but who was called back to work in an emergency. The operator lived up to that description; he interrupted the experimental proceedings, criticized the subject as well as others present, and behaved in a generally rude way.

All subjects were exposed to both fear and anger stimulations. About half received the fear stimulation first; the other half received the anger stimulation first.

Although results are not of primary concern to this discussion, it should be noted that Ax felt he had demonstrated a clear physiological difference between the two emotional states. Fear responses seemed to indicate an epinephrine-like reaction, while anger seemed to indicate a combination of epinephrine-like and nor-epinephrine-like reactions. It is worthy of comment that this interpretation of the findings suggests that the response measures themselves were not viewed as direct measures of a dependent variable, but as indices of more central physiological processes, the nature of which could only be inferred from available data.

The validity of this investigation depends to a large extent upon the degree to which the investigator was successful in actually producing the emotional states intended. The real independent variables were not the stimulus situations that presumedly produced these states but the subjects' probable responses to these situations. It follows that it would be highly desirable to know for certain whether the expected mediating responses actually occurred.

Subjects' remarks, made during and after the experiment, were used to illustrate the effectiveness of the stimulus conditions. No evidence was presented, however, regarding the number of subjects who made such remarks; and apparently no effort was made to obtain reliable numerical indices that might serve as measures of stimulus situation effectiveness. A somewhat disturbing specific aspect of the report of this study is the author's note that some subjects used "rather far-fetched rationalizations" to control their fear. As an example of this process, one subject is cited who did not report the shock to his finger because he thought it was part of the experiment.

These data can hardly be taken as evidence that fear was experienced. A highly suspicious critic might raise the objection that, if subjects are prone to rationalize their own feelings, investigators are even more prone to rationalize the feelings of their subjects; for scientists have a high stake in assuring themselves of the success of their experiments. Furthermore, he might point out that the particular subject who failed to report the shock to his finger was obviously not rationalizing anything—his belief was entirely correct.

Also, one cannot help wondering whether some subjects in this study, who were supposed to be frightened, might not have been made more than a little angry by the implied incompetence of an experimenter who would permit a short circuit to develop in high voltage equipment and who would seem to panic when it did. In the same way, it is not difficult to imagine that some subjects might have taken the allegedly incompetent polygraph operator's criticisms seriously. These subjects could well have felt something other than anger in response to the stooge's behavior (e.g., anxiety). It follows, then, that even if the findings are taken as demonstrating real differences between two emotional states induced by the stimulus manipulations, it need not be concluded that the differences are necessarily attributable to fear and anger, per se.

The study would have been improved if it had provided more systematic independent evidence of the specific effectiveness of the stimulus manipulations and of the steady stimulus state (the deception) in controlling the independent variable and other relevant mediating conditions.

A final important principle of design can be illustrated by this research. Ax mentioned that six subjects were excluded from the investigation because it was decided that they did not respond appropriately to the experimental situations. As indicated above, the reported criteria for exclusion were not very explicit; but it was made clear that exclusion did *not* take place on the basis of any observation of physiological records. To reject subjects because they did not respond physiologically would mean that the measure of the effectiveness of the manipulation of the independent variable is the same as the measure of the status of the dependent variable. The use of the same measure for assessing two variables would imply that there are not, in fact, two variables, but one. It would also eliminate any possibility, however remote, of discovering subjects who felt fear and anger without concomitant physiological reactions. Worse yet, it would suggest that responses which do not conform to the hypothesis may have been rejected simply because they did not support it; and, as has been shown, that would constitute a serious error of research design. Happily, such an error was not committed in this research.

Ax's study dealt with matters that are of considerable interest to the student of personality. Fear and anger are important affective processes, and a contribution to the understanding of these states constitutes a valuable addition to psychological science. But these

are emotions that usually occur outside the laboratory environment; they are a natural part of everyday living. Indeed, fear and
anger are so intimately a part of natural life that it seems impossible to produce them on command, so to speak, without resorting to
subterfuge. That is one reason why deception is such a common
feature of remote control researches.

Euphoria and anger. Another interesting approach to the
study of emotion is illustrated in a study by Schachter and Singer
(1962). This research was designed to test the hypothesis that cognitive factors are important determinants of socially induced emotional experiences. It was proposed that a state of physiological
arousal would be interpreted differently by subjects exposed to systematically different explanations for this state. When an appropriate, nonemotional explanation for the physiological condition was
provided, no affective response was anticipated. When no immediate explanation was available, subjects were expected to respond
sympathetically to emotional interpretations suggested by a well-
trained stooge.

For purposes of analysis, the production of a state of arousal in
this investigation may be considered to represent a manipulation of
the independent variable. The provision of various types of explanation for the aroused state and the attempt to induce emotional
experience through social suggestion may be considered to represent
manipulations of the cognitive and social conditions under which
the effects of the independent variable are tested.

The required state of arousal was induced by an injection of
epinephrine, described to all subjects as a "mild and harmless"
vitamin compound. A placebo condition (null standard), in which
the injection consisted of saline solution, was also included. Since it
is desirable to know how efficacious this manipulation was, it is
worthwhile to examine the means by which its effectiveness was
evaluated. Pulse rate was taken twice, before injection and after
almost all other procedures of the experiment had been completed.
Also, at the end of the experiment, subjects were asked to fill out a
questionnaire containing items dealing with physiological sensations. Data from all subjects were examined to determine the overall effectiveness of the injection. Group mean values indicated that
the injection had produced the desired effects, although five subjects were dropped from the epinephrine group because they dem-

onstrated no response to the substance. There were no significant differences between subgroups assigned to the various cognitive and social conditions.

To manipulate the cognitive conditions, the subjects who received epinephrine (all were male college students) were divided into three subgroups (probably on a random basis). Fifty were appropriately informed about the subjective effects to be expected from the drug (hand trembling, pounding of the heart, warmth and flushing of the face). Twenty-six subjects were misinformed about the effects of the drug; they were told to anticipate numbness of the feet, itching, and a slight headache. Forty-nine subjects remained ignorant, that is, they were told that the injection would produce no side effects. The 49 subjects in the placebo group were also ignorant. Apparently, no independent assessment of the effectiveness of the manipulations of cognitive conditions was obtained.

For the manipulation of social conditions, each subject was brought immediately after injection into a room with a stooge, who followed a prearranged behavior schedule, designed to suggest either a state of euphoria or of anger at the requirements of the study. Aroused subjects from all three cognitive conditions and subjects who had been administered the placebo (under ignorant conditions) were assigned to the euphoric interpersonal atmosphere. Subjects from the epinephrine-informed, epinephrine-ignorant, and placebo conditions were assigned to the anger-stimulating atmosphere. There were between 23 and 27 subjects in each group. The report does not specify whether the same stooges served to produce both atmospheres; it does mention that the stooge did not know to which of the injected groups any given subject belonged. The reason given for including the misinformed group in the euphoric atmosphere only was that it was intended to serve as a control for possible artifacts due to the nature of the instructions (i.e., cognitive conditions); it seemed unnecessary to include it in both atmospheres.

The dependent variable was assessed in two ways. The first assessment occurred during each subject's exposure to the stooge. Behavioral observations (taken through a one-way viewing screen) were recorded, and these records were coded according to a preestablished scheme for judging degrees of euphoria or anger. Interjudge reliability was evaluated for two experimental sessions of the euphoria atmosphere and three sessions of the anger atmosphere. These were deemed satisfactory. The second assessment occurred after the subject had finished his session with the stooge. He was presented with a questionnaire containing a variety of items. The crucial items, of course, were two that dealt with feelings of anger and happiness and five that dealt with physiological sensations. Two additional open-ended questions dealing with physical and emotional sensations were also included. The subject was informed of the true purpose of the experiment only after completing the questionnaire.

The behavioral situations, as well as the questionnaires, may be considered *tests*, in this experiment, since it is presumed that, except for differences in physiological state and cognitive preparation, all subjects, within any given group, responded to virtually the same stimulus conditions. The various responses to these tests constitute the observations upon which the measures of the dependent variable were based.

The findings generally confirmed the hypothesis, though not in all anticipated details. Aroused subjects in the uninformed (ignorant) group were "readily manipulatable into the disparate feeling states of euphoria and anger." Those who were correctly informed were "relatively immune to any effects of the manipulated cognitions." The interested reader may consult the published report for more specific information, since the statistical outcomes of this study are of less immediate interest than its design.

Though basically well-conceived, Schachter and Singer's research shows how involved a remote control study can become. In all, they employed seven groups of subjects, a total of 174, each of whom had to be seen individually in a complex experimental situation. (The investigators report seeing 185 subjects, one of whom refused the injection, thus reducing the total to 184. For some reason, their tables account for ten less than that number.) That is already a lot of work; but a real stickler for controls could still argue that it would also have been desirable for these investigators to have included an additional epinephrine-misinformed-angry group. A methodological purist could even insist that the placebo conditions in this study were incomplete, because they did not include groups who were told to expect side effects from their inert injections. Further, it might be considered essential by some to include in this investigation another set of null standards: groups of subjects, in all conditions of injection and of preparatory information, who are placed with a stooge who essentially does nothing.

It is perhaps necessary only to suggest that massive additions to the study would also be required if a critic insisted that more than one type of physiological activator or that different dosages and modes of administration of various substances should have been used. The vastness of the procedural implications of these suggestions should be obvious, especially when it is realized that all three conditions of information and both social atmospheres would have to be represented for each possible combination of the various activating agents, dosages, and modes of administration. This apparent endlessness of design requirements, if the study is to be above all possible reproach, is often characteristic of studies using the method of remote control.

As is also common in this type of research, these investigators discovered some things that had not been anticipated. It was noted, for instance, that subjects who displayed behavioral signs of anger while with the stooge seemed unwilling to admit such feelings on the questionnaire. There seemed to be no similar reluctance to express euphoria in both response modes. This finding obviously casts doubt on the validity of one of the important measures of the dependent variable. Another problem was associated with the process of injection itself. It seemed that the very fact of being injected offered all subjects a degree of appropriate cognitive structure for any experiences they might have. That is, all epinephrine-injected subjects were, in effect, provided with a nonemotional explanation for their somatic sensations by their very awareness that they had received an injection. This observation raises questions about the effectiveness of the remote control of cognitive conditions.

Difficulties of this sort are to be anticipated in research that attempts to operationize slippery, complex personality processes. It is typical of the human being to cope actively with his current situation; and the more open a research setting is to such reactions, the greater will be the variety and unpredictability of the specific techniques subjects will employ.

Some last words about Schachter and Singer's study. The

present analysis has stressed the importance of physiological arousal as the independent variable. As described, the research tested the proposition that physiological factors determine emotional states, but only when the person is predisposed to emotionality by virtue of his cognitive state and facilitating conditions in the environment. This approach is consistent with the apparent intentions of the investigators, who actually seemed to be combining two investigations into one report. One investigation examined the influence of physiological arousal on euphoria; the other examined its influence on anger. Each research was conducted under well-defined sets of cognitive conditions, and each employed an independent comparison (placebo) group.

Another analytical possibility would have been to consider social suggestion to be the *independent variable* and cognitive-physiological states to be the *research conditions*. (Cognitive states alone cannot be the independent variable for the study, taken as a whole, because these were not varied under nonaroused conditions.) This analysis would consider the research a test of the proposition that environmental variables (social suggestion) cause emotion, but only when cognitive and physiological conditions are appropriate. The research could thus be construed to be a series of studies of the influence of two kinds of social suggestion on emotional responses, each study conducted under one set of physiological-cognitive conditions (aroused-misinformed; aroused-informed; aroused-ignorant; nonaroused-ignorant). This design would call for direct statistical comparisons of the effects of angry and euphoric atmospheres, under each physiological-cognitive condition. The data were not, in fact, so treated; and such a formulation of the research problem therefore seems unsuited to the investigators' purposes.

A case can be made for considering this investigation to be an incomplete, factorial, multivariate design, in which somatic, social, and cognitive variables are all independent variables. Analysis of the study, on this basis, would be far too complex for consideration here and will not be attempted.

Threat and Perception

Much of the work on and controversy over research that proposes to demonstrate the influence of mediating processes on perception involves research designs that employ the method of remote controls. In a well-known experiment by Lazarus and McCleary (1951), for example, electric shock was paired with the presentation of five nonsense syllables (but not with five others) until conditioned galvanic skin responses were consistently obtained when the experimental syllables were presented without shock. The purpose of this procedure was to induce a state of "threat" in subjects when the experimental syllables were exposed. All ten syllables were then presented by tachistoscope in a final test period; and subjects were asked to report verbally which syllable had been flashed. GSR responses were also recorded, and it was shown that subjects often responded to previously shocked syllables on the GSR measure without being able to report a visual recognition of the stimulus flashed before them. The authors took this study to indicate that perceptual processes are subject to influences (e.g., needs) of which the individual may not be aware. They termed this effect "subception."

The manipulated variable is not so obvious in this study as in researches, like the one by Zajonc (1962), that use culturally "threatening" (e.g., penis, raped, vomit) and "nonthreatening" (e.g., candy, chair, child) words as stimuli to induce desired mediating states in the subjects. Nevertheless, the intentions of Lazarus and McCleary were made clear, not only in the report of their original experiment but also in their reply to Eriksen's criticism (1956) of their research.

Eriksen protested, in part, that Lazarus and McCleary had not proven the phenomenon of subception; they had merely demonstrated the existence of two concurrent response systems, each based on a different set of neurophysiological mechanisms. Furthermore, the two systems are differentially sensitive to stimulus characteristics; there are different numbers of response categories in each; and they are imperfectly correlated with each other as well as with the properties of the stimuli. Since both measures (verbal and GSR) can be taken to reflect only mechanical differences in response systems, there is no basis for supposing that one influences the other or that one is more basic than the other.

Essentially, these criticisms represented an effort to discredit the personality variables, used in the original investigators' explanation. It breaks down and peripheralizes the hypothesized causal connection between an aroused mediating process (threat, as reflected in the GSR) and a behavioral indicator of awareness (verbal response). By doing so, it makes the results consistent with a theoretical analysis that uses only stimulus and response terms; and it apparently eliminates the necessity to speak of mediating states or conditions.

Lazarus' reply (1956) to Eriksen constituted a general expression of the point of view of the personality theorist, as well as an answer to Eriksen's specific arguments. He pointed out that, although the index provided by the GSR measure is continuous (an important point in the attack on Lazarus' study), the nature of the process underlying this reaction is not known and may well be discontinuous. The real question, as Lazarus saw it, was not the statistical properties of the measures, but whether GSR responses mirror stimulus properties directly or whether they are best conceived to reflect more central processes, touched off by affective properties of the stimuli. The investigation was characterized, not as an experimental *proof* of subception, but merely as an "empirical model of what actually happens in nature." Finally, Lazarus observed that the question of whether mediating processes influence perception "cannot be decided solely on the basis of laboratory experimentation." It is common to discover that many theories can explain the same set of findings; and it is not surprising that this should also be true of the study in question. Arguments over the validity of *post hoc* alternatives is a fruitless playing with words, for the fundamental issue is the conception of human behavior that is adopted by the investigator. That conception is to be judged primarily by its usefulness as a generator of research and its consistency with empirical findings. Eriksen's arguments were taken to represent no more than a theoretical preference which is inherently neither better nor more poorly suited to the data than that which generated the investigation in the first place.

Expressed in Lazarus' reply is the personologist's interest in mediating psychological processes, his recognition of the inadequacy of laboratory methods for studying events as they usually occur in people's lives, and his rejection of any single, narrow theoretical point of view that is treated as if it were absolute truth instead of a conceptual convenience. Lazarus' statements provide an excellent starting point for our final overview and evaluation for the method of remote controls.

OVERVIEW AND EVALUATION

The characteristics of the remote control method are best evaluated in the context of their relation to the properties of the natural process method and the method of direct control. As previously indicated, remote control research in personality usually constitutes a compromise between the investigator's desire to study variables that have maximal significance for personality theory and his wish to satisfy the demand for a complete exteriorization of all variables.

The compromise may be justified on the grounds that it brings a greater degree of specificity and explicitness to the study of personality processes. Furthermore, it comprises a step in the direction of simplifying and purifying the experimental situation. If one can arouse stress, anxiety, or anger in a laboratory, at least the conditions under which the arousal took place are known and systematically controlled. The constant nature of the laboratory situation also tends to keep extraneous variables (e.g., variations in lighting, temperature, furnishings) constant for all subjects, thus reducing the probability of occurrence of chance nonrandomness on these theoretically irrelevant, but possibly influential, variables. It may even be argued that organized mediating processes are likely to display their effects most strongly in a laboratory, where response possibilities are limited and the influence of these processes is, therefore, necessarily channeled and more precisely focused than is usually the case in the natural environment.

The same compromise may be attacked on the grounds that, while specificity and explicitness are generally desirable in research, simplification and purification of the experimental situation are not. As personality processes become more subject to the restrictions imposed by the laboratory situation, they become proportionally less identifiable as real personality processes. To restrict behavioral possibilities is to limit the flexibility of the adaptive processes of the human organism; and these processes are the very essence of personality. To search for simplicity is to pursue a will-o'-the-wisp. According to this view, the ideal investigation of personality would be the one which is least controlled and best measured.

A particularly cogent argument that may be leveled against many remote control studies is that the very process of assessing the degree of effectiveness of the artificial remote manipulations often interferes with or blocks the operation of the process being assessed. A projective examination, used to assess the degree of hostility aroused by an experimental procedure, may provide just enough release of hostility to obviate whatever success the manipulation may have had. By the same token, it is difficult for a person to feel genuine love or affection when he is sitting in a chair, wired up to eight EEG leads and a multi-channel polygraph. It often happens that the requirements of good psychological measurement are highly restrictive. Many tests are frightening to naive subjects; and when that is the case, any other manipulated process is bound to be contaminated by the aroused fear.

The arguments for and against the compromise assume, of course, that there are such things as personality processes. Lazarus pointed out, however, that it is not likely that any amount of empirical data will prove or disprove the existence of personality, as most personologists understand that term. One's choice of conceptions of the human being is determined by far more complex considerations than those inherent in recorded observations of overt behavior.

Research as Models

Lazarus' statement makes another important point that may serve as a general guide to the resolution of the argument between those who advocate the laboratory and those who advocate nature as proper settings for personality research. It is that remote control experiments in personality are models, rather than proofs, of the operation of important psychological processes. Perhaps another way of saying the same thing would be to argue that these experiments merely *demonstrate* relevant phenomena. They use situations that are designed to function only as analogues of naturally occurring events; they do not, in fact, intend to produce events as they usually occur in real life.

This view of remote control research is probably the most useful conception of its value to personality theory that can be formulated. It recognizes that, by manipulating and controlling external features of the environment, the investigator is better able to standardize and communicate his procedures and results. Highly formalized operations are usually readily repeatable by others, so that replication of research is facilitated. It also implies one of the main advantages of analogic investigation: its convenience. It often is simply not feasible to follow subjects around all day in the hope that something will happen that makes them feel genuinely proud, angry, sad, or frustrated. It may be feasible, however, to set up a model of a situation that ought to produce feelings which are not too different from these, even if they are not quite as strong or complex as the real thing.

There are distinct advantages to the use of such empirical models in psychology, as long as their limitations are also recognized. A model is, by definition, useful only to the extent that its features parallel (albeit in simplified fashion) those of the real phenomenon it analogizes. The purpose of providing assessments of the effectiveness of remote manipulations in this type of research is precisely that of providing assurances that the model successfully accomplishes its purpose. If a subject is supposed to be frustrated in a negative way by a situation that merely delights him because it affords a challenge to his skill, it can hardly be said that his responses on a dependent measure demonstrate the effects of frustration on that variable. If a set of conditions designed to produce *compliance,* produce *resistance* instead, the model can scarcely be said to reflect reality with accuracy.

There are assuredly many problems involved in the construction of appropriate research models of a personality process. Not the least of these is the problem of recognizing and specifying the type of model that is being built. When mediating processes are being remotely controlled, several things must be explicitly specified. First, it is always helpful if a clear distinction is made between *variables* and *conditions,* although this may not be fully possible in some multivariate designs. It is almost always reasonable to ask, however, that the investigator provide a clear description of the components of the model he expects to employ. In remote control research, these components are conceptual in nature, inasmuch as they represent the mediating processes which are of interest in the investigation (e.g., frustration, threat, anxiety, cognitive dissonance). Second, it is necessary to provide a complete exposition of the environmental or organismic manipulations by which the various components of the conceptual model are to be set at known

values. Third, the assessments by which the success of these manipulations is to be evaluated must be specified. It must be established
that these are not, in fact, assessments of the dependent variable
and that they do satisfactorily fulfill necessary psychometric requirements. Fourth, the criteria by which subjects will be excluded
from the study, if they do not respond appropriately to the manipulations, must be explicit. These need not be determined in advance;
but it is usually better if they are. Fifth, the relationship between
the response measure and the dependent variable must be specified.
If possible, this relationship should be exhaustive, as far as the
particular investigation is concerned.

Finally, the investigator must realize that his construction of
the model is subject to question at any point. He is almost always
open to criticism from the "naturalist" that he has omitted something important, that his manipulations are too artificial, that his
measures are too focused, that he has not included necessary control
groups, or that his results are interesting, but not generalizable.
These objections are not necessarily as serious as they may sound,
for there are few experiments anywhere in psychology that cannot
be attacked in a similar way. They are effective only if the researcher fools himself into thinking that he has actually produced a
natural situation in his laboratory and forgets that he is merely
hopefully arranging the components of an artificial conceptual
system. Model construction and manipulation in theory or research
are surely not a simple solution to the empirical study of personality; but they are feasible if properly employed.

The proper construction and testing of research models can
have a variety of uses in personality research. There is, perhaps, no
other way of examining, under controlled conditions, phenomena
that are often only hinted at in the psychotherapeutic session or in
everyday experience. Well-constructed models have important didactic uses, too. The statement that "organized mediating conditions influence behavioral part processes" takes on additional force
if it is possible to refer to specific research efforts that have demonstrated this relationship in controlled experimental situations which
analogize the process and permit testing specific predictions about
behavior. The statement itself may be an assumption, rather than a
fact that is proven for all time by data; but it is certainly no worse off
in that respect than are all theories in psychology. If its value can be

demonstrated in laboratory studies, the theorist who advocates it knows that, while he does not possess absolute truth, he is at least not doing violence to reality.

References

American Psychological Association. *Ethical standards of psychologists.* Washington, D.C.: Amer. Psychol. Assn., 1953.

Ax, A. F. The physiological differentiation between fear and anger in humans. *Psychosom. Med.*, 1953, *15*, 433-442. (In Mednick & Mednick, pp. 273-285 [see References, chapter 1, above].)

Barber, T. X., & Hahn, K. W., Jr. Physiological and subjective responses to pain producing stimuli under hypnotically-suggested and waking-imagined "analgesia." *J. abnorm. soc. Psychol.*, 1962, *65*, 411-418.

Chapanis, Natalia P., & Chapanis, A. Cognitive dissonance: five years later. *Psychol. Bull.*, 1964, *61*, 1-22. (In Southwell & Merbaum, pp. 412-438, under the title: A critical evaluation of the theory of cognitive dissonance [see References, chapter 1, above].)

Eriksen, C. W. Subception: fact or artifact? *Psychol. Rev.*, 1956, *63*, 74-80. (In Mednick & Mednick, pp. 181-187 [see References, chapter 1, above].)

Festinger, L. *A theory of cognitive dissonance.* New York: Harper & Row, 1957. (See also extract in Southwell & Merbaum, pp. 378-397 [see References, chapter 1, above].)

Festinger, L., & Carlsmith, J. M. Cognitive consequences of forced compliance. *J. abnorm. soc. Psychol.*, 1959, *58*, 203-210.

Freedman, S. J., Riesen, A. H., Held, R., & Teuber, H. Sensory deprivation: Facts in search of a theory. *J. nerv. ment. Dis.*, 1961, *132*, 17-43.

Hall, C. S. A modest confirmation of Freud's theory of a distinction between the superego of men and women. *J. abnorm. soc. Psychol.*, 1964, *69*, 440-442.

Lazarus, R. S. Subception: fact or artifact? A reply to Eriksen. *Psychol. Rev.*, 1956, *63*, 343-347. (In Mednick & Mednick, pp. 188-192 [see References, chapter 1, above].)

Lazarus, R. S., & McCleary, R. A. Autonomic discrimination without awareness: A study of subception. *Psychol. Rev.*, 1951, *58*, 113-122. (In Mednick & Mednick, pp. 170-180 [see References, chapter 1, above].)

Schachter, S., & Singer, J. E. Cognitive, social, and physiological determinants of emotional state. *Psychol. Rev.*, 1962, *69*, 379-399.

Silverman, J. In defense of dissonance theory: Reply to Chapanis and Chapanis. *Psychol. Bull.*, 1964, *62*, 205-209.

SOLOMON, P., KUBZANSKY, P. E., LEIDERMAN, P. H., MENDELSON, J. H., TRUMBULL, R., & WEXLER, D. (Eds.) *Sensory deprivation.* Cambridge: Harvard Univer. Press, 1961.

SPEISMAN, J. C., LAZARUS, R. S., DAVISON, L., & MORDKOFF, A. M. Experimental analysis of a film used as a threatening stimulus. *J. consult. Psychol.*, 1964, *28*, 23-33.

ZAJONC, R. B. Response suppression in perceptual defense. *J. exp. Psychol.*, 1962, *64*, 206-214. (In Mednick & Mednick, pp. 155-165 [see References, chapter 1, above].)

10

Direct control of variables

The basic principles of the method of direct controls have been stated in the preceding chapter and need not be elaborated again. Briefly, the ideal form of the method is characterized by the fact that all variables and conditions are exhaustively identified with physical attributes or manipulations of the research situation and with aspects of subjects' responses that can be observed or counted with a minimum of investigator mediation. The two most important features of directly controlled research are its *tangibility* and its *sharpness of focus*. A third feature, *conventionalism,* derives from the first two but is not essential to the method.

Tangibility. Since the method of direct controls requires that every variable or process that might possibly influence the outcome of a research be describable in terms of stimulus conditions or investigative procedures, it demands complete tangibility in all aspects of a research effort. This demand usually leads to the production of highly explicit research reports; for if controls *are* variables, it is clearly necessary to describe these controls unambiguously. The tangibility, and subsequent explicitness, of direct control research are often cited as advantages of the method because they assure the reproducibility of most such studies; and reproducibility is a property that is generally agreed to be essential to all successful scientific investigation.

Sharpness of focus. Relatively pure applications of the method of direct controls tend to follow the rule of the single variable, often with the added proviso that variables must be as simple as possible. All undesired stimuli and responses are removed from the research situation, and interest is usually confined to studies that employ devices such as traditional mazes, Skinner boxes, and lists of nonsense syllables, which allow for relatively limited stimulus complexity and a reduced number of response possibilities. It follows, then, that this method is best suited to the study of relations among part processes. Indeed, the apparent complexity of some directly controlled research designs is not a function of concern with the intricacies of integrated psychological functioning but of elaborate efforts to prevent it. Simplicity of concept, sharpness of focus, and purity of the experimental situation are readily justified on the grounds that only under these conditions is precise knowledge of empirical events possible; and precision is the most commonly claimed virtue of the method of direct controls.

Conventionalism. A third, derivative feature of the method is that its consistent application tends to bring about standardization and uniformity of investigative procedures. The methodological ideals of complete control provide criteria by which research may readily be evaluated and criticized. These criteria, in turn, lead to the establishment of sets of more or less customary practices that come to be considered acceptable as research devices. Thus, the investigator who elects to use this method often finds it possible to define certain variables, such as stress, in terms of already established procedures, for example, the administration of electric shock. Similarly, hunger may be equated with a specific period of food deprivation; reinforcement may be identified as the administration of a food pellet or a smile, and so forth.

Few can deny the convenience and consistency that would ensue to research if a universal nomenclature and a common set of investigative procedures could be agreeably established. The question in psychology at the present time is not whether conventionalism has desirable implications, but whether the forms of standardization that are currently popular are the best or only ones required. This question will be dealt with later.

Reasons for Use

Varying degrees of commitment to the method of direct controls are possible. At one extreme, an investigator may choose to employ this strategy only because it provides a convenient and clearly communicated description of his work. All that is implied by such a choice is the investigator's willingness to act as if the total significance of a particular study lies in its physical and procedural structure. Personality theorists who use the method would probably do so at this level of commitment.

At the other extreme, an investigator may employ the method of direct controls because he feels that it constitutes the only legitimate approach to research. His choice may ordinarily be expected to involve some rather strong and pervasive beliefs about the nature of the scientific process and the obligations of psychological investigators in general (*cf.*, Bachrach, 1962). It is not necessary to examine these beliefs in detail, but it is helpful to consider the source from which disagreements over the proper use of the method generally arise.

Problems of inference. If the method of direct control is taken completely at face value and if its implications are carried to the extreme, it is necessary to conclude that its principles, like those of actuarialism, require the elimination of theory in the research process. Strictly speaking, there can be no conceptual formulation of a directly controlled investigation because there are no "rules of correspondence," by which abstract concepts are brought into a parallel, though inexhaustive, relationship with objective conditions or responses. There are only "identity statements," which define concepts completely in objective terms. This property of the method is sometimes idealized, on the grounds that it forces the investigator to make the meanings of his concepts operationally clear. Thus, it is said to increase precision and to avoid the dangers inherent in speculative or dogmatic theorization.

The desire for precision is commendable; but it sometimes appears merely to serve as a device by which an investigator avoids personal responsibility for possible errors of judgment that may occur when theory is used as a guide to research. If all concepts are empirically identifiable, it might seem that scientists would then be free from every possibility of offense; for all will agree that pure facts can never be wrong, and facts alone are communicated in direct control research. The trouble with this attitude is that it fails to account for the fact that theory is an integral part of all scientific effort. The difficulties that stem from speculation and intuition do not lie in theory, per se, but in the doctrinairism that arises when theory is confounded with operation, so that an effective distinction between the two becomes impossible. No research is completely exploratory in nature, and it is impossible to imagine that any study takes place entirely without conceptual guidance. Failure to acknowledge the existence of a theory or to accept hypothesis testing as a major scientific enterprise merely blinds one to his own biases. When that happens, an investigator becomes just that much more susceptible to the very confounding he is trying to avoid. Atheoreticism alone does not solve the problem of theoretical bias and distortion, it merely conceals it.

It might be held that the method of direct control is theoretically neutral: that it is only a method for collecting facts and that, as such, it has no implications for theory or inference. This is a legitimate conviction, but it is not commonly espoused. When a method is so often held to eliminate theory by its very nature, it can hardly be said to be indifferent to the issue (Plutchik, 1963). Needless to say, an extreme or exclusive commitment to direct controls is not advocated in this chapter.

EXAMPLES

Displacement and Conflict

In a research by Murray (1954), already discussed in the chapter on the natural process method, it was shown that a particular patient in psychotherapy tended to displace hostility away from its supposedly true object, the mother. This displacement appeared to take place along a gradient of personal importance. After expressing mild anger toward the mother, the patient, presumedly because of anxiety, next directed his hostility primarily to his aunt, and later to other less personally important individuals.

The explanation of these findings in terms of a learning theory analysis of conflict situations and of stimulus generalization led Murray and Berkun (1955) to study the observed therapeutic phenomena in a more directly controlled research. They therefore proposed a quasi-mathematical model of the conflict-displacement situation. Briefly, the model indicated that approach-avoidance behavioral tendencies, with respect to a goal toward which both tendencies have been previously learned, are a joint function of (a) the nearness of the behaver to the goal object and (b) the similarity of the goal object to the original. The authors inferred from this model that the greater the similarity of a given goal to the original, the less close to that goal the behaver would come before leaving the situation and choosing a less similar goal. By the same logic, a goal that is sufficiently dissimilar to the original might actually bring about the response toward which behavior was first directed in the earlier, conflictual learning situation. Should that response occur, it would bring about a rapid extinction (reduction) of the avoidance response; and the behaver should then approach the original goal much more closely if placed back into the initial situation.

The relationship between the model and the therapy situation was described as follows: the goal over which conflict was experienced by the patient was the expression of hostility toward the mother; nearness to the goal was represented by the strength or overtness of the hostility; similarity to the original object was presumed to be greater for the aunt than for others toward whom hostility was later expressed.

The actual investigation was conducted with 11 male albino rats, pretested for black, gray, or white preference in the experimental apparatus. The apparatus was a maze with three adjacent, parallel alleys (one was black, the middle one was gray, and one was white) so constructed that by jumping through windows, the rat could transfer itself bodily from one alley to the next at any of several points along the way.

The rats were trained to enter an alley corresponding to their original brightness preference and to traverse the length of the alley for a reward of food and water. During the first ten training trials, transfer from one alley to another was made impossible. During the next thirty training trials, the passages between alleys were left open, although the animals never used them.

Next came a series of avoidance-training trials, in which the rats were placed in the maze as usual (interconnecting passageways closed) but were shocked when they reached the food cup. Trials were continued until the animals stopped traveling more than 18 inches down the 48-inch alley.

Test trials followed. Passageways between alleys were opened, food was placed in the goal box of the alley on which original training took place, and each rat was inserted in the apparatus in the original starting position. No shocks were administered.

Analysis of group results indicated that the typical animal went part way down the original alley, demonstrated behavioral oscillation, moved to the adjacent alley, advanced a little farther toward the goal box, retreated, and jumped to the next alley—two steps removed from the original—where a goal-response was often made. On later trials, similar patterns were observed; but closer approaches to the goals in the first two alleys were then more frequently noted. The results were considered consistent with predictions derived from the model. Case material from the therapeutic record of a human patient was then presented to illustrate the operation of the conflict-displacement complex in a particular psychotherapy session.

The reader may have noted that despite its use of direct controls, this study was not an experiment. It was a test of rats' behavior under constant conditions. (The authors did report the results of one experiment, in which conditions were varied by placing food rewards in all alleys during the test trials. This investigation constituted only a minor part of the research report, however; and the results showed no differences between experimental and comparison groups.)

Murray and Berkun's study illustrates many of the points already raised and demonstrates the features and problems of the method of direct controls when it is applied to the study of processes of interest to the personologist. With regard to the feature of conventionalism, it should be noted that a number of standard procedures and operational definitions were incorporated into the research design. Behavior was examined in a maze, a type of apparatus that is highly familiar to most students of psychology. The traditional hunger drive and the conventional avoidance inducer, electric shock, were also used to establish what was to be called "conflict." Approach was taken, as usual, to mean movement toward the goal of food; avoidance was classically defined as movement away from the goal; and conflict was evidenced by oscillation between these two directional tendencies. Displacement was signified by the animal's entering a parallel alley, one or more steps removed from the original training alley. As is also usual, the required conditions for the test trials were established by uniform pretraining schedules. None of these operations or techniques is particularly new to students of learning, although their organization in this study must be regarded as ingenious and original.

The sharpness of focus of the study is evident even upon superficial examination of its design. The use of rats of a purebred, laboratory-raised strain, instead of persons, was almost certainly an attempt to control or eliminate the complexities of human constitution, the variations of human experience, and the rich behavior potential that characterizes people, all of which could be viewed only as contaminations in a study of this type. The maze itself, though more flexible than many currently in use, must also be regarded as a focusing device. Almost the only behaviors available to the rats were those few in which the experimenter was interested. It is nearly impossible to do anything in a maze alley but run back and forth or escape, if the animal is to behave at all. Furthermore, those few other activities that are possible (e.g., defecation, urination, trembling) were not observed or at least not reported, probably because they were not considered relevant to the hypotheses.

Indeed, in this study the intensity of focus was so strong that given the conditions of the investigation, it is hard to see how results other than those reported could have been obtained. The findings describe the not-too-surprising facts that rats exhibit avoidance responses to an alley in which they were previously shocked and that they tend to enter other alleys in fairly systematic fashion. Leaving the shocked alley is, by definition, displacement, and it is hard to see how any other response could have occurred in this apparatus. The systematic character of the displacement (the gradient) is relatively simply explained by the observation that it is doubtless easier for a rat to jump to an adjacent alley before he jumps to one that is farther away. (In this study, the importance of brightness—that is, "similarity"—cannot be judged, since the white, gray, and black alleys were evidently not interchanged.)

Even the fact that goal responses were made in displacement alleys may also be a function of the apparatus. Suppose that displacement were not possible, so that the animal had to remain in the original alley. In a condition of true, balanced (and not too severe) conflict the rat would be expected to approach the goal more closely on succeeding tries if only because his hunger (food deprivation time) increases automatically with exposure to the apparatus. Thus, he might very well exhibit the same behavior found by these investigators, but without displacement. If this is so and if the displacement itself is imposed on the animal by the very construction of the maze, then the total result of the study may be attributed entirely to artifactual causes.

Whether its findings are artifactual or not, however, this investigation still poses problems of inference. There is only one basis upon which it may be said that its findings are relevant to the study of personality; that is the basis of analogy. It might be said that the investigation does not, in fact, examine personality variables; it merely makes them tangible and analogizes them, in the same way that the theoretical model that was tested analogized the investigation itself. (*Cf.* chapter 9. Also, see Lazarus [1964], for an elaboration of the logic of experimental analogy, as specifically applied to the study of stress.)

A look at some of the analogies that must be accepted should set this argument to rest. Rats must be considered models of people. A maze must be analogized to life situations; and within the maze, approach and avoidance behavior must be accepted as equivalents to psychological conflict. Hunger must be equated with hostility, shock with fear of hostile impulses. Food must be considered the analogue of expressed anger, and alleys must become transformed into personally important people. Displacement of a central impulse must be converted into jumping from one pathway to another, and conditioning procedures must substitute for a lifetime of psychological development. It is possible that inference from such a model to the life situation of the neurotic person is perfectly reasonable; but the logic of the proposed parallels is scarcely compelling. From the point of view of theoretical significance, Murray's own intensive investigation of a single patient in psychotherapy, despite its lack of direct controls, makes more obvious sense to the personologist than the infinitely more precise examination of rats in a maze. Both researches may be fine pieces of work in their own right; and it is probably true that the construction of the rat study from the observation of a therapy case, via a behavioristic theory of learning, represents a good example of technical ingenuity and creative thinking. The intellectual process of relating these two studies to each other invokes a fine sense of esthetic appreciation, but it cannot be forcefully imposed by ordinary empirical or logical devices.

Operant Conditioning

While the study by Murray and Berkun attempted to deal with clinically meaningful phenomena by means of a directly controlled analogy, other studies deal in even more concrete fashion with matters that are presumably interesting to the personologist. Such investigations are generally founded on the logic of operant conditioning (Skinner, 1953; Skinner, 1963a; Skinner, 1963b), which promulgates the doctrine of reducing all psychological concepts to the description and specification of stimulus manipulations and overt responses.

An example of this type of research is the study by Rheingold, Gewirtz, and Ross (1959), on the conditioning of vocalization in infants. Twenty-two infants, all about three months of age, were observed for two days, to establish their "baseline" of vocalization, that is, the rate at which vocal sounds were produced without reinforcement. During the third and fourth days, vocalizations produced by the infant were immediately followed by a reinforcement. The reinforcement was administered by the experimenter and consisted of "a broad smile, three 'tsk' sounds, and a light touch to the infant's abdomen with thumb and fingers of the hand opposed." This constituted the *conditioning* period. During the fifth and sixth days, the *extinction* period, the experimenter leaned over the crib "with an expressionless face," as in the baseline period, and administered no reinforcement for vocalization.

The number of vocalizations produced under the three conditions were then compared statistically. The mean number of vocalizations was found to increase markedly from the baseline to the conditioning period, and then to decrease significantly from the conditioning period to the extinction period.

As it stands, this investigation shows that a smile, three "tsks" and a touch on the tummy, administered as soon as possible after a child makes a sound, increase the probability of his making more sounds than he did before, at least for as long as the reinforcement continues. What inferences are to be drawn from these findings?

The report of the study notes that "if the results can be extended to life situations," then responses of adults to behaviors of infants can be thought of as providing reinforcements for certain behaviors, thus influencing the development of the child's social responsiveness. It also suggests that since quantity of vocalization is manipulable by reinforcement, perhaps quality is also manipulable by these means; hence, one is led to suppose that the learning of speech could well be the result of operant conditioning. (Kerr, Meyerson, and Michael [in press] make a similar point, but they also note that operant conditioning is probably not the same process that occurs in natural speech development and is probably not feasible in speech therapy.) Similarly, many other kinds of behavior, such as "showing an interest in people, reaching out to them or turning away, perhaps even fear of the stranger," may be manipulated by reinforcement.

Three characteristics of this approach to the general problem of development should be noted. First, the infant is viewed as passive: his behavior changes only because it is shaped by environmental stimuli. Second, the approach is reductionistic: the meaningful implications that make it interesting are analyzed in terms of the simplest possible conditioning procedures; the complexities of the interpersonal relation between mother and child are implicitly reduced to an extension, by accretion of reinforced responses on the part of the infant. Third, as controlled as the method may appear to be and as concrete, specific, and precise as its findings are, its results have meaning for the study of personality only if one is willing to engage in a good deal of fairly wide-ranging speculation of the very type that the method of direct controls is often expected to eliminate. Having demonstrated that vocalizations can be conditioned by external stimuli, it is still a long logical way to the proposition that speech and socialization are products of this process alone. It is not easy to establish the validity of the implication that specific research operations in a study such as the one just cited fairly represent, albeit in simplified form, any very important behavioral interaction between parent and child. Neither is it easy to accept without question the notion that vocalization, per se, is the prototype of such important social attitudes as being interested in people or being afraid of strangers.

An interesting comparison between operant conditioning studies is afforded by the study cited above and one by Brackbill (1958) on the effect of reinforcement schedule on extinction of the smiling response in infants. Briefly, Brackbill conditioned two groups of infants to smile, after observing their base rate in a preconditioning session. One group was conditioned with regular reinforcement; the other was conditioned with irregular reinforcement. The reinforcer was a smile and thirty seconds of jostling and vocalization by the examiner. During the extinction period the infants in both groups were observed, to determine whether the irregularly reinforced group smiled more frequently for a longer time, as predicted. In general the results confirmed the hypothesis that regular reinforcement produces less resistance to extinction than irregular reinforcement.

The main characteristic of this experiment is that it was directly controlled from beginning to end. The research problem was stated in terms of relationships between stimulus properties (reinforcement schedules) and response frequencies (smiles), under standard conditions of training and observation. The results were also interpreted in these terms, and no further statements were made regarding the significance of the findings for mother-child relationships. Essentially, the study began with stimulus-response relations, that had been observed in other situations with other kinds of behaving organisms, and set about to determine whether similar relations existed specifically for infants with respect to a particular response. The findings were taken to imply no more than that there are certain consistent relations between stimuli and responses that can be demonstrated to exist with respect to infants as well as to other organisms. As seems only fit and proper, the reader was left free to speculate about or ignore the implications of these results for broader issues. It was not suggested that one group of infants had been made more cheerful and optimistic than the other, or that the findings showed the oral stage of psychoanalytic theory to be reducible, in essence, to the reinforcement of smiling responses. The study stayed within the limits of its method from start to finish and thereby made a specific contribution to a particular way of dealing with one of the many problems of psychological science.

Direct Controls in Clinical Situations

The discussion of this method would surely be incomplete if no mention were made of the uses of directly controlled methods in situations that require solutions to practical problems of behavior manipulation. The technology of operant conditioning has been found to be extremely valuable in some rehabilitation settings, where the principles of "contingent reinforcement" are applied to shape clients' behavior in desired ways, (Kerr, Meyerson, & Michael, in press; Meyerson, Kerr, & Michael, in press). Detailed examples of this approach are not presented here, though it is worthwhile to outline the essentials of this use of the method.

To shape behavior, it is necessary to identify the final act that is required from the subject and to discover an effective reinforcing agent, that is, a manipulable stimulus, the controlled administration of which tends to sustain subject behavior that approximates the desired act. For example, pieces of popcorn have been used as reinforcers in teaching a nine-year-old mentally retarded child to walk. Reinforcement was administered first for standing with support; next, for standing without support; next, for standing ambulation, however brief or crude, and so forth, until the child began to ambulate independently.

Applied in this way, the principles and procedures of operant conditioning have proven their worth in providing valuable adjunctive treatment methods in clinical practice. It is reasonable to suppose that response training influences and alters personality processes, but this possibility has not yet been thoroughly investigated. As currently employed, the methods of operant conditioning are not intended for use in testing hypotheses about personality; therefore they are not considered further here.

EVALUATION

Subject Matter

The best way to begin a final evaluation of the method of direct controls is with a consideration of the subject matter of psychological research. It is semantically confusing for all psychologists to refer to members of their research samples as *subjects,* for the word may have disparate meanings in different research settings. To the personologist, the ultimate subject of investigation is, or ought to be, the person whose psychological characteristics are being studied. Psychological processes, to the personologist, are conceptual tools by which persons are described and their behavior explained or predicted. The test of our understanding of these processes is therefore the degree to which they enable us to understand and deal effectively with our subjects, that is, people.

To many psychologists, however, the subject of an investigation is not the person as a complex of processes, but the isolated processes themselves. Whether or not a learning curve actually describes the behavior of particular individuals is of little or no concern in many researches. Deviations of individual scores from average values are considered to be not only uninteresting, they are taken to be evidence of poor control over contaminating conditions. Similarly, the psychologist who studies perception is not necessarily studying people perceiving; he often studies only particular kinds of responses to controlled environmental stimuli, and he may very well be inclined to feel that the participating organism is more a hindrance than a help to his efforts.

Some interesting ideas are touched off by Stevens' observation (1951) that the psychophysical experimenter often finds it useful to regard perceivers (persons) as "null instruments," devices that register the apparent equivalence of stimuli (pp. 36-37). When this is true, the investigator's problem is either to discover the sensitivity of these instruments to actual differences in stimulus characteristics or to use them for matching stimuli, the equivalence of which is otherwise unknowable (e.g., when are a given sight and sound equal in perceptual intensity?).

Given such a concept of research, it follows that the greater the similarity among the various null instruments that comprise the sample of perceivers, the more reliable empirical results will be. The best instruments are therefore those that display the least individuality; and the best conditions under which such research is undertaken are those which eliminate all stimulating objects except the particular ones to which the instruments are expected to respond. Since the subjects of this type of research are not persons or mediating psychological processes, but correlations between the physical properties of objects and specific overt responses, it is best conducted under conditions that minimize individual differences and unique experiences.

Psychologists who are interested only in object-response relations find the method of direct control extremely useful. It has been observed, however, that the possibilities of such "distally focused" research may be limited. "Because it only asks 'what' and not 'how', it cannot achieve complete determination. If it were to ask 'how', and if it wanted to describe completely the processes involved in a single concrete case of behavior, it would have to consider proximal and interior determinants; it is, in the end, even questionable whether it is possible to give a complete answer to the question 'what' without doing so." (Heider, 1959, pp. 76-77; orig. pub., 1939)

Advantages and Disadvantages

Viewed in the light of the personologist's interests and legitimate scientific concerns, some features of the method of direct controls appear to be somewhat less than completely desirable.

For instance, the precision of the method, that results from its sharpness of focus, is of little value to the study of personality if the only processes about which an investigator can be precise are unnatural, unreal, impersonal, or unimportant. The confinement of behavioral possibilities, the construction of restrictive environments, and the observation, no matter how objective, of limited aspects of complex processes, give much of this research an artificial quality that raises doubts about the applicability of its results to real people in real situations. The personality theorist is disturbed by the fact that such research so often demands a passive, docile subject, who is content to function only in response to the immediate situation, and who is either willing or can be forced to give up whatever impulses he may have to engage in independent, self-initiated activity.

Since personality theory sees the ultimate source of most behavior as existing within the person (which is not the same as saying that behavior is uninfluenced by environmental events), the personologist's preference is for methods that permit mediating processes to operate as freely as possible. Rigidly artificial laboratory situations so seldom do so effectively that they are not highly regarded by him as research devices. He sees little merit in precision, if it can only be achieved at the cost of the organized integrity of the experimental subject.

Similarly, although the conventionalism of the method of direct control seems to make possible a final standardization of definitions and investigative procedures, this same conventionalism, if carried to extremes, can all too easily degenerate into an unreasoned traditionalism, that is, a viewpoint that places a high value on specific procedures simply because they have been frequently used before. A correlated result can be the stifling of ingenuity and the blocking of investigative interest in new problems or techniques only because they have never previously been subjected to empirical study (Maslow, 1954, pp. 13-21).

Probably the only features of the method of direct controls that can be universally favored are its tangibility and its explicitness. It should be remembered, however, that neither of these properties is the exclusive possession of a particular research strategy. Partial or indirect indices of mediating processes, for example, are also tangible phenomena which may be described in detail; and it is by no means necessary to exhaust the meaning of a theoretical concept in a particular operation in order to be explicit about research procedures.

Conclusion

It is perhaps necessary to remind the reader that direct control research has a very definite place in the scientific examination of man. It would be as senseless to argue that pure stimulus-response relations are unimportant as it is to maintain that they are all-important. Difficulties and disagreements arise either when the

laboratory psychologist becomes too thorough and attempts to reduce all of psychology to correlations among directly controlled
events or when the personologist, on his side, attempts to eliminate
from consideration all the influences on behavior that stem from
the physical properties of the environment. Each protagonist then
seeks to establish the truth of his bias and the falsity of the other's;
and neither permits himself to become aware of the real strengths
and weaknesses of his own preferences.

It is not likely that either party to such disputes will ever fully
prevail, for there is, in psychological methodology, an inherent
dilemma (mentioned in the preceding chapter) that has not yet
been, and may never be, satisfactorily handled. It is that increased
precision is almost always gained only by sacrificing naturalness and
the individual integrity of the behaver. In the same way, an improvement in the probable real-life significance of an empirical investigation almost always results in a lack of certainty about the
precise nature of the events that are taking place.

In general it is probably best to avoid attempts to identify the
study of personality with research methods that require direct control of all variables. The effort to combine the requirements of such
methods with the tenets of a personalistic view of the human organism too easily leads to a blurring of the line between data and
conclusions. When this line becomes too vague, the investigator is
tempted not to perceive it at all and to engage in a form of thinking
that may lack the discipline necessary for scientific progress. The
personality theorist relies heavily on theory in everything he does,
from research to clinical evaluation. He must remain acutely aware
of this reliance; and his awareness is best assured through the use of
methods that require detailed explication of the total and reciprocal process of research development, from concept to response assessment and back.

References

BACHRACH, A. J. *Psychological research: An introduction.* New York:
    Random House, 1962.
BRACKBILL, YVONNE. Extinction of the smiling response in infants as a
    function of reinforcement schedule. *Child Develpm.,* 1958, *29,* 115-124.

(In Mednick & Mednick, pp. 127-135 [see References, chapter 1, above].)

HEIDER, F. Environmental determinants in psychological theories. *Psychol. Rev.*, 1939, *46*, 383-410. Also in G. S. Klein (Ed.), *Psychological Issues.* New York: Internat. Univer. Press, 1959. Part 3, pp. 61-84.

KERR, NANCY, MEYERSON, L., & MICHAEL, J. A procedure for shaping vocalizations in a mute child. In L. P. Ullman, & L. Krasner (Eds.), *Case studies in behavior modification.* New York: Holt, Rinehart and Winston, in press.

LAZARUS, R. S. A laboratory approach to the dynamics of psychological stress. *Amer. Psychologist*, 1964, *19*, 400-411.

MASLOW, A. H. *Motivation and personality.* New York: Harper & Row, 1954.

MEYERSON, L., KERR, NANCY, & MICHAEL, J. Behavior modification in rehabilitation. In S. Bijou, *Cases in behavior modification,* in preparation.

MURRAY, E. J. A case study in the behavioral analysis of psychotherapy. *J. abnorm. soc. Psychol.*, 1954, *49*, 305-310. (In Mednick & Mednick, pp. 414-422 [see References, chapter 1, above].)

MURRAY, E. J., & BERKUN, M. M. Displacement as a function of conflict. *J. abnorm. soc. Psychol.*, 1955, *51*, 47-56. (In Mednick & Mednick, pp. 422-433 [see References, chapter 1, above].)

PLUTCHIK, R. A. Operationism as methodology. *Behav. Sci.*, 1963, *8*, 234-241.

RHEINGOLD, HARRIET L., GEWIRTZ, J. L., & ROSS, HELEN W. Social conditioning of vocalizations in the infant. *J. comp. physiol. Psychol.*, 1959, *52*, 68-73. (In Mednick & Mednick, pp. 136-143 [see References, chapter 1, above].)

SKINNER, B. F. *The behavior of organisms: An experimental analysis.* New York: Appleton-Century-Crofts, 1938.

SKINNER, B. F. *Science and human behavior.* New York: Macmillan, 1953.

SKINNER, B. F. Behaviorism at fifty. *Science*, 1963, *140*, 951-958. (a)

SKINNER, B. F. Operant behavior. *Amer. Psychologist*, 1963, *18*, 503-515. (b)

STEVENS, S. S. Mathematics, measurement, and psychophysics. In S. S. Stevens (Ed.), *Handbook of experimental psychology.* New York: Wiley, 1951. Pp. 1-49.

11
The representative case·
A recommendation

Throughout the preceding chapters, attention has been directed to the analysis of commonly used research strategies for the study of personality. It is now appropriate to devote some space and effort to a consideration and exemplification of the properties of an approach that is not very popular but that may have considerable potential for personological research. It is the method of the *representative case*; and its essential properties, though not all of its technical complexities, are relatively easily specified. The method comprises an integration of the case study approach with natural process and remote control strategies. Its aims are to test deductively derived hypotheses, through the examination of single subjects, chosen for their specific appropriateness to the research problem of interest.

Representative case research begins, as does all research, with the statement of a problem. In this method the problem must be statable in theoretical or conceptual terms; for the purpose of the method is to confirm the descriptive, explanatory, or predictive utility of theoretical propositions.

The next step is to find or select a single individual for intensive study. This person constitutes the representative case, from which the method gets its name. The subject is by no means chosen at random; indeed, a great deal of information is usually needed about him to establish his representativeness with respect to the propositions to be empirically evaluated. Prior to the research proper, the subject is examined to determine his characteristic behavioral tendencies, with respect to the variables in question. Thus, for example, if the research concerns the dynamics of homosexuality, it must be known in advance how the particular subject expresses his own homosexual impulses. This knowledge permits the establishment of individually meaningful rules of correspondence, by which the effects of natural or remotely manipulated experimental processes may be evaluated.

Data collection then consists of observing and recording relevant responses of the subject to conditions that vary according to the dictates of the problem, preferably in as natural a fashion as possible. Individually appropriate rules of correspondence determine when conditions specified by the problem are met. For example, if a given set of mediating processes, such as aroused hostility toward females, is presupposed to increase a male subject's homosexual tendencies, it might be predicted that the behaviors associated with this arousal will increase following an argument between the subject and a woman. Ideally, it might be best to follow the subject about and to obtain measures when such an argument actually occurs in the course of his daily affairs. Whether that is possible or not depends on a variety of practical factors that are not always at the command of the experimenter. Most often, something short of the ideal must suffice. As one possibility, the subject might be asked to describe how he felt the last time he had an argument with his mother or sister (retrospective report). Another possibility would be to use remote manipulation. The subject might be purposely engaged in an argument with a female during the time when he is available for examination. Remote manipulation, though fraught with difficulties in group-oriented research, may be quite useful when a single person, about whom a great deal is known, is the experimental subject; for it is relatively easy to specify how similar environmental conditions have affected that person in the past and to assess the effectiveness of a specifically tailor-made situation in producing desired mediating states.

Data from these sources may then be treated statistically to determine whether predictions suggested by theory, and explicated by rules of correspondence, are borne out. Conclusions may then be drawn about the applicability of the concepts that led to the execution of the research, not only to the particular subject but to others who share his important psychological properties.

Objections and Replies

Two objections to the method come immediately to mind. One concerns the practical problems that are inherent in the conduct of such investigations. The other has to do with the smallness of the sample and the apparent lack of generalizability of the results. The first objection is easily answered. No one ever proposed that the proper study of personality is easy.

The second objection may be answered most conveniently by reference to an analogy. A chemist who wishes to study the properties of a compound or element need not concern himself with the number of samples of the substance on which his tests are run, as long as he is certain that he knows the identity of the particular material on which he is working and as long as his procedures are explicit and carefully followed. By the same token, a psychologist who wishes to study an important personality process, such as anxiety, need not concern himself greatly with the size of his sample, provided that his subject is appropriately selected and that he has procedures that enable him to recognize (i.e., measure) anxiety when it occurs in the person he is investigating. The logical basis for the study of single subjects will become clearer as this chapter progresses.

A third possible objection to the method of the representative case is somewhat more subtle than the first two. It is that the pre-study of an individual subject necessarily involves exposing him to situations similar to those that will later be used in the experiment proper. Thus, the experiment merely clothes already established qualitative observations with numbers and high-sounding theoretical terms. Predictions should be derived from theory and given a fair test; but if it is already known that a subject responds in a specific way to certain kinds of situations, and he simply continues to do so, no real test is involved.

The obvious answer to this argument is that all science proceeds in very nearly the same way. One observes natural phenomena and sees within them regularities that lead to the postulation of general principles. These principles are then stated in more precise and specific measurement terms and tested, essentially for their descriptive value, under specifiable conditions of observation.

Still a fourth objection to the method may arise from the suspicion that its very procedures make the representative case study subject to bias. For example, the intensive examination of a single person may alter the processes that are being investigated in him. The subject may not be anxious, for instance, until anxiety is called to his attention by an inquisitive examiner; or a person's response to anxiety may change as soon as he becomes aware of the fact that it is being investigated. Indeed, the investigative process itself may induce responses that confirm the psychologist's hypotheses but that are not consistent with the subject's usual behavior patterns.

This problem is real, but it is not unique to the representative case approach; it exists even in rigidly controlled laboratory experimentation on isolated events. There is as much to be said, for instance, against experiments in which the subject is told to learn a list of words. There is as much reason to believe that learning processes alter under conditions of concentrated awareness as to believe that personality changes when it is investigated intensively. The argument has merit and must be taken seriously, but the problems it poses are not characteristic of any particular research strategy.

The best answers to this objection are procedural. Precautions of technique can no more be ignored in the representative case method than in any other. Many problems can be avoided through proper consideration and elimination of sources of bias in the data by careful advance planning of research procedures. It is essential to this approach that data be high in immediacy, objectivity, and relevance. It is often necessary that a disinterested or uninformed person serve as data collector; and since the method frequently relies heavily on indirect measurements, independent raters or judges are commonly required. It is important also that the subject's situation be such that his personal desires to please or discredit the experimenter have minimal effects upon the outcome. It is not necessary that the subject be kept entirely in the dark about the project; in fact, his permission for such intensive investigation is usually required. However, he need not always be told the precise purposes of the study or the expected results; of course he should not if the research is predictive in nature. The importance of adequate measuring instruments need hardly be reemphasized.

Representative case research offers no easy solution to the study of personality. It requires careful planning and execution, as does all scientific investigation. But all its apparent difficulties are not entirely disadvantageous. For example, it may be considered restrictive that representative case research can be conducted only in situations where relatively continuous availability of data is possible. This makes it difficult to use in the university laboratory situation. At the same time, however, it suits the method well to clinical settings; and most existing examples of its use have been derived from that source.

Techniques

G. W. Allport (1962) has enumerated several data collection techniques that are suited to intensive individual research. He called them "morphogenic" techniques; and although he did not specifically advocate the method of the representative case, his suggestions may be quite useful in this type of investigation. It is not the purpose of this work to examine particular procedures in detail; but it will be helpful to consider several of Allport's recommendations briefly, if only to establish that the representative case method is not impoverished in technical possibilities.

The technique of *matching* requires judges to identify, in a pool of data, performances of the same person on different tasks or in different situations. This technique is especially useful for studying the degree of relatedness among a variety of individually expressive behavioral modes.

The technique of *personal structure analysis* is credited to Baldwin (1942) and calls for the use of a series of records of expressive behavior from the same individual (e.g., personal letters), which are analyzed for common themes and characteristics. *Central motif analysis* appears to have much in common with personal structure analysis, except that central motif analysis takes into account the whole life structure of the individual.

The *individual questionnaire* was suggested to Allport by Shapiro (1961), who proposed that custom-made questionnaire items be constructed for the individual case. Specific items are formulated on the basis of a five-hour intensive interview with the individual for whom the questionnaire is devised. The questionnaire then remains standard for that particular person, and it is readministered as necessary to evaluate changes or constancies in that person. (The use of Q-sort statements, employing the person's own words, or the use of individually meaningful concepts and scales in a semantic differential would exemplify somewhat more fully-developed uses of the same technique.)

Direct questioning is particularly useful for studying personal value systems. Allport argues that evidence derived from projective tests should always be supplemented by data from direct questions. Probably his caution should be extended to include all forms of indirect measurement as well.

The *self-anchoring scale* (Kilpatrick & Cantril, 1960) is a rating device in which the person is asked to anchor certain extreme judgments (on a scale from, say, one to ten) in his own value system. For example, the extreme points might be anchored by asking the person to describe the most extraverted and the most introverted ways of living he can imagine. The person may then be asked to select scale values representing his, or possibly someone else's, personal standing on the scale in the past, present, or future.

Some of the techniques advocated for morphogenic research may seem crude, and many cannot be fully understood without further elaboration of their particular features and dangers. The reader is encouraged to refer to original sources for more specific information about the ones that interest him. It should be remembered that if these techniques are unrefined, they are so only because they are seldom used. It is, in fact, impossible either to improve them or to judge their strengths and weaknesses adequately until they have been subjected to the ultimate test of extensive research application.

EXAMPLES

Idiopathic epilepsy. In a previous chapter (chapter 6), mention was made of a study by Bowdlear (1955) on the dynamics of idiopathic epilepsy. This investigation provides a good example of the method and problems of the representative case.

Bowdlear's report began with an exhaustive review of the literature on idiopathic epilepsy and a summary of its presumed psychodynamic properties, as suggested by previous authorities. It was noted that seizures have been assigned the contradictory functions of acting out feelings and of inhibiting expression of feelings. It was also noted that the importance of close interpersonal relations with parents and siblings had been emphasized by many authors. Certain kinds of specific life situations seemed particularly potent (for example, the seizure itself, heterosexual and homosexual activity, physical fights, and self-revelation). The specific feelings of hostility, sexuality, dependence, yielding, and dominance were stressed by many authorities.

The author then established that his particular subject, selected for investigating the validity of these propositions, met the criteria of the diagnostic category which he was to represent and about which the psychological literature had so much to say. Extensive case data were presented, covering the social and medical history of the individual, a twenty-eight-year-old male in a Veterans Administration Hospital; and it was concluded that he was appropriate to the purposes of the investigation. Additional case study information of a psychological nature was obtained from the patient's psychotherapist, who provided a comprehensive, though impressionistic, theoretical description of the subject's personality structure.

Hypotheses were then stated. These were divided into three groups, depending upon their source. The first group of hypotheses came from the literature; the second came from the therapist, and were based on his knowledge of the particular person being studied; the third came from the writer himself, as a result of his effort to integrate the generalities of the literature and the particularities of the patient.

The procedure of the experiment proper was designed to test the three groups of hypotheses by examining variations in the patient's descriptions of himself under a variety of instructional conditions. A Q-sort instrument was constructed for data collection purposes. Individual relevance of the items of the Q sort was assured by constructing the instrument from a pool of statements the patient himself had made about his feelings. Theoretical relevance was obtained by classifying these statements into 24 groups, representing six significant feelings, as the subject had expressed them toward four significant persons in his life. The persons were mother, father, and a particular brother and sister known to be especially important to the patient (he had eight siblings). The feelings were dependence on, hostility to, dominance of, independence of, sexual wishes toward, and yielding to. Each feeling was represented for each person, providing a cross-classification structure in the item sample.

Statements which had thus been classified were then further examined for appropriateness to the Q-sort method, and a revised item pool resulted from the process of culling out unusable statements. Finally, three items from each cell of the cross-classification were randomly selected to produce a structured Q-sort sample of 72 statements, which the patient was then to use in describing himself. The theoretical significance of the items was not explained to the subject.

Instructions for the various descriptions were designed to represent situations, the importance of which had been suggested by the various hypotheses of the study. There were, of course, a self-sort and an ideal-sort (describe how you usually feel; describe how you would like to feel). The other 23 sortings reflected dynamic situations, presumed to be important on the basis of theory and previously expressed authoritative opinion. Here are some examples: describe how you feel before a seizure; after a seizure; when you and your mother (father, sister, brother) have had a particularly good time together; when you have given in to your mother (father, sister, brother); just before (after) a fight; after sexual intercourse with a girl friend; when you worry about being a freak; when you worry about being a child.

Because of the already existing rapport between subject and therapist, the Q sort was administered by the therapist rather than by the experimenter himself.

Two forms of statistical analysis were employed on the resulting data. Analysis of variance was employed on Q-sort item placement scores to test for significant differences in descriptive usage of the various items, as a function of instructional sets. (The hypotheses predicted the outcome of these statistical tests.) Factor analysis (O-design) was employed to examine for congruencies and dissimilarities among overall descriptions, provided under the various research conditions.

It is impossible to present the statistical results, per se, without going beyond the purposes of this summarization. It is worthwhile, however, to mention briefly the conclusions that seemed warranted by the findings. The seizure seemed to represent for this patient an acting-out of dependency. It typically began with feelings of yielding that triggered hostility; after it was over the subject felt passive and submissive. Homosexual feelings also seemed to gain expression in the seizure, since they were strong preceding it, but not following it. Heterosexual feelings were generally uncomfortable for the patient and received some slight, but far from complete, reduction as a result of the seizure. Bowdlear felt that his findings "tended to complicate, rather than simplify, the dynamics of idiopathic epilepsy. The seizure did not have a single meaning for our subject" (p. 5, abstract).

There are several formal features of this study that deserve comment. First, it began with a problem that was defined by a medical diagnostic category, but about which a good deal of unsystematically tested theoretical material was available in the literature. For maximum probable meaningfulness of results to personality theory, this approach to problem selection often proves to be unfortunate, since medical diagnostic categories are rarely useful as indicators of psychological processes and organizations. The lack of systematic relationship between diagnosis and psychological organization in this study is additionally confirmed by the multiplicity of explanations of the seizure offered by authorities and suggested by the findings.

Research problems in personality are best selected for their psychological clarity; and representative case research probably proceeds best when psychological structure is its starting point. In this way, psychological (i.e., personality) variables, inferred to exist on the basis of preinvestigative information, are related, via hypothetically derived predictions, to specific behaviors in specifiable situations. Bowdlear's study was actually concerned with drawing inferences about the psychological characteristics of the subject, given the fact that this is a person who engages in an interesting form of behavior (seizures). It was therefore diagnostically or descriptively, as well as deductively, oriented. In this research, the specification of a variety of hypotheses constituted the explication of a number of sets of alternative possibilities for explaining the subject's seizure behavior. The investigator probably hoped that his data would enable him to find one set of explanations that would be so much more consistent with his results than the rest as to require rejection of the others. Instead, nearly all proffered explanations of the behavior appeared to be simultaneously appropriate. The dynamic theorist should scarcely be surprised at this outcome, for it has long been a tenet of such theories that a specific act may have a variety of underlying causes.

A second formal feature of the study is that although it employed a Q-sort instrument, it closely paralleled the factor analytic O-design, in which many measures are taken of the same subject on a variety of occasions. From a technical point of view, there is the question of the degree to which similarities or changes in the patient's descriptions were simply a function of repeated measurements with the same instrument. One way to deal with this problem might have been to have the subject redescribe his usual self at, say, every fifth sorting. Correlations among these descriptions, obtained under identical instructions but at different points in the series, would establish the degree of consistency of item placement as functions of time and of familiarity with the items themselves.

This problem in Bowdlear's study does not imply that correlations with time in representative case studies are always to be thought of as contaminations. Often, as in the next research example, time relationships are best left in the data. Attempts to design them out or to correct for them statistically would not make theoretical sense. For example, although it is logically possible to randomize the order of instructional sets, it is clearly best, from the point of view of research design, to ask the subject how he feels just before he has a seizure, before asking him how he feels after he has had a seizure. It cannot be argued that the influence of the first description on the second must somehow be eliminated or removed, since it is precisely this dependence that is of interest to the investigator.

Two other major features of this study have already been discussed and require only brief reemphasis. They are the stress on the relevance of the measuring instrument to the particular individual being investigated, and the meticulous care devoted to establishing a clear relationship between the uniquenesses of the patient and the universalities of the propositions studied. Bowdlear's research was not an idiographic study. It did not investigate the subject as a self-contained universe with its own laws. It saw the patient as a representative of a large class of individuals with similar behavioral characteristics; and it sought to learn about the large class by studying intensively one of its clearly identifiable members. The fact that the class itself is rather poorly defined, from a psychological as well as a somatic point of view (Tizard, 1962), does not alter the structure of the investigation, although it probably accounts in part for the lack of clarity of its results.

Neither did this investigation examine the selected patient as a *sample* of some broader universe. A proper sample, as that term is usually used in psychology, can be obtained only if every member of a class has an equal opportunity to be chosen for examination. By contrast, the subject in Bowdlear's study was purposely and deliberately picked, because he demonstrated that he displayed especially clearly the features in which the investigator was interested. Although he was not randomly selected from a larger population, it cannot be said that he unfairly represents one.

To convey the point more clearly, let us turn back to our chemical analogy. A chemist who wishes to study the properties of salt has every right to select, with considerable premeditation if necessary, the material he intends to examine, so that he may be sure his results will reflect the properties of salt more than of other contaminants. He is not censured for preferring crystalline salt that is relatively pure, to crude sea water for his research. No statistician would be likely, under these circumstances, to object to the lack of randomness in his sample selection. Like the chemist, the psychologist also has the right to select a subject who represents as clearly as possible the class of variables in which the investigator is interested. Random samples, as they are usually defined, are well suited to a variety of research problems in psychology (standardizing tests, for example); but their necessity in personality research has been grossly exaggerated.

Terminal illness. Certain experiences or events have such universal importance and yet are so particular and individual in their actuality that the method of the representative case seems suited to them by definition. Such an event is death. Despite its all-encompassing inevitability, there seems to be no better way to study the psychological significance of death than to examine the effects of its anticipation on a single dying person. The task has recently been undertaken by Zinker (1963).

The report of Zinker's work begins, as usual, with a review of the literature and a series of methodological comments that it would be best for the reader to examine himself, if at all possible. Briefly, he noted that the negative, disintegrating, destructive, aspects of the experience of anticipating death have been almost universally emphasized by students of the subject. Yet it seemed quite likely to the investigator that the prospect of personal death might serve as an organizing force for psychological growth in the structure of the individual. Essentially the problem of the research, then, was to examine the personality of a single person who was dying from cancer for signs of progressive growth or deterioration. Clearly, nature was taking care of the manipulation of the essential independent variable.

As a theoretical framework, Maslow's concept of a hierarchy of needs was selected (1954). The method of collecting raw data was straightforward. The selected patient was seen by the investigator approximately twice a week for open-ended interviews of from twenty minutes to an hour each. The interviews were tape recorded (of course, both the subject's and the physician's permission had been obtained for the procedure). Data from the 31 interviews were organized and quantified by means of a specially constructed Q-sort.

The Q-sort statements were designed by the investigator to express the five levels of needs proposed by Maslow (physiological, safety, belongingness and love, esteem, self-actualization) in terms that would be relevant to the particular patient being studied. Two independent psychologists, who were familiar with Maslow's system, were then given the items in random order and asked to identify each item with its appropriate need level. Final adjustments in item number and content reduced the Q sort to twelve items in each of the five theoretical categories.

Pilot studies, using interviews with patients other than the one specifically being investigated, established the reliability of the instrument and served to familiarize and train the judges in its use.

The judges then listened to the tape recordings of all 31 interviews with the dying patient, in random order. They used the *Q* sort to describe every interview in terms of the organization and degree of satisfaction of needs expressed in it. It was proposed that if the patient's psychological organization were deteriorating as death approached, needs that are higher on the hierarchy (esteem, self-actualization) would be progressively less characteristic of the patient as she became more ill.

Additional data on the subject included independent medical evidence confirming her physical deterioration, social- and medical-history reports, psychological ratings provided weekly by 14 non-psychologist hospital staff members who knew the patient well, and a follow-up questionnaire that was completed by 10 of the 14 staff members mentioned above.

As may be easily imagined, the statistical analysis of all this information is far too complex to be reviewed in this primarily methodologically oriented discussion. A brief summary of the author's conclusions is nevertheless in order.

The patient's motivational structure was found to be dominated by physiological and safety needs throughout the total period of the investigation. Physiological needs did become progressively more important over time, while esteem needs became progressively less important; but love and belongingness needs were found to be significantly more satisfied than all other types throughout the study. Frustration of physiological needs increased as death approached; but no changes in satisfaction or frustration of the other four need-types was observed. Despite minor observed shifts, there was no change over time in the values of a composite score, designed to reflect in a single index the level of need-maturity of the subject.

Zinker's work failed to establish that the anticipation of death was a positive growth experience for his subject; but his work raised serious doubt about the validity of any contention that dying is necessarily a seriously disorganizing psychological process. The psychological stability of his subject in the face of her physically deteriorating condition indicated to the investigator "the capacity of human beings to withstand conditions of extreme physical stress, and to maintain, even in the face of death, concern about the satisfaction of the broad spectrum of human needs, which go far beyond the alleviation of physical pain and the need for physical survival" (p. 184).

Zinker identified his study as idiographic, but it is not, in fact, so. As in Bowdlear's work, the research shows remarkable interest in and concern for the integrity of the individual subject as a unique person. It would be a mistake, however, to confuse this concern with a lack of interest in general psychological principles. The investigator's use of a conceptual scheme of motivation and his focus on a question, the answer to which is important to all persons, reveal the actual breadth of his interest. Essentially Zinker set out to discover whether the anticipation of death is necessarily a psychologically disorganizing experience, and he found that it is not. Thus, his work answered the question that was posed before data collection began.

This is not to say that the study solves all problems about the meaning of death to all individuals. Indeed, like most good science, it asks more questions than it answers. If the anticipation of death is not necessarily disorganizing, then it does not inevitably follow that all persons would remain integrated if faced with a terminal illness. Neither does the existence of stability in Zinker's patient indicate that dying may not, under some conditions, have a positive effect and induce psychological growth and maturity. What these conditions may be remains an open question.

The study also is not methodologically perfect in all respects. There are procedural criticisms to be leveled, particularly at the way in which raw data were collected. It is hardly likely that even a trained clinical psychologist could talk with a dying person twice a week for four months and present a completely neutral appearance at all times. And even if this were possible, the very presence of the psychologist necessarily introduces an unrepresentative feature into the situation; for it is well known that terminal patients are ordinarily left to die in isolation from other people. Furthermore, it might be noted that Zinker's patient was in some ways special. She had a long history of chronic illness, and her overall motivational organization did not show signs of a high level of maturity to start with. It may be that a person who has never developed higher level needs is less threatened by death than one who has.

Some of these criticisms, particularly those regarding subject selection, may be answered by further research on other terminal patients. Some could only be answered if a means were found for collecting data without the active participation of an interested investigator. None of the criticisms constitutes a valid attack on the method of the representative case as a research strategy; but they do illustrate the complexity of the technical problems faced by the personality theorist, even when his basic strategy is sound.

Drug effects. An interesting use of the single-case method is represented by Bellak and Chassan's description (1964) of a research designed to evaluate the effects of the drug, *chlordiazepoxide* on a patient in psychotherapy. This investigation was identified by the authors as a "feasibility" study and was intended to demonstrate the value of intensive experimentation with individuals in clinical settings.

Previous knowledge of the patient enabled the investigators to formulate eight variables (e.g., anxiety, confusion, depression) on which the subject's behavior could be rated by his therapist after each therapeutic hour. The study lasted for ten weeks, with one therapy session held each week. At every session the patient was given a bottle of pills to take during the following week. Double-blind procedure ensured that neither patient nor therapist knew whether the bottle contained the drug or an inactive substance. A balanced schedule of drug administration was also established which enabled the investigators to determine whether changes in rated behavior were due to the psychotherapy alone or whether they could, in fact, be attributed to the action of the drug. Though not designed to provide a final test of the effectiveness of chlordiazepoxide as a therapeutic agent, this research did establish its value as an adjunct to the psychotherapeutic process in the single case investigated.

Bellak and Chassan's discussion of the advantages and problems of the single case approach to the evaluation of drug effects is worthwhile reading for any serious student of psychology. Their method has a great deal in common with representative case experimentation, as described in this chapter. Its only deficiency is its relative lack of emphasis upon the care with which particular cases are selected for maximum relevance to theoretical problems. If a given substance is specifically claimed to reduce anxiety, for example, it would be critical to test it on a patient for whom anxiety is a major problem. It would also be useful, incidentally, to perform the same test on another, otherwise comparable, patient whose symptoms do not include anxiety as a major component. Bellak and Chassan probably presumed that any careful investigator would automatically consider these problems in the design of his research; and it would be nice to believe that this is so. Nevertheless, it does no harm to be cautious and to recognize explicitly that the success of representative case experimentation depends as much upon the properties of the case as upon the quality of the experimentation.

Dream interpretation.   The final example of the representative case method is nonquantitative and might well have served in a previous chapter to show how case materials may be used to demonstrate a technique. The subject is dream interpretation, and the reference is a book by T. M. French and Erika Fromm (1964).[1]

The relevance of this work lies less in the content of the dream material the authors' have analyzed than in the methodological proposals they have made. These proposals suggest, but unfortunately do not fully develop, an approach that may be useful in making scientific sense out of a wide variety of qualitatively important, but not easily quantified, materials, such as are often available to the personologist or clinician.

The method of dream interpretation proposed by French and Fromm begins with a frank admission that the initial measuring instrument is the interpreter's intuition. Reported dream material and the associations elicited later from the manifest content are approached empathically. Parts of the content that seem to make sense (presumedly in terms of some accepted theory of personality) are selected, and hypotheses are formulated as to their possible significance. Other available material is then checked for consistency with the various alternative hypotheses. Inferences which do

---

[1] C. S. Hall and R. L. Van de Castle have recently published a manual (*The Content Analysis of Dreams.* New York: Appleton-Century-Crofts, 1966) describing empirical and theoretical scales for scoring dream reports. Their book includes discussions of important methodological problems encountered in the use of indirect measurement techniques. These should be valuable to all students of personality.

not hold up under such scrutinization are abandoned and replaced with alternate possibilities. In short, evidence for testing the hypotheses, which have been derived from specified partial cues, is gathered from broader and broader clinical sources, until the propositional picture of the structure of individual personality is consistent not only with itself but, ideally, with all available relevant information. The advantages of the recommended procedure are essentially that it forces the interpreter to specify the empirical basis for his intuitions and that it sharply discriminates between the process of inference, by which hypotheses are generated, and the process of deduction, by which they are evaluated.

Thus far, there is nothing especially exciting about this proposal. It is simply an advocation of the method of internal consistency, that has long been highly regarded by clinical psychologists as a means of deriving from complex data an integrated picture of an individual subject (see, for example, Garfield, 1963). Although it proposes to test hypotheses, the hypotheses it has available appear to have little general theoretical significance. The authors themselves stated that their method "is an art that must be learned"; and the critical empiricist wonders whether it is not also, perhaps, a dogma. At least he may doubt that it is science.

If the technique suggested were nothing more than a matter of finding consistencies, it would be entirely unsatisfactory as a research device. Every personality theorist knows, or should know, that the same set of clinical materials can usually be explained in a variety of ways. The critical point, of course, is the stage at which explicit theoretical formulations enter the interpretive picture and permit a conceptually directed extension of the content of statements made about the subject, beyond the limits of immediately available information. If this extension takes place in sufficiently rigorous fashion, it may eventuate in a test of the theory from which it was derived, by predicting the behavioral effects of specific life events on the individual.

French and Fromm (1964) used extending concepts such as "cognitive structure" and principles such as "the basic problems of each individual are the problems in mutual adaptation of the groups to which he has belonged," (p. 58) and "once one has been committed to it, an affective charge must be discharged in overt activity, appear in consciousness, or find outlet in the activation of physiological functions" (p. 70). Others may not feel that these particular constructs and principles are the most productive of rigorously derived hypotheses, but that does not constitute a criticism of the method, as such. It does suggest that personality theory has a long way to go before it can meet the methodological demands of the strategies it has available. French and Fromm were acutely aware of the problem of semantics and commented upon it at length (pp. 118 ff.).

The difficulty with the technique proposed by these authors lies less in its basic logic than in its promulgators' failure to elaborate to a researcher's satisfaction (a) the necessity to objectify as fully as possible the final tests of interpretive hypotheses and (b) the even more crucial necessity to specify exactly the relation between the evidence obtained from a particular individual and some more generally applicable principle or law of human behavior. Unless deductions from the formulation of an individual's personality structure lead to predictions of behavior that can be wrong as well as right, the deductions are useless. Predictions must be explicit and capable of being incorrect. Furthermore, the investigator must know in advance the precise nature of the criteria by which he will decide whether the events he anticipated actually take place. At the same time, each prediction should have some bearing upon an important theoretical issue. If it were found, for example, that a particular patient exhibits a fear of insects, it might be proposed that this individual provides a good test of the hypothesis that such fears are based on anxiety over relationships with the mother. It might then be demonstrated by empirical methods that the arousal of a conflict with the mother produces a correlated increase, specifically in the fear of insects, but not, say, in the fear of guns or weapons. One might also attempt to demonstrate the unidirectionality of the correlation by showing that an arousal of the fear of insects does not necessarily cause the patient to feel more disturbed about his mother. Such experiments are not beyond the possibilities inherent in most clinical situations, and they could fit well into the methodology of the representative case.

It may be argued that the demonstration that conflict with the mother produces a fear of insects in one person offers very little proof that this relationship is universally valid. We have dealt with this argument before and will therefore dispense with it quickly. (It is mentioned again only because it is so frequently raised, and always with an air of finality that seems to indicate that counter-argument is obviously useless.)

If such investigations do not prove their points beyond all possible doubt, they certainly do nothing to discredit them. The intensive test of a theoretical proposition in an individual case, providing it is properly done, is far more rigorous and demanding than the survey of a thousand people with questionnaires that ask how they feel about insects and about their own mothers. There can be no doubt that to establish the general usefulness of hypotheses such as those suggested above requires the accumulation of consistent data from many individuals. The important point, however, is that in the representative case method each individual, as an individual, constitutes one full and complete test of the universal proposition. Other cases that are added later are not to be construed as increases in sample size, but as replications of an experiment that is capable of standing or falling on its own merit as a scientific enterprise.

EVALUATION

No method of science is so perfect as to incorporate answers to all the problems that vex the psychological investigator. Criticisms of the examples, considered in the preceding section, have already suggested many of the specific difficulties inherent in the representative case approach. There is no need to elaborate further, in this general discussion, the host of practical and procedural details that must be satisfactorily handled before such an investigation may be considered satisfactory as a research effort.

The representative case method is certainly no panacea, nor is it equally suited to every purpose the investigator may devise. In all fairness, however, it should also be noted that the method's potential cannot now be fairly judged, since its promises and prospects have not yet been taken sufficiently seriously or employed in the conduct of many meaningful and well-designed investigations. Representative case research is far from popular in psychology today, and examples of its use are few and far between in the literature.

The reason that the method has been avoided is not that any serious consideration of its characteristics or results has led to a carefully deliberated rejection of its tenets. Most likely, it has gone unused because very little systematic thought has been given to the methodological needs of the personality theorist (the contributions of Allport [1962], of Stephenson [1961a; 1961b; 1961c], and of Chassan [1960; 1961] are noteworthy exceptions); and the method itself has therefore simply gone unrecognized. Modern psychology has a research tradition that places highest value on the study of isolated part processes in large groups of persons without identity. Even the contemporary study of individual differences is not the study of individuals, but the study of group variances, as measured by scores on tests designed to measure specific functions, rather than the organizational particularity of the individual human being (Ross, 1963).

Any assessment of the value of the representative case method must remain incomplete until the trend of psychological research preference changes or loosens sufficiently to permit the approach itself to become more adequately tested and its results to be more frequently publicized than is presently the case. In the meantime, the best that can be done is to attempt to anticipate some of the general problems that may appear and some of the questions that may be raised about the method's utility. To accomplish this, it is well to begin with a reconsideration of the types of research purposes the method is designed to serve.

Purpose. The representative case method is a strategy by which meaningful psychological propositions, of interest to the personologist, may be confirmed or disconfirmed without destroying the integrity of the individual subject.

Although the purpose of this method is not to provide a mechanism for the study of isolated processes, as such, that does not imply that part processes cannot or should not be studied in individuals. Many of the procedures by which verbal learning is still studied were developed late in the nineteenth century by a single investigator, Ebbinghaus, who used himself as his only subject (Boring, 1950, pp. 386 ff.; Mednick, 1964, p. 58; Murphy, 1949, pp. 174 ff.). This use of individual subjects, though valuable and important, is not of major concern to the personality theorist, since it obviously does not deal with matters that fall within the province of his concerns. Other examples of the use of single cases in psychological research have been reviewed by Dukes (1965), who has found

246 studies in the relevant literature in the past 25 years. Dukes feels that "the usefulness of N=1 studies in psychological research seems . . . to be fairly well established" (p. 78); but it should be noted that few of the studies he mentions actually fit the model of the representative case method, as it is outlined here.

The general purpose of the representative case method is essentially to solve problems in personality theory; but the requirements of a good problem in personality research are more easily stated than they are fulfilled. This is so partly because the state of personality theory itself is not yet such that empirical questions may be stated clearly and unequivocally. Partly, also, the difficulty of fulfilling the requirements of a good problem is inherent in the complexity of the subject matter and the practical difficulties one meets with when attempting to conduct suitably controlled experiments in the field. As already suggested, a good problem is statable in theoretical terms. It may have any of a number of original sources: a practical situational difficulty that stimulates the investigator to theoretical formulations of an abstract nature; a set of intuitively interpreted qualitative clinical materials that suggest the special research value of a particular patient or client; a derivation from theory that calls for a particular kind of person to serve as research subject if the validity of the derivation is to be empirically established, and so forth. Whatever its genesis, the problem must eventuate in a series of clearly stated hypotheses that can be related, through acceptable rules of correspondence, to observable events.

As proposed here, the representative case method is deductive in character. It presumes that previous research or experience has already enabled the investigator to restrict the focus of his concern to specific and statable aspects of his subject's behavior, aspects which are assigned theoretical relevance in the statement of the research question itself. Single, selected cases may and should be used for inductive purposes in other methods (case studies, factor analysis); but representative case research accepts the dictum that the ultimate test of the usefulness of a generalization is its ability to predict as yet unobserved events in particular cases, under known conditions. The statement of the problem to which a particular representative case research is directed should therefore take into account this essential characteristic of the method.

As far as a single investigation is concerned, then, the problem begins with a theoretical statement that defines a presumedly important personality process or organization and that states how this process or organization will be significantly affected by alterations in the conditions under which it normally operates. The conditions which are to be altered in the experiment proper may be either external or internal (although they will probably most often be the latter), but the nature of their expected effect must be clearly statable. It is insufficient, for example, to hypothesize merely that usually repressed impulses are expressed under conditions of free association. One must be prepared to show (a) how repressed impulses are to be distinguished from unrepressed impulses before the actual investigation begins and (b) how the expression of these impulses is to be recognized when it occurs.

It is also desirable that the statement of the problem include a description of the conditions under which expected effects should *not* occur. Thus, the statement that repressed impulses are expressed in free association (assuming that repression and expression are identifiable when they occur) might well be supplemented by a statement that they are not expressed, say, in ordinary social conversation. This particular problem might benefit from some further specification as well. Although most therapists might presume to know exactly what constitutes free association, some further thought on the subject suggests that almost any definition of this term could easily be elaborated and questioned. For instance, a condition of free association probably does not exist if the subject is seated alone before a tape recorder microphone in an otherwise bare and empty room, even though the verbal instructions he may receive are identical to those he would be given by an interested and attentive therapist. Furthermore, the willingness of a person to engage in free association may well be a function of his peculiar purpose in participating in the research. A college sophomore compelled to serve as a research subject may be far less willing to open up to free association than a neurotic patient desperately seeking help for his suffering.

The first of these considerations suggests that environmental manipulation may have testable effects on the productivity of a given subject in providing expressions of repressed impulses. Some of these manipulations might well be included in the research design. The second consideration indicates that the very statement of the problem implies the need for a particular kind of subject if the hypothesis is to be given a fair and adequate test. A subject who is highly resistant to the expression of repressed impulses under all conditions is not likely to prove any more satisfactory than one who expresses repressed impulses at the drop of a hat. A measure of *repression level,* taken before the experiment begins, might then serve to establish the suitability of a given subject for the research proper. Better yet, for a single subject, it might enable the investigator to predict which impulses would achieve expression under specific sets of environmental conditions.

Many more possibilities could be imagined and many more difficulties stated without exhausting the matter of problem selection. The general points may be summed up briefly, however. They are (a) that the problem must be related to a consistent theory of personality; (b) that it must permit the parallel statement of all its important concepts in terms reflecting known characteristics of the particular subject and measurements or manipulations of observable conditions and events; and (c) that it must yield predictions of outcome which will enable the investigator to judge the success or failure of his theoretical effort.

Variables and Conditions

Since the language of research so frequently employs the terms *dependent* and *independent variables,* it is well to examine briefly how these apply to the representative case method.

Throughout this presentation of research strategies, a distinction has been maintained between the *conditions,* under which a research is conducted, and the *independent variables,* that are of major predictive concern to the investigator. Research conditions are usually controlled, either by holding them constant or by assuring randomization of their effects on the dependent measure. Independent variables change in ways known to the investigator and are presumed to work their influence on the research outcome in predictable fashion, according to the dictates of the theory to be tested.

In representative case research, some of the most important conditions of the investigation are the characteristics of the subject selected for study. Advanced examination of the subject not only establishes his appropriateness to the experimental problem but also specifies the important relevant aspects of the psychological context in which the research is embedded. Except for changes that are predicted by theory, in response to independent variables, it is usually presumed that this context (i.e., the subject) remains essentially constant throughout.

The independent variable (or independent variable complex) constitutes those alterations in the subject's situation that are presumed to produce systematically related effects on his personality or overt behavior, per se.

The dependent variable comprises the indexed or directly measured processes that are presumed to be predictably affected by the independent variables under the conditions of the research. In two of the examples in this chapter, the indices of personality processes were organizational in character; Q sorts were used to examine changes in patterns of feelings or motivational structures. Since personality is, itself, an organizational construct, this seems eminently reasonable; but it is not essential to the method. Highly specific measures of part processes may be employed to advantage in certain research contexts, such as, for example, those that might deal with the influence of variations in anxiety level on learning or perception.

In the hypothetical study on repression, suggested above, variations in conditions defining free association would constitute all or part of the independent variable complex. The dependent variable would be the measure of expression of repressed impulses. The conditions of the study would be the relevant psychological attributes of the subject himself; it would be necessary to describe which impulses he represses and how deeply he does so.

In representative case research, an undeniable relationship commonly exists between research conditions and measures of the dependent variable. It is precisely this relationship that makes it possible, in principle, to overcome certain objections frequently raised about personality research in general. These objections take the form of the criticism that since personality processes are well known to express themselves in various ways, through many different kinds of specific behaviors, research on these processes is patently impossible. After all, one cannot study a central process that is not consistently tied to specifiable and observable behavioral manifestations. If extraversion manifests itself in everything the extravert does, then anything he does becomes proof of his extraversion; and, by virtue of the observation of his overall activities, it is impossible for him to be anything but what he has been called.

Representative case research proposes to answer such objections by specifying in advance exactly how the individual subject does and does not manifest the processes being studied. This specification, which amounts to a description of research conditions, also delineates the measures of the dependent variable that the investigation requires. Suppose that, in our hypothetical study of repression, it is known that the particular subject being investigated typically manifests (expresses) his repressions somatically, perhaps in increased palmar sweating or gastro-intestinal discomfort. Knowledge of this fact enables the investigator to establish rules of correspondence between his central dependent variable and measurable responses of the subject. He is not thereby saying that all repression in all persons is manifested by these signs, he is merely saying that it is so manifested under the conditions of this particular experiment.

It may be objected that the results of such a study are applicable only to persons whose repressions are manifested somatically; and if research on this problem were to stop after the intensive study of only one person, the objection would be entirely valid. Here, however, is another situation in which an apparent disadvantage actually constitutes a special merit of the method. Suppose that the first study of the influence of free association on the manifestation of repressed impulses were successful. The investigator's next step should be, as it usually is in science, to repeat his research under a new set of conditions. In the method of the representative case, the phrase "a new set of conditions" means, specifically, "with another subject who manifests his repressions in a different way."

If the general hypothesis is confirmed again and again, regardless of the variability in individual modes of expression of repressed impulses, it begins to take on the appearance of a generally applicable law of behavior. If it is (as psychological propositions usually are) sometimes confirmed and sometimes rejected, the investigator will be in a position either to modify his thinking or to state more clearly the conditions under which the hypothesis does and does not provide a useful model of psychological events.

The experimenter as a variable. Another set of problems may arise from the possibility that in intensive case studies results are likely to be as much a product of the investigator's personal influence on the subject as of the properties of the subject himself. As with several other criticisms, already mentioned, this difficulty is not exclusive to any single method of psychological investigation. It is likely to be present in almost any research that involves direct interaction of investigator and subject, however formal it may be. The outcomes of learning, verbal conditioning, and photograph rating experiments have been shown to be affected by differences among experimenters; and it seems highly probable that other kinds of psychological research results are similarly affected as well. Not even the much respected double-blind technique is immune to bias from this source; and experimenter expectations have also been shown to influence the outcome of studies in which rats, rather than human beings, have served as subjects (McGuigan, 1963; Rosenthal, 1963).

McGuigan called "alarming" the possibility that experiments exist, which have used multiple data collectors without controlling for experimenter variables (p. 422). He further cautioned that the question of generalizing from a single experimenter experiment "can assume nightmarish proportions" (p. 427). He recommended that when more than one data collector is used, the investigator should (a) specify the techniques employed to control experimenter characteristics, (b) report the results of data analysis as a function of experimenters, and (c) test the interactions between experimenters and treatments (p. 427). Rosenthal recommended sampling experimenters and purposefully introducing experimenter biases as means for controlling the nature and degree of their effects. These suggestions have merit and should be taken seriously in the design of all research that employs large numbers of subjects and/or data collectors.

It may seem that the problem of experimenter bias is insurmountable in the representative case method. Many psychologists would themselves agree that personality is largely a function of interpersonal processes. That being so, it follows that the interpersonal character of much representative case research is bound to cause it to be unusually sensitive to experimenter influence. In the present chapter this criticism was raised specifically with regard to Zinker's study (1963) of the woman with terminal cancer. At that point, as elsewhere, certain procedural necessities were suggested for minimizing these effects.

Aside from specific procedural possibilities for reducing bias, however, there is a more general, but less obvious, aspect to this emphasis on experimenter variables that must be considered. In representative case research it is no more necessary to sample data collectors than to sample subjects. With respect to the selection of a person for intensive investigation, it has already been pointed out that the process is not one of random sampling, but one of measuring and choosing a person for known and relevant psychological characteristics. The same must often be true with respect to the experimenter himself.

Just as the subject constitutes an important set of conditions, under which the research is undertaken, the data collector often constitutes an equally important set of conditions, the properties of which must be known and specifiable in the report of results. In Zinker's study, for example, it would have been desirable to describe in some systematic way the interviewer's mode of approach to the patient, his purposes in conducting the interviews (beyond that of merely collecting information), the range and type of his previous experience with terminal patients, his prior expectations with regard to the outcome of the study, and so forth. It would doubtless be helpful to future investigators to know these facts; for their explicit presentation would enable those who might wish to replicate the investigation to state more exactly their degree of success in reproducing the essential features of the original study.

Furthermore, in representative case research the experimenter not only constitutes some of the conditions under which the investigation is executed, but he is also frequently identified directly with the manipulation of the independent variable. An example may make this point clearer. If the independent variable were free association, it would certainly be necessary to specify the personal characteristics of the investigator that qualify him to conduct free association sessions. As far as possible, it would also be desirable to identify, in general terms, those personal and interpersonal characteristics of a data collector that would encourage free association and to measure these characteristics during the course of actual experimental sessions.

These design requirements may not be so difficult to fulfill as they may sound, at least at the level of first approximation. One could certainly specify in advance that an investigator who feels that free association is a worthless therapeutic or investigative device or who has not had extensive previous, supervised experience with the method would be unqualified to manipulate the independent variable. Similarly, it could be fairly clearly stated that the lower the rating a data collector receives on a measure of "authoritative communication" during experimental free associations, the more he meets the criteria of the study. In short, it may often happen that the investigator himself becomes as much the subject of representative case research as the person being investigated.

Perhaps the most important point to be remembered about representative case research, when problems of sampling arise, is this: ordinary methods of psychological investigation prescribe that large samples substitute for knowledge; if we measure something poorly in one case, we attempt to improve our precision by averaging uncertainties over many cases. By contrast, the representative case method prescribes that measures be definite, or at least that definite commitments be made to them, so that intensive knowledge (which derives from measurement) will make large samples unnecessary. This prescription of the method must often apply to knowledge of the data collector as well as to knowledge of the subject himself. If it be argued that existing measuring instruments are too poor to justify this approach to personality research, the objection is not to be leveled at the method, but at the state of instrumentation in which the study of personality currently finds itself.

Another important point, implied in all this, is that continued investigation, in the representative case method, does not comprise a simple adding together of cases, all of which are treated or evaluated in precisely the same way. It implies studying and treating individuals as individuals, with the guidance of general theoretical concepts and with an eye to the continued improvement of the empirical applicability of these concepts as more cases are investigated.

A Final Note

H. A. Murray (1963) has called for an integration of experimental and personological approaches in psychology; and there are few who could object to so desirable a goal. Murray has presented certain "strategic, methodological principles, or aims" as guides for achieving this end. These are worth a brief review. The first is, "Make the experimental conditions as natural as possible." The second is (in abbreviated form), "Aim at a temporal, holistic model of the observed event." The third is, "Assume that every psychological variable is a hypothetical (theoretical) construct, the activity of which can be inferred only on the basis of one or more of its subjective and/or objective manifestations." The fourth is, "Attempt to explain the reactions, especially the variant reactions of every individual subject."

The first of these principles is self-explanatory, in terms of what has already been said in this volume. The second principle calls for the simultaneous and synchronized recording of the manifestations of all relevant variables, so that sequential and concomitant variations will not be missed. In the context of the present chapter, this principle can just as well be taken to imply, more broadly, that the wholeness and temporal consistency of the individual subject are the starting and ending points as well as the media for all personological investigations. The third principle stresses the necessity for the personologist to deal with theoretically central events, largely by processes of indirect measurement. Finally, the fourth principle states the aim toward which all research in personality theory is oriented: "to attain the enviable position of being able to predict the critical reactions of each individual subject with a fair measure of accuracy and precision."

The method of the representative case seems ideally suited to these principles; and the principles, in turn, express with force and clarity the desirable properties of all good research methods in personality.

References

ALLPORT, G. W. The general and the unique in psychological science. *J. Pers.*, 1962, *30*, 405-421. (In Southwell & Merbaum, pp. 244-258 [see References, chapter 1, above].)
BALDWIN, A. L. Personal structure analysis: A statistical method for investigating the single personality. *J. abnorm. soc. Psychol.*, 1942, *37*, 163-183. (In Southwell & Merbaum, pp. 258-275 [see References, chapter 1, above].)

BELLAK, L., & CHASSAN, J. B. An approach to the evaluation of drug effect during psychotherapy: A double-blind study of a single case. *J. nerv. ment. Dis.*, 1964, *139*, 20-30.

BORING, E. G. *A history of experimental psychology.* (2nd ed.) New York: Appleton-Century-Crofts, 1950.

BOWDLEAR, C. M. Dynamics of idiopathic epilepsy as studied in one case. Unpublished doctoral dissertation, Western Reserve Univer., 1955.

CHASSAN, J. B. Statistical inference and the single case in clinical design. *Psychiatry*, 1960, *23*, 173-184.

CHASSAN, J. B. Stochastic models of the single case as the basis of clinical research design. *Behav. Sci.*, 1961, *6*, 42-50.

DUKES, W. F. N=1. *Psychol. Bull.*, 1965, *64*, 74-79.

FRENCH, T. M., & FROMM, ERIKA. *Dream interpretation.* New York: Basic Books, 1964.

GARFIELD, S. L. The clinical method in personality assessment. In J. M. Wepman, & R. W. Heine (Eds.), *Concepts of Personality.* Chicago: Aldine, 1963. Pp. 474-502.

HALL, C. S., & VAN DE CASTLE, R. L. *The content analysis of dreams.* New York: Appleton-Century-Crofts, in press.

KILPATRICK, F. P., & CANTRIL, H. Self-anchoring scale: A measure of the individual's unique reality world. *J. indiv. Psychol.*, 1960, *16*, 158-170.

MASLOW, A. H. *Motivation and personality.* New York: Harper & Row, 1954.

McGUIGAN, F. J. The experimenter: A neglected stimulus object. *Psychol. Bull.*, 1963, *60*, 421-428.

MEDNICK, S. A. *Learning.* Englewood Cliffs, N. J.: Prentice-Hall, 1964.

MURPHY, G. *Historical introduction to modern psychology.* New York: Harcourt, Brace & World, 1949.

MURRAY, H. A. Studies of stressful interpersonal disputations. *Amer. Psychologist*, 1963, *18*, 28-36.

ROSENTHAL, R. On the social psychology of the psychological experiment. *Amer. Sci.*, 1963, *51*, 268-283.

ROSS, A. O. Deviant case analysis: Neglected approach to behavior research. *Percept. mot. Skills*, 1963, *16*, 337-340.

SHAPIRO, M. B. The single case in fundamental clinical psychological research. *Brit. J. Med. Psychol.*, 1961, *34*, 255-262.

STEPHENSON, W. Scientific creed—1961: abductory principles. *Psychol. Rec.*, 1961, *11*, 9-17. (a)

STEPHENSON, W. Scientific creed—1961: centrality of self. *Psychol. Rec.*, 1961, *11*, 19-25. (b)

STEPHENSON, W. Scientific creed—1961: philosophical credo. *Psychol. Rec.*, 1961, *11*, 1-8. (c)

TIZARD, BARBARA. The personality of epileptics: A discussion of the evidence. *Psychol. Bull.*, 1962, *59*, 196-210.

ZINKER, J. C. *Terminal illness as a source of personality change in a woman suffering from cancer.* Cleveland: Depts. of Psychology, Highland View Hospital & Western Reserve Univer., 1963.

NAME INDEX

Page numbers in parentheses identify citations in Reference lists.

265

SUBJECT INDEX